RE-THINKING MISSIONS

✠

RE-THINKING
MISSIONS

A LAYMEN'S INQUIRY
AFTER ONE HUNDRED YEARS

By

THE COMMISSION OF APPRAISAL
William Ernest Hocking
CHAIRMAN

HARPER & BROTHERS PUBLISHERS
New York and London
1932

Directors of

LAYMEN'S FOREIGN MISSIONS INQUIRY

BAPTIST COMMITTEE
Albert L. Scott, *Chairman*

Charles C. Tillinghast   Wilfred W. Fry
Wm. Travers Jerome, Jr.   Geo. W. Bovenizer

CONGREGATIONAL COMMITTEE
Franklin Warner, *Chairman*

Frank E. Barrows   Mrs. Allen H. Nelson
Arthur D. Williams   Mrs. Ozora S. Davis

DUTCH REFORMED COMMITTEE
W. Edward Foster, *Chairman*

A. P. Cobb   Wm. E. Reed
Simeon B. Chapin   Mrs. Malcolm James MacLeod

EPISCOPAL COMMITTEE
Stephen Baker, *Chairman*
Senator George Wharton Pepper
Geo. W. Wickersham
Lincoln Cromwell
John E. Rousmaniere

METHODIST EPISCOPAL COMMITTEE
Frank A. Horne, *Chairman*

Mrs. Francis J. McConnell   W. F. Bigelow
George B. Hodgman   George S. Hawley

PRESBYTERIAN COMMITTEE
James M. Speers, *Chairman*

Ralph W. Harbison   George H. Richards
Mrs. John H. Finley   Holmes Forsyth

UNITED PRESBYTERIAN COMMITTEE
Frederick C. MacMillan, *Chairman*

J. A. Gibson   Ralph Croy
George Ramer   J. H. Lockhart

CONTENTS

Foreword

IT IS doubtful whether any enterprise dependent entirely on continuous giving has so long sustained the interest of so many people as has the foreign mission. Its continuity has not been that of invested funds, but of perennially renewed sacrifice springing from persistent belief in its objects. In an era during which channels for giving to beneficent purposes have multiplied almost beyond reckoning, this enterprise has until very recent years not only held its own, but shown remarkable growth. Relying as it has upon the steadfastness of certain attitudes of mind and will, its very magnitude has rendered it vulnerable to any change which might affect those attitudes. In the last few years there have been signs of such change. The old fervor appears to have been succeeded in some quarters by questionings if not by indifference. Subscriptions have been falling off. Problems of the utmost gravity face mission boards in nearly all fields. There is a growing conviction that the mission enterprise is at a fork in the road, and that momentous decisions are called for.

In January 1930, a group of laymen of one denomination met in New York to consider these problems. It appeared to this group that the situation demanded a new and thoroughgoing study of the basis and purport of missions and of their operation. But since these questions were of common concern to many churches, invitations were sent to laymen of other denominations to join in the study. As a result, seven denominations, each unofficially represented by a group of five men and women, joined to constitute the thirty-five Directors of the Laymen's Foreign Missions Inquiry. These denominations are Baptist (Northern), Congregational, Methodist Episcopal, Presbyterian Church in U. S. A., Protestant Episcopal, Reformed Church in America, United Presbyterian. The chairmen of the denominational groups form an Executive Committee of seven.

Since the Inquiry was to include an objective review of the presuppositions of the entire enterprise, it was felt essential that it should not be carried on through agencies committed to its promotion. The initiative, direction and personnel of the Inquiry must therefore be independent of the mission boards. At the same time it was equally essential to have their full and hearty cooperation: the problems were common, the skilled knowledge and experience were theirs. This cooperation has been given without stint and has facilitated every step in the planning and execution of the Inquiry during the two years of its work. The same is to be said of the International Missionary Council, both in America and in England. In preparing our way in India, British members rendered especially gracious aid.

It was decided to restrict the Inquiry to India, Burma, China and Japan. It was evident that there were two types of work to be done. There must be an impartial and scientifically directed accumulation of data so that the judgment reached should be based on pertinent and accurately stated facts; and there must be an appraisal of these facts in the light of the widest possible consideration of the meaning of the mission enterprise and of the world conditions in which it is now, and is to be, carried out. It was believed that with the aid of data already available a corps of men and women especially trained in such study might in the course of a year provide in outline the requisite factual basis; and that directed by this work a second group might during another year of thought and observation reach well-founded judgments, not on the entire work of missions, but on those critical questions which are determining the attitude of the laymen of our churches and of the wider public.

The first stage of the study was placed in the hands of the Institute of Social and Religious Research. Beginning late in 1930, the Institute sent a corps of research workers to the designated fields under the supervision of Galen M. Fisher, General Director. The group in India and Burma was headed by C. Luther Fry, that in China by H. Paul Douglass, and that in Japan by Harvey H. Guy. An extraordinary work was achieved within the time prescribed. By September 1931, printed reports were placed in the hands of the Commission of Appraisal, together with much supplementary matter indicating a widespread interest on the part of missionaries and nationals in the undertaking, and a sympathetic recognition of its timeliness and value.

The second stage of the Inquiry was entrusted to a Commission of Appraisal of fifteen members, the Commission now reporting. The terms of reference of this Commission are defined in the following statement of its purpose:

"To aid laymen to determine their attitude toward Foreign Missions, by reconsidering the functions of such Missions in the world of today. With this general aim,

a. To make an objective appraisal of their activities in the fields visited;

b. To observe the effect of Missions on the life of the peoples of the Orient;

c. In the light of existing conditions and profiting, though not bound, by missionary experience, to work out a practical program for today, offering recommendations as to the extent to which missionary activities of every sort should be continued or changed."

In choosing the Commissioners, the Directors of the Inquiry were guided by the view that each member of the Commission should weigh the general problems confronting missions, and that each should also have a special concern in some aspect of the work of missions—evangelistic, administrative, educational, medical, etc. There was no thought of a mechanical division of mental function as between the finders of fact and the Commission of Appraisal. The preliminary judgments of the earlier workers have been of the greatest service to the Commission, and the Commissioners extended by their own travel their basis of fact and observation. Without the prior study by the Institute, itself a significant work of research, the labors of the Commission would not have been possible. Certain members of the staff of research, Orville A. Petty in India, and Harvey H. Guy in Japan, accompanied the Commission and rendered invaluable aid in planning its work. D. Willard Lyon, although not a member of the research staff, placed his wide experience and acquaintance in China at the disposal of the Commission while in that country.

The Commission sailed from New York in September 1931, reaching Bombay on October 23rd. After three months in India and Burma a week was spent in Kandy, reviewing findings for these countries. Leaving Colombo on January 31st, the Commission arrived in Hong Kong, February 10th. The two and a half months spent in China were during a period of public agitation, yet it was possible for the Commission to spend three useful weeks in mid-China, with headquarters in Shanghai between March 11th and March 25th. Several members went as far west as Hankow. On March 27th the office staff moved to Peiping, and then to Nara, Japan, setting up headquarters there on April 26th. Five of the Commission proceeded to Nara by way of Manchuria and Korea. Remaining in Japan until June 9th, the Commission sailed to Honolulu, where between June 17th and July 1st it made the preliminary sketches of the Report herewith presented.

The method of work was to hold group conferences in the larger cities with representative bodies of missionaries, Christian nationals, and non-Christians, and then to disperse for the more intimate conversations which a large group cannot carry on. There were many individual interviews and many studies by twos and threes. For these personal and detailed inquiries, which often took our members into rural and industrial districts near and remote, the Commission was organized into a number of committees representing the different aspects of mission work. The formation of these committees varied somewhat in the different countries. The final organization was as follows:

1. The Mission and the Indigenous Church
2. Primary and Secondary Education
3. Higher Education
4. Literature

5. Medical Work
6. Agriculture and Rural Life
7. Industrial Developments
8. Women's Interests
9. Administration and Organization

Special attention was also given to Music and Liturgy in all three countries. It will be evident in view of the number of committees that in general each Commissioner served on more than one committee. Even so, there were various phases of mission work which we should have been glad to disengage for separate committee study had our personnel permitted. At the close of our stay in each country, each of these committees brought before the Commission an account of its findings. These regional reports are presented to the Directors as informal studies, forming the background of, and giving illustrative material for, the condensed statements presented in this Report in the several chapters of parts two and three. While the authorship of these chapters is in the several committees, each chapter has been carefully considered and approved by the Commission as a whole.

It would obviously be impossible to mention, still less adequately to thank, all those who have aided our work. We are under special obligation to the National Christian Council in each country. We are indebted for courtesies extended by officials of the government in each country, and for the invariable hospitality of the missions, churches, schools, hospitals, and individual missionaries, to whom in many cases a double request had come as the Inquiry passed through its two stages. Many nationals and foreigners also, not connected with missions, many of other faiths, taking a broad interest in the problems of the Inquiry, have placed at our disposal time, thought, and hospitality. Nothing that could have been done has been left undone by the Directors and Sponsors of the Inquiry in their unrestricted provision of facilities for our work; and they have done what is more difficult, they have at every point protected the complete independence of our judgment.

All labors of thought which deal with problems of this magnitude must of necessity be cooperative. The success or failure of the Commission was from the start dependent on its fortune in bringing the riches of many other minds and of a long history to bear upon its work, including many important results of earlier studies and conferences. We have at no time been unaware of the magnitude of our task, its immense responsibility, and our own inadequacy. We have been fortunate in the many helpers who have extended our mental reach. To those best acquainted with missions, it will be apparent that our proposals lie in well recognized directions of advance and that they call far less for innovations than for the emphasis and encouragement of tendencies already present in the field and at home.

One of the chief advantages enjoyed by this Commission has been the circumstance that it includes contrasting views in the interpretation of Christianity and therefore of Christian missions. With less of a gamut it would have been by so much less representative of the membership of American churches. These differences are to some extent differences of expression, to some extent differences of substance. Such differences are not unimportant. We have not been under the illusion that the matters on which men agree are the only matters of value— on the contrary when religious issues are clearly defined, they are the most important issues of human life. To some of our members the enduring motive of Christian missions can only be adequately expressed as loyalty to Jesus Christ regarded as the perfect revelation of God and the only Way by which men can reach a satisfying experience of Him. To others, this motive would best be called the spirit of altruistic service, the desire to share with all mankind the benefits and the ideals of a Christian community. To still others, it would best be named the desire for a deeper knowledge and love of God, seeking with men everywhere a more adequate fulfilment of the divine possibilities of personal and social life.

These views are not mutually exclusive: no one statement is likely to exhaust the aim of a great enterprise. In so far as the differences are those of language, some prefer the words which unite the present with the earlier language of the Christian world. Others desire to avoid the language of tradition, not as untrue, but perhaps as obscurely figurative or symbolical, and for this reason an obstacle to the spontaneous recognition of the majesty of that Figure to whom men's thoughts return as by a natural instinct of the heart.

Retaining these differences, the members of this Commission unite in the judgments set forth in this book. In these judgments it is not presumed that all personal views are fully expressed, but to them each has given of his strength. And welded by the common purpose and experience, the result is a significant body of agreement, which we trust may afford a firm basis for reinterpreting and redirecting one of the noblest expressions of that undying hope of the soul, the spiritual unity of mankind.

WM. ERNEST HOCKING, *Chairman*
FREDERIC WOODWARD, *Vice-Chairman*
CLARENCE A. BARBOUR
EDGAR H. BETTS
ARLO A. BROWN
CHARLES P. EMERSON
MRS. WM. ERNEST HOCKING
HENRY S. HOUGHTON
RUFUS M. JONES
WILLIAM P. MERRILL
ALBERT L. SCOTT
HARPER SIBLEY
MRS. HARPER SIBLEY
HENRY C. TAYLOR
RUTH F. WOODSMALL

September 17, 1932

NOTE.—Chapters I to IV inclusive are interdependent, and should be considered as a whole.

PART I

GENERAL PRINCIPLES

CHAPTER I

The Mission in the World of Today

IT IS no new experience for Christian missions, least of all for Protestant missions in Asia, to be questioned. In the very position of foreign missions, as guests and for the most part uninvited guests, among people of other ways and faiths, they are used to glances which ask, Why are you here? They have had to make their own friends and create their own welcome. It is one advantage of their exposed situation that they are spurred so constantly and so deeply to re-think the meaning of the faith they recommend.

There are now other questions being put to them, not by the nationals where their work lies, nor by official visitors from the churches at home, but by the turn of the times. Have these missions in some measure finished their work? Are there new channels for what they have been bringing? Is there a decline in their value to the Far East, in view of vast changes since their early days in the relations of peoples and the means of intercourse?

Our Commission has brought to a group of Protestant missions in the Orient questions of this sort—not its own questions, we repeat, but the questions of the time—expressed by laymen of the several churches concerned. This Commission has been instructed to be thoroughgoing in its inquiry, and objective in its attitude. It was asked to consider whether these missions ought any longer to go on. And if they ought, whether it should be with great change, or little change, or none. By an objective attitude was meant not a coldly critical attitude—it was at no time forgotten that the mission is a work of devotion and must be judged with devotion—but an attitude which endeavored to consider always the greater interest rather than the lesser, the good of humanity rather than

3

the growth of a special movement. We were to remember not only the devotion in the field, but also the sacrifices at home, and to consider whether this great effort was being, as well as we could judge, most wisely directed and to its noblest ends.

To reach a satisfactory judgment on these far-reaching questions placed a double requirement on the Commissioners. Without a sensitiveness to the inner spirit of the mission, they could not so much as see what is there: the mission has many critics who know nothing of what it is all about. On the other hand, one who is too much absorbed by the sanctity of this inner spirit is disqualified as a judge of these questions: when piety is judged solely by piety, its works will always be found good—there is no real appraisal. It was necessary to be able and willing to recognize factors in the total situation, if they existed, which would in time make the Christian mission an irrelevant and intrusive method of furthering the highest spiritual interests of mankind.

As to the first and most searching question put to us, whether these missions should in our judgment any longer go on, we may say that this question has been with us, honestly and objectively entertained, throughout our inquiry. As the inquiry closes, we may confess that this formidable question has not proved to be highly significant. It is somewhat like asking whether good-will should continue or cease to express itself. Like other works, organized by men's hands, missions might conceivably ossify in unadaptable forms and deserve to perish. But at the center of the religious mission, though it takes the special form of promoting one's own type of thought and practice, there is an always valid impulse of love to men: one offers one's own faith simply because that is the best one has to offer. It is always reasonable to ask whether this good-will might take quite different shape: but to ask whether it should cease to operate would seem to suppose that the very substance of friendship among men and races might somehow be mistaken.

That these missions should go on, with whatever changes, we regard, therefore, as beyond serious question. In the field, one finds here and there concrete obligations assumed by our institutions to the peoples of the East which could not fairly be abandoned. One finds also beginnings of good work which it would be a pity not to continue and develop. There is much mission work which excites no such feeling. But of the rest, arousing in the observer a perpetual wish for more funds so that it might be done better, there is enough to bankrupt Christendom. There is in this fact, however, no ground for a renewed appeal for the support, much less for the enlargement, of these missions as a whole in their present form and on their present basis. This Commission makes no such appeal. In our judgment, there is not alone room for change, there is necessity for change, in respects which our report will indicate; and the effecting of such change should be the condition for every further enlargement of the enterprise.

Any appraisal, and especially any that calls for change, implies some standard of judgment, some criterion. By what standards should missions be judged? The measures are peculiarly elusive. In a sense, "objective" judgment is impossible: one is bound, with a mission as with a person, to see beyond what it is to what it is aiming at; one must, to be fair, credit it with its ideal.

On the other hand, this ideal, which furnishes mission as well as person with its own standard of self-judgment, gives a clue to the standard to be used by others. One must judge the mission first by its own intention: what is it really trying to do, how far does it achieve this object? There is a further question, whether this ideal or object meets the situation. One has to consider the fit between the mission and its environment, the targeting of its aim; then, its yield, its keenness of self-criticism, its readiness to adjust. Is it capable of lending a good hand in the work of the world as that work changes shape? In some degree the mission enters fields of action, such as the education of youth, works of healing and social service, where secular measures of worth and of effect exist. It has no wish to evade, it invites, judgment by those measures where they apply.

But we have to remember that no judgment can be either objective or sound which should see only visible things, consider only measurable results, or envisage only the present moment of world history. It may be well to begin our report by a glance at the sweep of the idea of missions in religious history, endeavoring to bring into clearer definition the fundamental motives which have brought them into being and actuated their labors.

1. The Motives of Missions

Among the great religions of the world there are some, like Hinduism, Judaism, Shinto, in which the local accent is strong: they have grown up with and have followed each one the fortunes of a particular race or nation. Their membership is defined by that group. The genius of such religions would not require nor permit them to conduct missions to other races or nations, without a change in their original conception, such as occurred in Judaism after the Exile. But most of the great religions, especially those which have owed their inception to the work of individual founders, Buddha, Jesus, Mohammed, have been missionary religions.

In dealing with missions, then, we are dealing with one of the major manifestations of the religious spirit. Our immediate concern is with but a fragment of the total fact. We are concerned only with Christian missions; and within them, only with Protestant missions of today; and with only a segment of them as they appear in the Far East. But the part cannot be judged without a sense of the whole: whatever these contemporary American missions in Asia may mean, that meaning is a part of the life and purpose of the whole movement.

The motive of all religious missions is an ardent desire to communicate a spiritual value regarded as unique and of supreme importance. It is an integral part of the passion for "saving" men and peoples, and implies a peculiar sense of the tragedy and danger of the unsaved.

To any one, man or church, possessed of religious certainty, the mission in some form is a matter not of choice but of obligation. If there is any truth or value in religion at all, it is for all men. The questions religion deals with are not questions which admit local or national answers: Is there some *right* way of life? How can human beings overcome evil, misery, fear? Can our courage toward the great world be more than animal spirits or a whistling in the dark? What are the ultimate powers or realities of that world? Do they care for us? Is there a career for individual persons beyond what is seen? Is there any deep-lying justice in the workings of destiny, here or beyond?

Men have always known that happiness is something deeper than good fortune, that it has something to do with what we can believe about the total frame of human living. The way to happiness is far more obscure than the way to pleasure or success; men grope for it through a common fate and darkness, knowing it to be the chief of all treasures, the issue of life or death for what we call the "soul." If one has on these matters some insight still more if he has enlightenment, certainty, peace—is he not under an inner compulsion to give what he has found without limit? Just this has been the experience of the great founders of religion: they have been teachers of men, moved by compassion, seeing the multitudes devoid of guidance or led by blind guides. They have spent themselves speaking to their own people; and they have left behind them an impulse which has moved on steadily across boundary after boundary. Religion becomes potentially universal in range as it becomes aware of its own inner logic.

This general principle explains the historic spread of the great faiths. It may not offer a sufficient reason for what are now called "foreign missions," in which the impulse to communicate one's way leaps abruptly from a place where its work is unfinished to remote fields where every barrier of custom, language, race makes understanding difficult. It hardly gives adequate reason for our being in Asia with several thousand propagandists for our form of faith.

Missions to remote foreign fields have not always been regarded as the immediate duty of the church. Leaders of the Reformation seem to have felt no impulsion to wander far from Europe. Luther saw that the Gospel was spreading: *that,* he thought, was the important thing; the rate and direction he could leave to God. Christ's injunction, thought Melancthon, had been given to the Apostles, and had already been fulfilled by them. It required two centuries for Protestantism to arouse itself to any general concern for the "foreign field" as we now know it. These earlier leaders were, no doubt, preoccupied with the affairs of the church in Europe. But their attitude makes it evident that the foreign mission implies some further motive than the general responsibility of the church for extending the area of its labors. The question continues to be asked, Why go so far when there is so much to be done at home?

To us it seems that this further motive in the early days of the Protestant missions was primarily the sense of the greater need of the Orient, and the greater return for a given effort. The pioneers were moved by the disturbing sense that many in Asia had not so much as heard the Gospel: millions of souls, believed to be in danger of eternal death, might be given the opportunity of life; there was but one way, the way of Christ. There was need for haste.

Mingled with this concern for individuals, there was the appealing vision of the world-wide Church. It was well to have many centers from which local extensions might begin. Around this picture of the universal Christian community gathered obscurely all that we now think of as preparation for world unity in civilization. We know that to effect an understanding in religious matters is to pave the way for an understanding in other matters. The world must eventually become a moral unity: to this end, it was necessary that the apparent localism of Christianity should be broken down. It must not be thought of as solely the religion of the West. It was because Christianity is *not* western, but universally human, that it must be brought back to the Orient and made at home there.

Let us add that one further motive always joins subconsciously with any impulse to give to others; that is, the impulse through expression to achieve one's own growth. We are so made that the communication of thought and feeling not alone relieves but develops the self that communicates. Those who give most, learn most definitely what they have. Especially if one communicates a faith believed to have universal fitness, this fitness can hardly be said to have been tested until the faith has been conveyed to peoples of highly different mold; the fact that remote regions are profoundly different adds to the stimulus, and so to the desire to converse with them and to reach a basis of unity. If it had no such impulse to enlarge its touch with the whole gamut of human type and culture, the church at home would confess its inherent provincialism and lack of vigor, and must suffer from a sense of the unreality of its own professions.

Thus if one asks why these American churches have entered Asia with their thousands of representatives of the Christian interpretation of life, the historical answer must include not only a concern for the spiritual welfare of the Orient, but also a fundamental groping toward the moral unity of the world, and a regard for the inner health and truth of the existing church.

The mixture of motives. In the actual practice of missions the motives we have been speaking of are necessarily affected by the instruments through which they operate. There is a human aspect of the mission, which, as in all work which takes the name of religion, stands out sharp against the ideal background and becomes the target for a type of caustic comment usually uninformed or oblivious to the substantial realities of the undertaking. It must be taken for granted that whatever the powers or defects of the individual missionary, they will affect his manner and his capacity to transmit his gift.

If he is imperious, dogmatic, vain, narrow, his love of man may still be genuine, yet it will be colored by personal arrogance. The history of missions has plentiful examples of such mixture of motive. With the legitimate motive have been associated such traits as love of adventure, ambition, the impulse to dominate or to impose one's type of mind on others, the "predatory temper," the will to power. There is some reason to think that the psychological type most likely in the early days to feel the call to mission work, was self-confident, temperamentally certain, and occasionally self-assertive. Heroes of the missions have usually been men of native force who would probably have made their mark in any calling. Loyola never lost the spirit of a military commander and transmitted it to his Jesuits: in him it was transformed into an intense zeal for good, but not without an equally intense zeal to do this good by promoting his own religious type and organization. It is futile to imagine that such mixtures of motive can be eliminated from any work carried on by human agencies. It is enough if the legitimate motive can be kept dominant, and enough truth be told to chasten the excesses of the intrusive self.

One particular association deserves notice. The three bursts of Christian mission activity, after the first or apostolic epoch, have been contemporaneous with periods of military, exploring, or commercial activity. The expansion of Christendom between the fifth and the tenth centuries into the Germanic world was on the whole a semi-political and more than semi-forcible conversion of tribes and peoples: it was the original mass movement. The Catholic missionary orders of the sixteenth century accompanied the explorer-conqueror or preceded him. The Protestant missionary of the eighteenth and nineteenth centuries followed in the wake of trade. This association with conquest or gainful adventure has frequently been read to the discredit of the sincerity of the missionary; or again, he has been considered a dupe or tool of national or commercial self-interest.

Such interpretations overlook the obvious and natural for an artificial explanation. The missionary was presumably a person, from among the religiously inclined, who was also disposed to adventure and sensitive to the currents of expanding geographical interest. He was prepared to endure hardship as a good soldier of Christ, and was prepared to do so together with the other hardy spirits of his age: he had his share of their intrepidity. If he has been aware of the elements of greed or cruelty attending the advance of the trader or conquistador, he has commonly done what he could to check or mitigate them, even in ages when these things were taken as hard necessities. He has usually been a person of passionate devotion to the people among whom he moved and of intense loyalty to his conception of the way of Christ. He has been—and this function has grown in importance in recent years—an unofficial representative of the interests of the common people of his district; and has not infrequently incurred the displeasure of the interests engaged in their exploitation. He may well be, amid settlers, diplomats, and traders the one person who by his position, detached from self-seeking, speaks out for humanity and justice.

It is undoubtedly true—as a fact discovered after much experience of the effects of missions—that their work has tended to create a receptivity to the products and ideas of the country of their origin. And once this is perceived by interested agencies, it is impossible to say that this relationship has never been exploited; in point of fact, the preaching of Christ has at times been the prelude or the pretext for exploitation by other hands, in ways which the missionary, as a rule, has been unable to prevent. But we can say with conviction regarding the Protestant missions studied by us that, while they are necessarily subject to political regulation by the government under which they work as well as by the requirements of their own citizenship, their missionaries are in no sense apologists for, nor promoters of, any political or economic system, or interest: they are there in the interest of religion and its applications, nothing else. If they are in any respect unfree, it is through deference to the authority of the organization as represented by the board, not through any personal compromise with Mammon.

The fact that material and other aspects of western life are in the field constitutes a special reason for the missionary's presence. For if any aspect of western culture—commercial, scientific, political, industrial, military—is to be recommended to other parts of the world, it is imperative that the religious aspect should also have its expression, and an adequate expression.

We may assume, then, that the primary motives of foreign missions have been not alone legitimate, but in an eminent sense noble. No movement so far-reaching, so persistently re-newed during two thousand years, can be supposed to spring from an impulse essentially fallacious or quixotic or selfish. It is precisely for this reason that the work of appraisal tends to rest less upon the originating motives than upon what these motives have brought to pass. Let us consider briefly what the contemporary observer sees and learns of the missions in operation.

2. Missions as Seen by the Observer

Of the external aspect of missions as we find them today, much might be said. We must be content here with touching upon three points which bear most directly upon our study, the visible activities and properties of missions, their results, and their personnel.

Activities and properties. As a colony of the church, the characteristic activity of the Protestant mission is the religious service with its preaching and personal appeal. Much of this work is carried out in remote districts, in hundreds of small outpost stations, meagerly equipped and under conditions of hardship, though improving roads in all countries make communication with larger centers more regular: remote stations are not as a rule to be thought of as isolated stations. Village work is usually carried on from town and city cen-ters, where the larger churches with their associated institu-tions, Sunday schools, kindergartens, training places for religious workers, centers of social work, resemble similar churches in America. There are many more institutions not directly connected with churches: schools, colleges, hospitals, traveling dispensaries, agricultural stations, publishing houses, social settlements. With the thousands of westerners, men and women, engaged in the work of these institutions, are asso-ciated other thousands of nationals. The missionary outside any of these institutions is an exception.

THE MISSION IN THE WORLD OF TODAY 13

There are contrasts among these exceptions. One finds among them some of the finest spirits who come to mind, men with those traits of greatness and originality which have made it hard for them to fit into the usual institutional mold, doing striking and important work. There are many others whom we would class as misfits, unable to cooperate, running more or less individual ventures, more often than not a discredit to the name of Christianity in the East. One of the problems of the future mission is that of enlarging the scope of its institutions to give the deservedly honorable place to the former group, retaining instead of losing their outstanding powers, and at the same time relieving the mission field of the latter group.

All of this work implies tangible property, land, buildings, equipment. One's mind reviews the multitude of impressions made by these mission properties in the Far East. Some few stand out by their dignity and beauty. Most of the schools are well and substantially built in the western manner, requiring western care. Of the city churches, the same can be said: they stand as a rule strong, high, uncompromisingly western, fitted to our modes of worship, too expensive in upkeep, and too alien in conception, to be handed over with confidence to oriental use. Outlying institutions frequently reveal the effort of the mission to do much with inadequate means. As a mark of a passing era, the high compound wall still encloses many of the older institutions, protecting and at the same time insulating the mission from the life around it. Distinction of design is exceptional in town or country. Remembering that such distinction and beauty come from the heart and imagination, and need not be a costly luxury, the impression remains that—with certain notable exceptions—we have much to learn from the Orient as to the part which the loveliness of nature and expressive architecture have to play in the worship of God.

Results. It would be natural to attempt an appraisal of the value of missions chiefly on the basis of their results.

The difficulty with this method is that the results of missions, particularly of present-day missions, are highly intangible. There are striking results of the earlier work of missions, when they were in many ways the chief bearers of western culture: of the beneficence of their work in spreading ideas and forming personalities one can speak with unstinted praise. In the founding of institutions of religion, there are also results which can be expressed in statistical totals, as of accessions to membership. Such numerical totals, considering the time of mission activity and the progress made by other religious movements under comparable conditions, are not impressive. Of Protestant Christians, India counts very roughly 2,000,000 out of 300,000,000 people; China, 400,000 out of 400,000,000 people; Japan, 160,000 out of 65,000,000 people. As a comparison one sect of Shinto in Japan, during a period of growth of some fifty years, claims an addition of over 4,000,000 to its membership. But these figures are of little value in any of the countries, partly because they include many merely nominal Christians (or nominal Shintoists), and partly because the influence of the Christian mission far outpasses the showing in church membership.

The presence of Christianity in any land, as a subject of discussion, affects the thought of many who never enter a church. A few notable personalities among the Christians give the Christian way of life a serious hearing among wide circles. Education in Christian schools and colleges leaves its mark upon many citizens—though the significance of this mark for the run of students is, we judge, easily overrated. Christian modes of worship and theology call out an answering activity on the part of the non-Christian religions. Mission philanthropies and hospitals spread the good repute of the Christian attitude to human need, and in their more experimental ventures serve as incentives to much social betterment. Christianity is, in brief, a powerful ferment in any community, when it is presented by persons who command the respect of that community. It continues to bring into Oriental life legitimate aspects of western civilization which, because of their different mental pattern, still stir constructive social thinking. Nobody knows when or where an *idea* is going to bear fruit: its effect is necessarily invisible and may be long latent. But we can be sure that wherever there is a strong group of persons in active and friendly intercourse with their Oriental neighbors, there ideas are silently at work, penetrating the community. Such a group is itself a success of the mission. Hence the estimate of the value of the mission turns largely on the estimate of the personnel and of the motives which determine the relations of missionary and people.

Personnel. We speak of the aggregate number of missionaries in these countries, as if it were a large total. Dispersed as it is among the vast populations of the East, it is in reality a comparatively small society, so distinctively and absorbingly occupied as to be referred largely to itself for companionship. In the planning of work there is a general tendency to lay out a maximum, with the result that most missionaries are overworked, and as a rule must be prepared to do substitute duty for others at need. There are very few lazy missionaries, and few who can specialize steadily on one thing.

Of these thousands of persons, there are many of conspicuous power, true saintliness and a sublime spirit of devotion, men and women in whose presence one feels himself at once exalted and unworthy. It is easier to say this, than to say the rest of the truth; the greater number seem to us of limited outlook and capacity; and there are not a few whose vision of the inner meaning of the mission has become obscured by the intricacies, divisions, frictions and details of a task too great for their powers and their hearts.

It is unreasonable to expect an undertaking calling for so many people as do these Protestant missions, to command a greater proportion of the ablest men and women than, let us say, a college or a business enterprise in America. We must expect the mission to show its proportion of second-rate work and of second-rate personality. We must also give due weight to the consideration that in all religious work a simple and earnest spirit inspired by love will be significant without talents which stand high in ordinary rating.

With due regard to these considerations it is still necessary to say that the human side of the mission, as we find it today, seems on the whole unduly weak. For there are two things which we may rightfully demand of the mission personnel. First, that in those services where there is a recognized standard of efficiency, as in teaching or medicine, the mission staff shall stand well. Second, that in the essential service of interpreting Christianity to the Orient, it shall not too far fail of its great theme. In neither of these respects can we speak of the total impression with the high enthusiasm we should like to offer. No one can fairly expect adequacy in meeting the infinite requirements of an ideal task: the sense of deficiency is the daily torment of every honest soul which engages in such work. But we feel that the Christian view of life has a magnificence and glory of which its interpreters, for the most part, give little hint: they seem prepared to correct, but seldom to inspire; they are better able to transmit the letter of doctrine than to understand and fulfil the religious life of the Orient.

We believe that these lacks are traceable in part to certain auspices under which the missionary does his work—deficiencies of leadership, or professional biases, or incidents of inept organizational machinery. There are two traits occasionally found which illustrate this point, tending to diminish his effectiveness: invidious comparison and subservience to organization.

Since the value of one's work is proportionate to the need of the people, the missionary in dealing with his sending bodies has a temptation to exaggerate the need, in part by dwelling on the unfavorable aspects of the culture in which he is placed, in part by minimizing the worth of the religions there prevalent. In his reports and letters he has often unduly blackened the picture of his environment. He has to resist a sort of professional interest in deprecation. If this interest becomes confirmed in a certain lack of magnanimity toward the life about him, his power to serve that life has ceased.

Again, as a member of a church, sent out by a church, the missionary is prone to conceive his task as primarily that of promoting this organization. His board, as a rule, embodies and intensifies this conception; and the missionary is likely to be dominated by the expectations of his board. Every human organization has its hunger for influence, funds, membership; tempts its servants into ways of ambition within its ranks, and into a reputed "loyalty" which involves petty competition with other organizations of similar aim. The trail of self-interest within the organization lies like a sinister shadow over many phases of mission work within our purview; we shall have occasion to note it at various points.

One relatively minor point may serve as illustration: the organization tends to obscure the natural interest which should direct the missionary to the field of his work. In the apostolic age there were no board missionaries. There were leaders and teachers who in their own hearts found special reasons at special times for journeying to special places: they would make the visit, teach the new Way, get together a group of adherents, leave some local person in charge, and then proceed elsewhere or return home. Paul was not a "foreign missionary" after our present pattern. Today we attempt to assemble a group of young candidates for mission work in general, and then by some joint process of decision in which the program of the board mingles in varying degrees with prior interests of the individual, the young person is "assigned" to a post. In not a few instances, this means that the organization has come between the man and his impulse; and that he arrives at his work with a deficit of individual volition. Robert Morrison chose China, Grenfell chose Labrador, on the ground of a specific interest in the place based on specific knowledge: it is this sort of relation which promises the best, and which our machinery tends not so much to thwart as to dispense with.

These two occasional traits are obviously shadows of mental attitudes which in some form are necessary. Unless there is need on the part of those among whom he lives, the missionary has no reason for being there. And to "get rid of organization" is neither possible nor desirable: it is a question of the right place and the right use. Nevertheless, the conditions of the missionary's task and training are affecting the type of person offering himself.*

Our judgment of the possible future value of the mission movement depends, more than upon any other factor, on the question whether there is a real likelihood that either through changing the conditions of work, or through improvement in quality, the personnel of missions can be materially strengthened.

3. Changes Affecting Missions

But the personnel of an enterprise is in all cases a response to the inherent appeal which that enterprise at any time presents. It is useless to call for stronger men unless the task is such as to command the interest of such men. The crucial problem, then, is this: whether the motives which animated the inauguration of the Protestant missions a century or so ago remain in full force, in view of the changes which have taken place since their inception.

Of the many changes in the world during the past century, a century of sweeping changes in the life of the Orient as well as in the life of the West, three are peculiarly pertinent to the mission enterprise, an altered theological outlook, the emergence of a basic world-culture, the rise of nationalism in the East.

a. The altered theological outlook. It would be a poor compliment to our theological insight if a hundred years so full of intellectual development, of advance in scientific thought and of philosophical activity, had brought no progress in the conceptions attending our religious experience. The bases of that experience belong to the eternal and unchangeable things—since it is precisely the function of religion to bring man into the presence of the everlasting and real.** But since religion is not isolated from the rest of our mental life, there will be changes in every living religious system, in its

* The problem of personnel is considered more fully in Chapter XIII.
** It is the folly of "modernism," so-called, to overlook this, the most important aspect of religious truth.

symbolical and imaginative expression, and in its adjustment to the developing body of scientific truth, as the rest of our world-view changes.

Of all changes in the world, a theological change will bear most directly upon the missionary motive. If the conception of hell changes, if attention is drawn away from the fear of God's punitive justice in the everlasting torment of the unsaved, to happier conceptions of destiny, if there is a shift of concern from other-worldly issues to the problems of sin and suffering in the present life, these changes will immediately alter that view of the perils of the soul which gave to the original motive of Protestant missions much of its poignant urgency.

Generally speaking, these changes have occurred: Western Christianity has in the main shifted its stress from the negative to the affirmative side of its message; it is less a religion of fear and more a religion of beneficence. It has passed through and beyond the stage of bitter conflict with the scientific consciousness of the race over details of the mode of creation, the age of the earth, the descent of man, miracle and law, to the stage of maturity in which a free religion and a free science become inseparable and complementary elements in a complete world-view. Whatever its present conception of the future life, there is little disposition to believe that sincere and aspiring seekers after God in other religions are to be damned: it has become less concerned in any land to save men from eternal punishment than from the danger of losing the supreme good.

b. The emergence of a world-culture. At the opening of our period there were many cultures, and the cleft between the Orient and the West was especially deep. But the impact of the West on the East has ceased to be the intrusion of an alien civilization. There never was that complete contrast which romantic writers and statesmen liked to imagine. It is now recognized throughout the Orient that there are sciences and arts, originating in the West, which are the Orient's own, in the sense that like mathematics they are not local in their nature but universal, the natural property of the human mind.

The East has therefore begun its own work of selection, distinguishing between civilization and western civilization. The result is the establishment of certain common properties in science, technology, trade, literature, art, as the basis of city life the world over; and through the spread of literacy, with the agencies of news-transmission, these are gradually becoming the property of the villagers of the world as well. The basic fund of common experience, the stuff of human brotherhood, assumes a steady growth.

Elements of democracy and of belief in general education appear in every nation. The extreme diversities in standards of living are challenged and must diminish by degrees. Women in every land become an active part of its mental and social resources. In problems of livelihood, production and distribution, the statesman and the economic scientist join forces, seeking principles of world-wide application.

With this attitude toward the problems of society, including those of the family, of health, of population, there goes a loosening of the authority of mere custom. Superstition disappears upon simple contact with the rational habit conveyed by this world-culture. There is a real danger that the sound elements of tradition will be discarded with its abuses, and that nothing will be adequate to take the place of the restraints of the older cultures, which however misconceived, at least maintained a social order.

There is a tendency for this world-culture to commit itself to secularism. If science and industry, or if the dictates of economy, are assumed to supply all that is needed in the guidance of life, as in certain varieties of Marxian doctrine, secularism is the consequence. But this result is neither inherent in the drift of world-culture, nor, in the main, likely to prevail in any country we visited. There is in all these countries an interest in the ethical elements of social order, a disposition to give those elements an important place in general education. There is also generally speaking an openness of mind to the view that whatever is valid in morals needs something of the nature of religion to give it full effect in the human will. In many quarters one finds the idea expressed that this religious

ingredient will not be identical with any of the positive religions now offering themselves; that there is a simpler, more universal, less contentious and less expressive religion coming into
human consciousness which might be called the religion of the
modern man, the religious aspect of the coming world-culture.

These changes have in their sum a decided bearing upon
the value of foreign missions. Many elements of progress formerly dependent on mission effort are now more effectively promoted by other agencies. Science and the scientific habit of mind
dispel superstition more certainly and finally than does the mission. The spread of education, the emergence of womanhood,
the promotion of general concern for the lot of the common
man, all these are now taken up in some degree by various secular and general interests or by other religions. The question
arises whether these agencies, now working together with the
mission, can or should in time displace it.

On the religious field, the missionary is under necessity of
presenting his case with much fuller mental equipment. He
has to address minds sophisticated in regard to religion, not
amenable any longer to the authoritative mode of approach,
even when this is enforced by distinguished personal qualities.
He must be prepared to deal with the critical thinking whose
outcome is secularism, and what is perhaps even more severe
a test, with the thinking which tends to the simple non-
partisan religion of the modern man.

With these changes there arises also a renewal of the question why the missionary need leave his home to convey his
message. The old impediments to communication are gone;
travel for purposes of inquiry is abundant; students from
Asia penetrate the western world; there is no important idea
which is not now an item of world-knowledge, including the
knowledge of the Gospel. And as for that concrete and personal
illustration of the meaning of religion, which so far exceeds
the mere statement of doctrine, Asia has now the facilities and
the disposition to go to Christian lands and gain, with perhaps more natural exemplification, the spirit of what it desires. Many of her Christian leaders are now so bred, an alter-

native which could not have been foreseen by the early Protestant missions. It is to be noted that the world-culture of which we speak now propagates itself; it is taken because it is consciously wanted; its influence widens in spite of a highly critical attitude to things western, and any deliberate effort to "sell" it would work against its acceptance. There is reason to believe that the spread of religion is in a different case, and requires different methods; but to many contemporary minds the burden of proof seems to rest upon the missions.

The general drift of these changes is certainly not to enhance the value of the foreign mission, and certainly not to cancel it. It is to require a sharpened definition of that function, to call for a higher standard of qualification, and to make evident the temporary character of many services which missions have rendered. It places clearly upon the defensive much of the mediocre work which is now proceeding upon momentum without regard to the changes in the mental and spiritual environment.

c. *The rise of nationalism in the East.* While the nationalism of the East is being developed in more or less deliberate reaction against western domination and cultural control, it has ceased to be hostile to the spread of world-culture, and may even be considered a phase of that movement, inasmuch as national distinctness is one of the characters of the modern world. There was a period when this was not realized, and the growing national feeling tried to preserve itself by antagonism to the flood of international idea and practice. The Boxer Rebellion in China may be considered the last serious act of such resistance. The newer nationalism is inclusive, not exclusive; it has learned to take what is universal, not as western, but as its own, and upon this basis to cultivate and strengthen its own distinctive tradition and art. Hence the oriental states are, or are becoming, self-conscious and self-directing members of the world-community.

There is a natural exaggeration in the national temper, which can hardly be expected to disappear until the desired self-sufficiency in economic as well as political and cultural matters becomes much more nearly realized. This exaggeration, rendering these lands supersensitive toward any formal dependence upon the West, also leads, on the part of many influential spirits, to a crying up and stimulation of local goods, philosophies, arts, religions, literatures—an important development, which may recover some of the losses due to the period of self-deprecation which marked the first contact with the West. With it, however, has come a disconcerting consciousness of the defects of western culture, much sharpened by the Great War, and a much more critical attitude toward our institutions, our democracy, our education. The failure of Christianity to dominate our economic and political life has brought about widespread skepticism regarding the value of our religious professions, if not of our religion itself.

Under these circumstances, the connection of Christianity with western life, formerly a matter of prestige, now has its disadvantages. For the sake of securing for Christianity a fair hearing it is necessary to separate it, as far as possible, from *our* history and our promoting agencies and to present it in its universal capacity.

4. *Temporary and Permanent Functions*

What is the total incidence of these changes upon the work of missions?

The fundamental motive, the imperative of sharing whatever certainties we have in the field of religion, remains. The changes we have noted tend, with one exception, to lessen the apparent need, and certainly the insistent urgency of haste, of the work of the foreign preacher and philanthropist.

That exception which has appeared to some to call for increased mission activity, is the danger of the loss of traditional restraints as the spread of world-culture undermines the sanctions of ancient custom and religion. The problem is real and imminent: a true and profound insight into the religious bases of social order should be genuinely helpful, if it were to be had, and were ready to meet the mind of Asia on its own ground. It must be remembered, however, that the forces which now discredit the old religions are tending to discredit all historical religion; that Christianity, as such, has still the disadvantage of a foreign tinge, and that the ethical situations to be relieved, such as are involved in the dissolution of the ancient family system, require a more intimate sympathy with the spirit of local life than our missionaries usually have or than can easily be gained by any visitor. It will require far more than the indication of a need of this kind, momentous as it is, to furnish an argument for the continuance of foreign missions, unless there is carefully considered change in the outlook and preparation of missionaries.

The other changes all tend to remind us that a mission, by definition, is intrinsically temporary.

A mission is presumably charged with a specific undertaking; that work may be finished. In the case of a religious mission, its Gospel may be proclaimed, its centers of religious life established. The time comes when these centers must be left to develop according to the genius of the place.

If the object of the mission were to be conceived in terms of a total conversion of Asia to Christian membership, the achievement would be indefinitely remote. In our belief, such an objective is an improper one for any foreign group. The "foreign" mission must regard as its task the planting of a seed, not the final growth of a tree.

In the nature of the case, it is peculiarly difficult to discern the right moment for this transfer of initiative. The missions themselves are at a disadvantage for perceiving it, inasmuch as their occupation and mental bent make them perpetually aware of new types of good work to be done, which call for indefinite expansion. Further, as a large undertaking, comprising thousands of careers naturally pressing forward within it to continuance and growth, it would not be surprising if the mission body tended to be self-preserving and self-developing in its view of its future functions. In spite of these facts, we have found not a few missionaries and mission administrators who believe that the time for this transition, in the countries visited, is within sight. This is sometimes interpreted as a defeatist temper. In our opinion, it is the reverse.

We believe, with this group, that the time of transition is now foreseeable. We do not mean that this moment is now here in any country; it is near in Japan; it is more remote in China and in India. Further, it is differently timed for different aspects of mission work in every land: some parts of this work should doubtless go forward, while other parts may be transferred. We mean simply that the time has now arrived, hastened no doubt by the events we have recounted, for preparing the future transition.

We would define this transition, not in terms of retirement nor primarily in terms of "devolution," but as a *change from the temporary to the permanent functions* of these representatives of Christianity in foreign lands.

For there is a permanent function of promoting world understanding on the spiritual level, a function which increases rather than diminishes in importance as civilization becomes more complex. The role of religion in establishing a civilization and in keeping it sound is not fully understood; but that it has such a role is now generally recognized. The development of true religion has become a matter of conscious and public concern in all civilized countries, including those we have visited. And in this development, there is an earnest desire to hear the voice of Christianity.

We cannot hesitate to respect the equally strong desire that growth in true religion shall not mean spiritual dependence on foreign thought or institutions. It is our part to relieve the consideration of Christianity from this handicap, and to present it for judgment on its merits. We must maintain the point of view of world-culture, and the common need of mankind. Temporary in the animus of missions is the presumption that the great and imminent need is solely on the side of the receiving land. It is incumbent upon us to acknowledge, without blindness to the special problems of Asia, our common need of salvation, the common drag toward paganism and indifference, an incomplete grasp of our own faith in matters affecting individual and social conscience, our need to confer in the search for a deeper view of religious truth.

On such a basis, there is no country in which men and women who can vigorously express the meaning of Christianity in life and in word will not be welcomed, and able to make invaluable contribution to the creation of the ideals for the next generation. We need look forward to no time when the authentic spirit of Christ, if freed from hampering organizational purposes, will be an undesired visitor in any land. It can be recognized by non-Christians as well as by Christians; which is one reason for suggesting that such representatives should be selected in part by invitation.

We conceive, then, a change in the conception of the foreign mission, in which functions and methods appropriate in earlier days shall gradually give place to permanent functions and methods. In the era of church-planting, it was natural that many persons of various degrees of equipment should be sent from abroad, aggressively promoting the local church; it was natural, too, that with a strong sense of the superiority and sufficiency of their own culture they should have tried to sever all association on the part of their converts with old custom, thought and religion. In the coming era, which might be pictured as an era of foreign service or ambassadorship, it will be natural, rather, to maintain in foreign lands a relatively few highly equipped persons, acceptable to those lands as representing the Christian way of thought and life, holding themselves ready to give advice and counsel whether to the local church or to other leaders of religion and thought, sympathetically concerned with the problems of changing local culture, and trying to minimize the strains of an abrupt breach with tradition. During the period of transition, there will be not only much thinking but much experimenting to be done, in bringing a religious outlook to bear on the problems of social life; and there will probably be no time in which the participation of the mission in such experiment will not have its place. It will also be a permanent function to maintain some institutions for the higher study and interpretation of Christian civilization, serving as liaison with scholarly interpreters of the Orient.

Whether this change in the conception of the mission should involve a change of name, as to one suggesting the foreign service of the Church, we need not advise: words will acquire their own connotations. But there can be nothing temporary in the need for the health of the Church that it have a permanent and even growing international function. The loss of the ideal of the Church universal, and of the place of continued labor and sacrifice for that object, would mean the sterility of the Church. On the other hand, the type of intercourse we view as permanent should mean not alone the continuous enlivening of the churches at home and abroad through conversation with each other, but also the promotion of world unity through a spread of the understanding of the vital elements of all religion.

The conception of these permanent functions will develop as our discussion proceeds: a closer study of the relation between the mission and its environment of other religions will throw further light on them. It may be useful here to draw up in a schematic and therefore somewhat artificial form a contrast between the two conceptions, emphasizing the fact that it is not a question of abruptly displacing one by the other, but of a growing of one into the other. (See following page.)

Temporary Functions | Permanent Functions
Church planting | *Foreign service; ambassadorship*

1. Sending many persons of various equipment to preach widely so that the message shall have been heard.

        1. Maintaining a relatively few highly equipped persons, representing the Christian way of thought and life, acceptable to or invited by the foreign land.

2. Aggressively promoting the local church through efforts actuated from the home churches.

        2. Standing at the service of the local church for advice and counsel, as well as of other leaders of thought and religion.

3. Expounding single-mindedly the Christianity and culture of the West; and tending to sever converts from old contexts in order to establish a distinctive body of local Christians.

        3. Studying sympathetically the problems of the changing local culture; trying to preserve what is valuable in the past of the people, and to minimize the dangers of abrupt break with tradition.

4. Carrying on educational and medical work primarily as a means of evangelizing and building up the Christian community.

        4. Carrying on pioneer and experimental work in education, medicine, rural development and other social applications of the Christian view of life, primarily in view of the emerging needs of the foreign land.

5. Training nationals as leaders who will in time replace the missionaries.

        5. Maintaining institutions for the study and interpretation of Christian civilization, of philosophy, theology, comparative religion, both for the higher training of qualified Christians, and as places of liaison with scholarly inquirers and interpreters of the Orient.

        6. Seeking through such intercourse a deeper grasp of the meaning of Christianity; promoting world unity through the spread of the universal elements of religion; enlivening the churches at home and abroad through rapport with each other.

CHAPTER II

CHRISTIANITY, OTHER RELIGIONS AND NON-RELIGION

AT THE beginning of our century of Protestant missions, Christianity found itself addressing men attached to other religions: its argument was with these religions. At present, it confronts a growing number of persons, especially among the thoughtful, critical of or hostile to all religion. Its further argument, we judge, is to be less with Islam or Hinduism or Buddhism than with materialism, secularism, naturalism. The growth of this third factor, non-religion, alters the relation of the other two: Christianity and the environing religions face at the same moment the same menace, the spread of the secular spirit; the former opponents have become to this extent allied by the common task. It is not surprising if our missions find this realignment difficult, perhaps embarrassing; it compels a thorough re-analysis of the purpose of missions in reference to other faiths. Let us first note how this situation has come about.

1. Growth Within the Mission

In returning, much altered in aspect, to the continent of its origin, Christianity was not approaching lands barren of religion. They were lands, not alone the ancient birthplace of great religions, but until recent times, sources of new religious movements. In all of them to this day religion is naturally a theme of ordinary conversation, the devotion of lives to religion usual and honored, the willing acceptance of privation and suffering in pursuit of religious experience prevalent. The very multiplicity of gods, temples, places of pilgrimage, observances, might serve as a rough index of the large place of religious themes in the daily life of these peoples. Their backwardness in terms of science and its applications was due

29

in no small part to this preoccupation. Our own type of civilization, when oriental peoples came to know it, appeared to them as material and secular in comparison. They were, like the Athenians whom Paul addressed, "very religious", and in much the same sense.

Our missionaries did not at first approach them with the Pauline tact or understanding, by picking up the thread of their religious quest, and carrying it on to a further stage. They were repelled by the external strangeness, the plural gods, the idols, the devious elements of superstition, fear, baseness, priestly corruption. If there was a lotus arising from the slime, they were not sensitized to perceive it—that was not their business. It was their defined charge to win souls from this context to a new discipleship, and to create a church.

Their attitude had all the strength of single-mindedness and clear-cut challenge; it saved a quantity of toil in examining the precise nature of the situation from which men were being rescued. It was sufficient to be sure of one's own ground without cumbering one's mind with the endless variety of error into which uninspired human ingenuity could stray. "If any man be in Christ, he is a new creature," presumably also a transplantable creature whose best attitude to his own past is a clean breach. It was advisable, at times imperative, to remove the convert to the mission compound, where he could be protected from molestation, and where his habits could be remade from the ground up, on the pattern of the western-Christian modes of living.

This clean-breach method, experience has now amply shown mistaken. Its uncompromising attitude toward local tradition, social scheme, religion, required heroism in the convert and found its heroes. But its cost in human suffering was like the cost of mediaeval surgery, and its results were mixed with failure. It was a cruel pedagogy, which required pruning down to the stalk the earlier growths of the spirit, and checking the momentum of an ancient current of life. If a new idea is to take sturdy root it should make a maximum use of whatever kindred ideas have been there before: the life that begins with an amputation can seldom reach full vigor. Further, the dependence on the mission produced by this system could hardly be overcome. For the made-over individual was out of working relation with the rest of his society. The mission was forced to assume some responsibility for his livelihood and even for his marriage within the Christian group. The position of these uprooted Christians was the more unhappy since their tutors in the faith were seldom inclined to admit them to social equality.* They were commonly brought from the lower walks of their own society into a new self-respect; but with this came also a new subordination, inconsistent with the growth of leadership. The missions have gone far in reading these lessons—farther in Japan and China than in India—and in revising their procedure.

But the central lesson they were slower to read, though they might have been led to it by their own faith that God has not anywhere left himself without a witness. It was hard for the missions to mix with their absorbing interest in rebirth a practical recognition that the surrounding religions were religions, and as such were ways to God. Their very compassion led them to hold these "false" religions responsible for the defects of oriental society and custom, the counterpart of an equally hasty social theory which made Christianity responsible for all the advantages they felt in western life. Nevertheless, this same humanity of spirit was bound in time to make its own observations: there was the genuine piety of many a soul around them, and an occasional life of distinguished spiritual quality whose sources were worthy of consideration and respect. The conviction makes its way that here also there must be something to build upon, and something to understand, if one is to speak to the soul of Asia.

But further, the mission is impelled by the requirements of simple truth. For after all, "we *are* brothers in a common quest, and the first step is to recognize it, and disarm ourselves of our prejudices."** It is a matter of truth: not because the

---

* Except in Japan, where our missions came late (1859) and for a time on suffrance of a strong government. Notice boards prohibiting Christian preaching were not removed until 1873.
** C. B. Olds of Okayama, "A Venture in Understanding."

assertion of likeness, where likeness exists, is any truer than the assertion of the difference that also exists. But because, having, by long habit, been dwelling on points of contrast, the mission requires a special leaning to reach the point of justice. Moreover, it takes a determined effort, armed both with sympathy and with analysis, to see through the diversities of language, of symbol, of observance, to the identities of meaning. This effort has long been incumbent upon us: it speaks but sadly for the candor and perspicacity of this present religious age that these barriers of expression, all but banished in the scientific unity of mankind, should still hold kindred spirits apart in the field of religion.

2. *Changes in Non-Christian Religions*

While this slow change of attitude has been going on within the mission, the environment of other-religion has itself undergone momentous changes. The Hinduism, Islam, Buddhism of today are not those of a hundred years ago.

They have been stirred, and no doubt stung, by the presence of an aggressively critical Christian movement. They have responded not merely by defensive argument or counter criticism, but by various movements of internal reform. Other reforms have been undertaken in entire independence of Christianity.

These religions have been further and more deeply shaken by all the events connected with the spread of world-culture. The scientific and critical temper of that culture is in a peculiar degree deadly to their authority. What becomes of the issues between the merits of one sacred text and another when the sacredness of all texts is being denied? Why compare Mohammed and Buddha, when all the utterances of religious intuition are threatened with discard in the light of practical reason? It is no longer, Which prophet? or Which book? It is whether any prophet, book, revelation, rite, church, is to be trusted. All the old oracles are seeing a new sign: the scorn on the faces of students who know the experiments in anti-religion in Russia and non-religion in Turkey, and the actual religionlessness of much western life. The chief foe of these oracles is not Christianity, but the anti-religious element of the philosophies of Marx, Lenin, Russell. The case that must now be stated is the case for any religion at all.

Those changes in the theological atmosphere which have affected us, come upon these religions far more abruptly, snatching them suddenly from the restful gloom of mediaeval discussions into the harsh demands of the utilitarian day. The ranks of students and initiates thin out. Here and there one detects a note of despair: can the re-orientation be accomplished so swiftly without disaster?

But these problems are not alone the problems of other religions. For since the same world-change has entered the sphere of the Christian Church and of the mission, they, too, must deal with their own question of life and death: they, too, must state the case for any religion at all. Thus it is that Christianity finds itself in point of fact aligned in this world-wide issue with the non-Christian faiths of Asia. It is an alignment which creates no new truths and solves no problems of religious difference. It simply shows how necessary it has become for every religion to be aware of and to stand upon the common ground of all religion.

3. *Creative Relationship Emerging*

There are thus several factors conspiring to one end: namely, *the necessity that the modern mission make a positive effort, first of all to know and understand the religions around it, then to recognize and associate itself with whatever kindred elements there are in them.*

Vigorous beginnings of this process are now taking place in various parts of Asia. The following account of the opening of "A Venture in Understanding" will indicate better than any words of ours the sort of change, initiative and discovery that is involved:

"An effort that we are making in this direction here in Okayama is worthy of attention I believe, not so much for what it has accomplished as for the evidence it gives that a new attitude is developing. It has grown out of the belief that we all, Christians, Buddhists, Shintoists, or whatever other faith, have much to learn from each other and much to contribute to each other. Also we feel that if we spiritual leaders are to accomplish anything constructive for the good of society as a whole we ought first to get together as religionists and come to know each other sympathetically.

"With the conviction that this could be done, I set out first, then, simply to get acquainted with some of the best representatives of the several religious sects that were operating in our city or its immediate vicinity. I called first on the leading priest of the Shin sect, visiting him in his temple, where we had a delightful conference together for two hours or more regarding the deeper spiritual values of our lives. We had not gone far in our talk together before it became evident to me that here, so far as I was concerned, was an unworked mine of spiritual possibilities, and, so far as he was concerned, a readiness, yes, a hunger, for something more than he had yet got. Thinking there must be others like him also, I at length, with some hesitation, suggested the possibility and the desirability of our getting together, a few earnest spirits of us from the different sects of the several religions represented in the community, with the frank and avowed purpose of sharing with each other as friends the deepest spiritual experiences of our lives as they had come to us through our several religious faiths. The suggestion met with his instant approval, and thereupon we together formulated a plan and made out a list of those who might well be brought into such a group. They must be kindred spirits, not argumentative, not intrenched in prejudice, for all discussions must be on the plane of experience rather than of dogmatism or theory, and there must be no furtive effort at propaganda. Everyone must be honest with himself, not surrendering his faith or softening down his convictions, but outspoken and sincere, holding to what he believed to be the truth and ready to declare it, and yet maintaining a tolerant and open mind. Those were hard conditions to fulfill, so our men had to be chosen carefully. But we made out our list; one each from five of the leading Buddhist sects in Japan, since all happened to have representatives in Okayama,—Shinshu, Shingon, Zen, Tendai, and Nichiren,—and besides them, one pure Shintoist and three Christians of whom one is a well-known pastor and social worker, one a prominent layman, equally well-known and respected, and myself, an American missionary.

"I then proceeded, as I found time, to call on the men whom we had listed, visiting each in his temple or home or office, and in every case I was most cordially received, everyone of them with undisguised enthusiasm acceding to our invitation to join the group."

4. *The Ultimate Issues*

The direction of growth, here indicated, may appear so natural that the extent of the implied change of attitude is not realized. Our account has not yet brought forward the most powerful of the reasons which have inspired the long hesitation, namely this: that the friendly recognition of other faiths means to many Christians in the mission fields and at home an essential disloyalty, a compromise with error, and a surrender of the uniqueness of Christianity. Not to examine their position would leave our work unfinished.

The original objective of the mission might be stated as the conquest of the world by Christianity: it was a world benevolence conceived in terms of a world campaign. There was one way of salvation and one only, one name, one atonement: this plan with its particular historical center in the career of Jesus must become the point of regard for every human soul. The universal quality of Christianity lay not alone in its valid principles of truth and morals, but in an essential paradox, the universal claim of one particular historic fact: the work of Christ. General principles may be reasoned out, and perhaps proved, so that all men must accept them. But particular facts cannot be proved: they must be recognized. Hence, in respect to its central fact Christianity was necessarily dogmatic—it could only say *Ecce Homo,* Behold the Man; and it was committed to a certain intolerance, beneficent in purpose—in the interest of the soul it could allow no substitute for Christ. It came to proclaim truth, which is universal; but its truth was embodied in a particular person and his work.

With respect to the religiousness of other religions, this quality was not so much questioned as held of doubtful value. In the field of religion, it was felt, the only strong and lasting power is the power in which truth is clearest. An obscurer version might become just the betrayal of the whole cause. There was undoubted piety and virtue at the heart of the Russian Church; yet these virtues did not save it from that cleansing of the Augean stables which was due, and "religion" was condemned with the corrupt organization. If in the Orient, the word "religion" to the coming generation is to mean Hinduism or Buddhism, perhaps the whole affair will be relegated to the dust heap; perhaps this is precisely what is happening. In that case, the hope would be that Christianity, instead of tying itself to the sinking hulks, would hold itself clear and give a distinctive version of what religion, in its purity, may mean.

It is through such reflections that those in the mission field who now face toward tolerance and association have their own qualms. They feel, and their critics feel still more keenly, that the presentiment of impending re-orientation introduces an element of uncertainty or hesitation into the whole enterprise. If we fraternize or accept the fellowship of the alien faith, what becomes of the original hope that Christianity will bring the world under its undivided sway? If that objective is surrendered, has not the nerve of the mission motive itself been cut?

Personal uncertainties are reflected in group divisions in the field: there is a party of advance toward fraternity which feels the drag and insulation of the right wing; there is this party of the right, conservative and loyal, which feels the overtures of the liberals toward the ex-enemy as a treasonable abandonment of the cause.

5. *The Principle of Growth*

In meeting this problem, we may at the outset point out one principle which all may accept. The more of religious insight there is in any group of mankind, the more favorable the conditions are for one who has further insight to contribute. It is not what is weak or corrupt but what is strong and sound in the non-Christian religions that offers the best hearing for whatever Christianity may have to say.* Christianity first appeared within Judaism, and spread first among those who were well prepared for its teachings.

If there were not at the core of all the creeds a nucleus of religious truth, neither Christianity nor any other faith would have anything to build on. Within the piety of the common people of every land, encrusted with superstition as it usually is, and weighed down with vulgar self-seeking in their bargainings with the gods, there is this germ, the inalienable religious intuition of the human soul. The God of this intuition is the true God: to this extent universal religion has not to be established, it exists.

Upon this theme, the great religions have made their elaborations. They have mixed true discernment with much vagrant imagination: but there is no doubt that they have used the real foundation and have made, on the whole, genuine advances. Confucianism in Japan improved upon primitive Shinto, contributing order, rationality, social definition; Buddhism adds to both a greater cosmic depth and a more searching appeal to the motives of the heart. Christianity, however unique its message, has nothing to gain by disparaging the degree of this progress. So far from taking satisfaction in moribund or decadent conditions where they exist within other faiths, Christianity may find itself bound to aid these faiths, and frequently does aid them, to a truer interpretation of their own meaning than they had otherwise achieved.

This seems to us peculiarly the case in China, where the life of the older religions in the main runs low, and where many

* Note the illustration, p. 34.

of the spokesmen of national feeling are beginning to adopt
and proclaim the view that the Chinese as a people are temperamentally matter-of-fact, secular-minded, ethical rather than
religious. We venture to believe that Christianity will not be
strong in China until it penetrates more deeply into those
special needs of the Chinese spirit which these older religions
have met. The fate of religion in China, in any time we can
now foresee, depends chiefly on the fate of these religions: for
it is they that to this people must long continue to represent
their sacred history. We can reach the hundred thousands, but
not the hundred millions except through their media. The
great need of China is for interpreters capable of perceiving
its deep-running spiritual life, and with all else that they
bring, laboring with infinite patience and love to preserve the
treasures within the old inheritance.

In general, to recognize the best is to strengthen the best.
For whatever is genuine in the non-Christian religions, the
consistent and the auspicious attitude for the Christian teacher
is not alone acknowledgment, but an earnest desire to make
the most of it, not the least. But this principle leaves three
questions unanswered: What shall be the attitude of Christianity toward the errors of non-Christian religions? What
toward their borrowings from Christianity and their new
growth? What of the uniqueness of Christianity and of its
message to the Orient? We shall discuss the first two of these
questions in the present chapter, the third in the chapter
following.

6. The Attitude Toward Error

a. The errors. In all the great religious systems of Asia one
learns to make distinctions—and is prepared to find them very
wide—between the religion of the people, the religion of the
priestly class and of the professional holy men, the religion
of the scholars and reformers, and the religion of the intelligent laity. Of these, the religion of the priesthood is in general the least edifying: there are always exceptional men, but
the priestly average is not much better instructed nor more

spiritual than it is required to be by the intelligence and conscience of the public with which it deals. And except in Japan, the requirements of the mass of the people are those of an uninstructed peasantry. The priesthood has a vested interest in the maintenance of all the beliefs which sustain the observances of the temples: it is recruited and trained with these observances chiefly in view. If the religion is a state religion, its priests will be also trained with a semi-political role in view, almost invariably resulting in the degradation of religion. There is many a Hindu scholar who has no personal contact with the worship of the temples. There are Buddhist monasteries in China and Japan where the business of the temple is in another world, mentally, from the adjacent business of the library, the school and the hall of meditation. As long as Asia may be obliged to accept for its peasant masses the twin curses of poverty and ignorance, so long must we expect to find the third curse, the unspiritual priest.

It is always possible that the right attitude toward an ecclesiastical system, as distinguished from the religion it frames, may be one of clear hostility. There are times when the policy of implacable antagonism is the way of true friendship to the religious interest itself. The decision will depend in each case on the degree of health within the system. In Hinduism, the power of the priestly class and its general influence are probably more deplorable than those of the corresponding class in the old regimes of Russia and Turkey. The motives for purging the temples are proportionately great. But there is a question for the Christian at this point: Is he the qualified and appointed judge?

He has to remember first of all that there are forces within Indian life occupied with just this problem, laboring with competence and understanding for reform from within. He must consider that no great system lives through the centuries on the strength of its diseases, but on the strength of some fitness to the total civilization: until he has thought through this function he should hesitate to adopt an iconoclastic view. It would be a sad error of judgment if, at the moment of a strong and promising movement of internal renovation, the

Christian Church should aim at destroying or displacing the old structure.

It is clearly not the duty of the Christian missionary to attack the non-Christian systems of religion. Nor is it his primary duty to denounce the errors and abuses he may see in them: it is his primary duty to present in positive form his conception of the true way of life and let it speak for itself. Nevertheless, it is more respectful to non-Christians, as men, to criticize plainly whatever deserves criticism, especially when it touches the kernel of the religious life, than it is to be silent. Gandhi has recently said "My fierce hatred of child marriage I gladly say is due to Christian influence . . . Before I knew anything of Christianity, I was an enemy of untouchability . . . My feelings gathered momentum owing to the fierce attack from Christian sources on this evil." What is necessary is that the missionary should realize that in his criticism he is joining Hindus in rectifying abuses which have invaded the structure of their religion. And further, that the Hindu can do far more toward any such reform than can he, the Christian, as an outsider. The Christian view may aid in resolving a Gandhi to an act of mercy in the slaughter of a suffering cow: but Gandhi's deed will do more to revise Hindu custom than all the criticisms of all the Christians.

The Christian will therefore regard himself a co-worker with the forces which are making for righteousness within every religious system. If he can in any way aid or encourage these forces, he will regard it a part of his Christian service to spend thought and energy in this way.

Desiring to be considered a co-worker rather than an enemy, he will especially refrain from misrepresentation abroad of the evils he desires to cure, and more particularly from dwelling on these evils without mentioning also the efforts being made by nationals to correct them.

7. Superstition

The problem of "superstition" deserves a special note: for to many minds this word summarizes the evils which, in the mission fields, Christianity is especially called to combat. And, unquestionably, if one were to assemble the superstitions of the world the peasantries of Asia, together with the Christian peasantries of Europe, would furnish a rich array. It is important to gain a clear concept of superstition, and then to recognize that superstition is not a peculiarity of any special type or tradition in religion: it is a phenomenon of a low stage of general enlightenment and attends every religion in such stages.

Superstition is the reliance on spiritual forces to do work proper to physical forces; it is a degradation of the spiritual to the level of the mechanical; it is a gratuitous invitation of conflict between religion and science; it is an illegitimate expectation of, or belief in, miracle, a faith in occult or magical connections between circumstances (like numbers, acts, days) and human fortunes not casually related thereto. It applies to meaningless taboos, to the special potencies of material objects and places as charm or shrine, and to acts of petition designed to bring the divine power into the service of the petitioner's personal advantage.

At present the most effective influence combating superstition is the spread of general enlightenment, especially of the scientific habit of mind in the treatment of disease, in agriculture, in dealing with personal and political fortune. This has been the case in the history of Christianity, and will be true in other traditions.*

Christianity can aid in the struggle to eliminate superstition from its own and other systems

* It is especially true in China, where the scientific consciousness has in historic times been little cultivated. In the great Confusian renaissance of the Twelfth and Thirteenth Centuries, with its slogan "Go to the things and study their causes," the only significant research was historical and philological—humanistic in the literary sense. China has made many remarkable observations on natural phenomena, and many of the great inventions, but has produced no single scientific treatise. This lack of theory has restricted the development of her marvellous discoveries. And the primitive state of scientific thought (due to an exclusively literary training) has retarded the maturity of religion. Without strong science, no strong religion.

1. By promoting the scientific habit of mind, and demonstrating its own fearlessness in presence of science;*

2. By making clear what the function of religion is, in completing the unfinished world-view of science, adding the element of value and meaning which science, taken alone, would omit;

3. By working with enlightened members of all faiths for a non-superstitious conception of providence and prayer.

8. *The Attitude Toward Reform*

b. Growth in non-Christian religions: borrowings. Whenever two vigorous religions are in contact, each will tend to borrow from the other—terms, usages, ideas, even gods and articles of faith. After centuries of such borrowing they show strong resemblances, like Taoism and Buddhism in China, while holding to some precious points of difference. Commonly the borrowing is without acknowledgment: each religion takes what it can use from the other, or from the common fund of popular usage, and gives it a turn and a derivation suited to its own history. So Christianity in its early days adopted Christmas tree, or Yule festival, or imagery from the mysteries, or philosophical tools from the stock of Greece and Rome. Sometimes the new acquisitions are merely set up outside or loaded into the general warehouse without logical regard to what is already there: Hinduism has frequently added to its inner variety in this way. Sometimes they take root and grow on the existing stock, because they belong there by natural stages of advance.

In the presence of Christianity, it is not surprising that the living religions of the East should grow in this way, especially Hinduism and Buddhism. They are not as a rule averse to acknowledging the debt, even while claiming that what they borrow is their own by right. In this way, little by little, much of Christianity is assimilated by these religions without calling it Christianity. Not merely modes of worship, preaching,

* Prof. Carter Speers' laboratory in Lahore is an effective illustration of this point.

Sunday schools, hymns, popular fables, but aspects of the conception of God, ethical notions, the honoring of Christ, may be taken over.

What should be the attitude of the Christian mission to this process? At best, it would appear to be a striking success of its own work: a transfer of the substance apart from the name. With what are we concerned except for the spread through the world of what Christianity *means*?

Nevertheless, there are misgivings. In part from a fear that the adoption will be imitative, unreal, or half-understood, leaving men satisfied with what resembles Christianity without its reality. In part from a very different fear, namely, that the adoption will be real as far as it goes, the non-Christian religion thereby receive new vigor, the contrast between it and Christianity be lessened, the motives which have led its members to come over into the Christian fellowship correspondingly minimized. Those who feel this latter fear are evidently thinking in terms of competition. We have in mind a missionary who defines the God of Islam as a God of power, whereas the Christian God is a God of love. He is accordingly disturbed when he finds a Moslem teaching that the compassion of Allah is the same as the love of God: he inclines to cry plagiarism! and to warn all Moslems that the idea of God as loving Father is Christian and private property!

The situation is particularly pointed in Japan, where Buddhism with a keen, aggressive, well-equipped leadership shows the greatest readiness to appropriate Christian ideas and practices. If this means an advance in true religion among the Japanese people, how can the Christian have anything but welcome for the result? Yet the numerical advance of the Christian organization is retarded by this very success: hence there enters an element of rivalry. To those primarily interested in the extension of church membership, this growth within Buddhism is likely to be read as a challenge calling for something like a counter-aggression. Concern for the institution here threatens to part company with concern for the souls of men.

It is time for the Christian movement to have overcome these unworthy fears springing from a sense of proprietorship.

The unique thing in Christianity is not borrowable nor transferable without the transfer of Christianity itself. Whatever can be borrowed and successfully grown on another stock does in fact belong to the borrower. For a part of the life of any living religion is its groping for a better grasp of truth. The truth which rectifies the faults of any religious system is already foreshadowed in its own search. Hence all fences and private properties in truth are futile: the final truth, whatever it may be, is the New Testament of every existing faith.

We desire the triumph of that final truth: we need not prescribe the route. It appears probable that the advance toward that goal may be by way of the immediate strengthening of several of the present religions of Asia, Christian and non-Christian together. The Christian who would be anxious in view of such a result displays too little confidence in the merits of his own faith. Whatever is unique in it, and necessary to the highest religious life of men can be trusted to show its value in due time and in its own way. Meantime, if through growing appreciation and borrowing, the vitality of genuine religion is anywhere increased he may well rejoice in that fact. He will look forward, not to the destruction of these religions, but to their continued co-existence with Christianity, each stimulating the other in growth toward the ultimate goal, unity in the completest religious truth.

We bear in mind that while, through this process of growth, the several religions become more alike in one way, there is also the process of eliminating superstition and abuse which makes them more alike in another way. The modern spirit is a severe surgeon to much that once characterized these religions: silent and massive alterations of taste among the people are disposing of ancient crudities and indecencies; pious frauds find the sources of their incomes drying up. Just as human sacrifice has gone, and sacred prostitution has all but gone, so other practises become felt to be anachronistic or revolting to common consciousness and vanish from all the cults. The way is long, and a new patience is needed; but we can desire no variety of religious experience to perish until it has yielded up to the rest its own ingredient of truth.

9. *What These Developments Call For*

But there is certainly something to be done by Christianity in the Orient in response to the new growths in the non-Christian religions. We see in it no call for a renewed rivalry or counter-aggression, but rather for something far more difficult, namely, *deepening our grasp of what Christianity actually means*. There is reason for desiring this, in the Orient and at home: for everywhere Christianity is suffering from the poverty, the rigidity, the inertness of the conceptions which Christians have of its significance; everywhere Christians are called upon to search the sources of their own faith. Let us indicate certain ways through which this desire may be realized, and in so doing illustrate more nearly what we conceive emerging as a permanent function of the mission in the modern world.

Almost everyone now agrees that religion cannot be handed on as a finished doctrine, without renewal of insight by those who undertake to transmit it. But the ways of this renewal are various, just as the meaning of Christianity may be realized in different ways, in thought, in application to conduct, in immediate personal experience. None of these ways can be safely omitted.

Christianity, therefore, cannot afford to leave to Buddhism or to Hinduism the arts of meditation. It may well be that Buddhism depends too much on meditation as the way *par excellence* to enlightenment. If so, it is the corresponding error of our Protestant ministry, mission or other, that it depends too much on activity as the way to retain the meaning of its faith. It is one of the strengths of Christianity that it is disposed to run out into action. It expects to be applied. But it has the defect of its strength. Our ministry grows dull by too great business. It forgets, or its institution forgets, the irreplaceable uses of leisure in the search for a new stage of truth.

We would commend to the Christian Church a serious inquiry into the religious value of meditation, and a study of the ways in which a further place for this function can be brought into the Christian life, without falling into the common abuses of monasticism.

One of the securities against an empty mysticism is that, along with meditation (or alternating with it) should go the discipline of thought. If Christianity is to get a better hold on its own meaning, it must make a place for explorative thinking; and the same is true if it is to aid in any work of interpreting other religions. The danger of the time is not merely a failure of spirit, it is as much a failure of ideas and of the power of discrimination. To deal with the problems set by naturalism to all religious world-views, clarity of analysis is essential. To define identities among the religions, and to see where the real issues lie, requires practice in the use of concepts and familiarity with their history. Philosophy is not religion, nor any equivalent therefor: but no religion can do its work in the modern age without all the tools of reflection. Not everyone is obliged to do this special work; but to some of the missionary personnel, and to such oriental Christians as have aptitude for such studies, there should be provided opportunity for advanced work in logic, philosophy, theology, the history of religion. Christianity is not equipped to meet and converse with the religious leaders of the Orient until it can enter competently into their world of thought.

10. *Instituting the Sharing Process*

But perhaps the chief hope for an important deepening of self-knowledge on the part of Christendom is by way of a more thoroughgoing sharing of its life with the life of the Orient. Sharing may mean spreading abroad what one has: but sharing becomes real only as it becomes mutual, running in both directions, each teaching, each learning, each with the other meeting the unsolved problems of both.

That the non-Christian religions do contain elements of instruction for us, imperfect exponents as we are of the truth we have, cannot be doubted. We have just illustrated this in what we have said of meditation. There are many other respects in which we may well be the learners. Buddhism's un-worldliness, in many ways a disadvantage, still represents an ingredient of all true religion, prominent in early and mediaeval Christianity, from which the "social gospel" may become too far estranged. And with it goes an undeviating concern for metaphysical truth which we of the West have been tempted at times to abandon in the interest of "practicality". In this, it may be Buddhism that is truly practical: for it is the depths of the universe which most directly stir the depths of selfhood, and the stability of the inner life is the source of all strength for outer action. It is Zen Buddhism, we remember, a cult of quietude and discipline, which has given to Japan so many strong men in public life.

One great reason for the presence of Christianity in the Orient is an interest in its own developing interpretation, as it could hardly grow in America alone, through free intercourse with various other types of religious experience. The relation between religions must take increasingly hereafter the form of a common search for truth.

It is our view that this function should be in part performed through a type of institution distinct from and supplementary to the present type of teaching mission.

We have in mind the establishment of centers here and there as persons and occasions offer, for the avowed purpose of facilitating such cooperative religious inquiry through give and take between persons of various faiths.* We are not thinking of institutions which bind and hold men together in unions of fixed membership; such institutions exist, and they have a way of going dull. We think rather of places fitted for hospitality toward persons desiring to come and go freely, where men concerned with these themes may meet one another, per-

---

* Germs of such a plan are found in various places. The ashram of India has occasionally, in very simple and natural form, embodied something of this conception. Tagore's institute at Santiniketan and Gandhi's at Sabarmati naturally bring together those concerned to learn of these men; Tagore's ashram includes an especially notable group of scholars. E. Stanley Jones conducts a seasonal ashram. We have spoken of the work of C. B. Olds of Okayama, which has not yet deposited itself in permanent form, but which has the idea and the spirit.

haps live together for a time, eat together, study together, work together, and also have plenty of opportunity for solitary thought and reading. As the function is a natural one, there have always been ways, more or less adequate, of providing for it.* It is now time to do it well.

Doing it well would imply a place where quiet and retreat are possible. At the same time, it might with advantage have a special activity of its own, bringing together a nucleus of permanent personnel. It might be a place of study and research such as we have suggested. But the business of the place would be conversation, ample, repeated, unhurried, with intervals of reflection and work.

Out of these conversations and thoughts there should come, in the first place, a steady growth of mutual understanding and respect among these seekers of various faiths; then that deepening of self-knowledge which is inseparable from a better knowledge of others; and from time to time, as the supreme success, the birth of an idea which shall stir and strengthen religion in the race.

We turn to consider our third problem in this field, the uniqueness of Christianity and its message to the Orient.

* Anticipations of this function may be recognized in certain hospitable activities of Catholic hostels and hospices, and in Buddhist monasteries here and there. They have often maintained in atmospheres tense with authority and finality, not alone the open door for inquirers, but also the open search for truth in live heads and liberal hearts.

CHAPTER III

1. *The Uniqueness of Christianity*

THE uniqueness of Christianity is in no way compromised by the developments we have been describing. To recognize the basis of agreement among the great religions is at the same time to clarify the points of difference. As in personal intercourse individuality is sharpened, so the association of religions in any common cause makes salient the individuality of each.

In respect to its theology and ethics, Christianity has many doctrines in common with other religions, yet no other religion has the same group of doctrines. It would be difficult to point out any one general principle which could surely be found nowhere else. But there is no need—it is a humiliating mistake—for Christianity to contest priority or uniqueness in regard to these general ideas. As we were saying, there is no property here: what is true belongs, in its nature, to the human mind everywhere.

From this treasury of thought, however, Christianity proffers a selection which is unique. The principle of selection is its own peculiar character: its individuality lies in the way in which it assembles and proportions these truths, and lends to them clarity, certainty, exemplification and therefore power. Its features, like the features of a person, are unmistakably its own.

It is of the essence of Christianity that its central teachings are simple.

It was one aspect of the genius of Jesus that amid a rich store of earlier codes and doctrines he discerned what was

49

essential and brought it to brief and forcible expression. The essence of the law he states in the two great commandments; the essence of right conduct in the Golden Rule; the essence of prayer in the Lord's Prayer; the essence of theology in the picture of God as Father; the essence of the social ideal in the vision of the Kingdom of Heaven among men.

Christianity is not an easy teaching; but the qualifications for grasping it, the ear to hear and the will to obey, are primarily moral and were first achieved by untutored fishermen; whereas its difficulties are said to be chiefly for those who, ruled by their possessions or entangled in affairs or befogged by seeming wisdom, find it hard to return to the direct intuitions of childhood.

If, then, the Orient is anywhere unresponsive to our complex theologies (and here we think especially of China), the implication may be not that the Orient is dull toward Christianity, but that these complexities are too little Christian, too much the artifacts of our western brains.

The simplicity of Christianity is a part of its uniqueness.

It is evident that much of the spiritual value of Christianity in the Orient is its power of release from the intricacies which have grown up within the great polytheistic systems. There is a conservative impulse in religion which has its own justification, but which, in retaining primitive practices and ideas, frequently incongruous with one another, accumulates confusion by its very loyalties. This is especially true of Hinduism. The presence of even a small Christian community, holding to its few essentials of religion, ensures that these same essentials will do a persistent work of sifting within these conglomerate traditions of Asia.

The Christianity which thus works silently, by the inherent power of a valid focus, within these ancient bodies presupposes a Christian group which maintains its own distinctness. When simplicity is merged with complexity, simplicity is lost. There must be a group of believers who can illustrate the "pure instance" of an Oriental Christianity.

And further, only a religion whose first principles are capable of the simplest formulation can become a religion for the modern man, whether in the Orient or elsewhere. The religion which assumes too much knowledge of the supernatural realm, its system of heavens and hells, or its inner mechanisms of eternal justice, can no longer be a living issue.

But the uniqueness of Christianity does not consist solely in its interpretation of religious truth. It consists also, perhaps chiefly, in those things which make religion different from all philosophy,—its symbolism, its observances, its historical fellowship, and especially the personal figure to whom it points not alone as founder and teacher, but as its highest expression of the religious life. In these matters Christianity is necessarily unique.

In them it is also rich. The great simplicity of its doctrine is not inconsistent with wealth in symbol, imagery and story. Religion has to speak to the emotions and the will, not to the intellect alone. Further, the historical and imaginative elements of religion are not mere illustrations or adornments of faith; they are parts of its meaning. When religious truth is drained off into a set of propositions divorced from their emotional setting, it is somewhat less than true. The narratives and parables of the Gospel, unique in the sacred literature of the world, have probably influenced the lives of men far more than the exacter formulations of faith.

In general, our Protestant churches, as compared with Roman Catholic and Buddhist have made too little of the concrete and poetic elements of religion, conveyed through all the forms of art, through local setting and ritual expression. To the Oriental this lack is an impediment; for the symbolic and personal expression of religion is his native channel for appreciating it.

Symbols without explanations run to theological mummery; explanations without symbols run to philosophical dry bones.

Into the person of Jesus, as the central symbol as well as the central historic reality of their faith, Christians are prone to compress its entire meaning. Hence it has been customary for Christian bodies in announcing their message to mankind to say compactly, "Our message is Jesus Christ."

This language, full of meaning as it is for those who already know what Jesus stands for, is of course full of mystery for those who do not. To the average Oriental, without further explanation, it could mean nothing. Even to many a contemporary in the West, unused to the language of the churches, it means little more than a current phrase marking loyalty to a tradition somewhat undefined in his thought. In our own effort to present the message of Christianity, we desire to use the privilege of laymen in avoiding as far as possible the language of the unexplained symbol. We believe it to be one of the necessities of the present hour that Christianity should be able to make more immediate connection with common experience and thought. Especially in addressing the Orient it is imperative that we present our faith in terms which those wholly unfamiliar with the history of Christian doctrine can understand.*

2. *The Message for the Orient*

To a world of men preoccupied with the struggle for living amid the actualities of physical facts and laws and of social relations Christianity, with other religions, declares that the most real of all realities, the most momentous for human concern, is the unseen spirit within and beyond these visible things, God.

For Christianity, God is not far off; but in all our actions we are dealing with him whether we know it or not; in plowing, sowing, reaping; in the work of home, shop, office; in

---

* In our statement we shall dwell little on those contrasts between Christianity and other religions which scholars have been at so much pains to define. The growth within these religions, the new knowledge of their history, the arrival of new sects within them, make such contrasts always insecure. We shall rather attempt to give a positive account of the way in which Christianity meets the issues which Oriental religions raise, with incidental reference to broad diverging tendencies. It is not necessary that Christianity should announce, define and insist on superiorities at this point and that: it is necessary that it be certain of what it lives by, and live by it.

effort and rest, in success and failure, God is present, imperceptible, forceless, all-powerful. He is an undiscerned strength to those who serve their fellow men. Those who ignore him fail of truth and build on what is perishable.

Though God is everywhere present, Christianity holds that God is also One; so that in the world there is one purpose and one divine power with whom we have to deal,—not many.

Christianity is prepared with the polytheistic faiths to see God in varied aspects. Since he is present in all events, the sensitive soul, whether seer or poet or peasant, may perceive him at many turns and in many guises: the richness of life is enhanced by these numerous meetings. Those are the poor, for whom the shell of finite appearance never breaks.

But in all these myriad discernings the being of God is not dispersed, nor his character varied. If there is a God in the pain or in the terror of the world, it is the same God as appears in its beauty: this is the only hope for the ultimate conquest of evil. Nor are these events in which God appears removed from the realm of natural law: to the unity of nature corresponds the unity of the divine will. It is only through this unity that the sciences are freed for their full work, unhampered by threatened intrusions from the supernatural.

Though the world is a world of law, the supreme law of the world is not physical but moral. The reality of men and of societies consists not in wealth and force but in their inner moral quality; it is this which governs their destiny. This truth is common to the great religions.

For Christianity, this means that God is a self, not an impersonal principle of moral order. With Buddhism, Christianity would assert that at the heart of all happening in the universe there is a rigorous law of moral consequence, holding over from the visible to the invisible reaches of destiny. With Buddhism also, this law of retribution is subject to a higher principle, admitting release. For Christianity this higher principle is a personal love, actively seeking to win the human soul to a new relationship with itself, and therewith to right-eousness and peace.

For Christianity, the truth that God is holy as well as loving implies that he is not capricious, nor vengeful in his justice, nor moved by desire to which men can minister except by in-ward fidelity and love. He is therefore not to be moved by gifts and sacrifices, nor in need of conciliation: he can be worshipped only by pure and sincere hearts.

Christianity does not disapprove of nor dispense with visible symbols to aid the worshipper in the direction of his mind. But, as we conceive it, it rejects the identification of any of these material objects with deity. It is opposed to the belief that any such object or place or personal relic can be a source of divine or miraculous power.

Nevertheless, Christianity believes in the real presence of God in personal life and teaches that the highest privilege of religion is a direct experience of companionship with God and union with his will.

In this experience, the Christian finds what in the Orient is often sought as "realization". But Christianity teaches that this union with God is a result, not of a special and difficult technique, nor of asceticism and the abandonment of human ties; but rather of a pure devotion to God's will which is at the same time and inseparably a love for the divine possibilities in other human beings, one's brothers.

Hence religion cannot be realized by solitary self-discipline alone, but by active loyalty to some person or cause in which the welfare of men is involved. God's Kingdom, to the Chris-tian, is to be established among men; hence he is never free to give over the course of human affairs to forces of evil or disorder.

On the other hand, the realization of human welfare re-quires the deepening of the self by reflection, meditation and self-mastery. Hence practical religion tends to be an alternate or double process of withdrawal from the world and immersion in the world, of prayer and social activity.

The proportions of these two phases will vary widely with individual need. There are persons who may well give themselves very largely to the life of meditation, if only its results come eventually to the common good. There may be others chiefly given to "service", if only that activity reverts to its moment of the realization of meaning.

If Hindu, Buddhist, or Taoist tend to exalt the ideal of the secluded and ascetic life to the detriment of the realization of God in human affairs, the practical spirit of the age may in reaction tend to identify religion with social performance. It must be emphasized that activity runs shallow, loses zest, meaning, and ultimately effect; and social efforts lose their power to cohere; unless they return from time to time to recruit the springs of the will in communion with the Great Will.

Christianity refers its conception of God, of man, and of religion to the teachings and life of Jesus.

It believes that in the course of history the insistent problems of religion came to Jesus with peculiar clarity and force, and that he gave answers to them which, because of their simple and essential nature, may be taken as final. Further, he exemplified his own teaching in life and death, and affords to all men who come to know him the most transparent and accessible example of a life lived greatly through immediate union with God. Because this career was given wholly to manifesting the meaning of religion, and was carried through under the severest tests, it stands as a unique support to all who subsequently desire to carry out the same venture. After him, they can never be alone, whatever their hazards. He becomes in spirit their companion and master.

To many Christians, the life of religion becomes a life of actual fellowship with Jesus conceived as a living spirit, the Christ; and through union with him they are united with one another in the Church, the body of his followers. Christians differ in the metaphysical meaning to be assigned to this per-

son and to this experience of union. To many of them the
Christ fuses with the conception of God; and Jesus is called
in a unique sense the "Son of God" or the "Incarnation of
God". These doctrines may mean a profound spiritual union
of the will of Jesus with the will of God; for others, a more
literal identity, attested by miracle in his birth, deeds, death
and resurrection. It is not our function to limit the range of
these differences of conception, but rather to draw attention
to the fact that they exist, and that beneath them are under-
lying agreements, belonging to the essence of Christianity, as
a positive and historical religion.

3. The Message for the Orient: Ethical and Social

Since Christianity unites the love of God with the love of
men, its theology at once flows out into a conception of
rightful human relationships.

The great religions agree that it is the office of religion
in human affairs to make prevalent the spirit of sympathy and
love. To some of them, this spirit operates in a realm of illusion where in the end no private interest matters, and no private self is real. Compassion and kindness are chiefly disci-
plines for destroying in oneself the root of selfishness, thus
overcoming the moral illusion of separate selfhood.

To the Christian also, selfishness is the enemy. But the love
of men which destroys its root is directed to real issues. For it
holds that each individual soul matters in the sight of God,
and that those who love men are but perceiving their true and
absolute worth. The idea of the immortality of the soul is the
measure of the soul's intrinsic dignity. This conception of
the worth of the individual person becomes in personal life
the final basis for self-respect and for inescapable responsibility; in social life it builds the structure of rights and also of
duties.

For Christianity, the spirit of love is the guiding principle
in meeting all specific ethical problems.

With the instinctive life and its perversities,—with greed,

lust, anger, pride,—the teachings of Jesus deal expressly and poignantly. The Sermon on the Mount translocates the issues of right and wrong from the outward act to the inner motive. Adultery is identified with lust. Property, however lawfully owned, is a danger to the soul: its health demands a moral freedom from all possessions, an absence of anxiety for the morrow. The problems of injury and wrath are not solved by the legalities of justice: the enemy is to be loved, and to the smiter one must turn the other cheek. Epoch-making dicta for the dispositions of the heart; their clear radicalism flows from an unerring sense of what things are first in the values of life.

These same sayings become the basis for an inward renewal of social life. They do not contain specific solutions for the social problems set by pugnacity, property, and sex. There is nothing in their authority to spare Christians who would apply them the effort of thought.

In the practices of Christendom which stand in glaring contrast to the words of the Sermon on the Mount, there is ground for humiliation. Our message to the Orient must be accompanied by our confession: the standards we profess are not the positions we have attained. In many ways Christianity is farther beyond the behavior of the Christian world than it is beyond the behavior of portions of the Orient.

At the same time it should be said that our departures from the literal injunctions of this Sermon are not wholly matters of bad conscience: those words do not define, and were not intended to define, our social ideals. "Take no thought" can not be used as a maxim for the economic life of man in the society of today. "Turn the other cheek" is not a solution for the problems of legal and political justice. The spirit of love alone does not meet the immediate problems set by national aggression or by competition. Side by side with the great sayings of Jesus which declare the dangers of passionate impulse, and the primary importance of "the Kingdom of God, and its righteousness," there are others which declare the moral value of an abundant life, implying the full development of human nature: the Sermon on the Mount is not the whole of his teaching. There must be a right use of sex, of pugnacity, of wealth. These right uses are, for our time, problems incompletely solved. They are problems for all the great religions, especially for those which like Christianity, Buddhism, the Vedanta, see the necessity for an inner renunciation and detachment before human desires may safely be given freedom to weave their fabrics in the world of experience.

While these problems are being worked out, the spirit of their solution is present. Through Jesus and through such wills as his, God works throughout human history bringing men toward unity in a love which is universal in its sweep.

This spirit establishes and makes sacred the family tie. It extends beyond the family to the nation and to other social groups, as far as they are ready to admit love and justice as elements of control. It extends to the most difficult international and inter-racial adjustments, as humanity learns what righteousness requires in the conduct of world affairs.

Christianity regards no human grouping as sacred in itself: none can command absolute loyalty. The stability of them all—family, economic order, nation—is conditional upon the loyalty of each member to something beyond the group itself, the spirit of love and justice, which is God. In this sense, it is the law of history that men and groups must lose their lives in order to save them.

4. The Aim of Missions

The message presents a way of life and thinking which the Christian conceives, not as his way alone, but as a way for all men. It is a way which may enter without violence the texture of their living and transform it from within. As Christianity shares this faith with men of all faiths, they become changed into the same substance. The names which now separate them lose their divisive meaning; and there need be no loss of the historic thread of devotion which unites each to its own origins and inspirations.

The goal to which this way leads may be variously described, most perfectly perhaps in the single phrase, Thy Kingdom come. This is, and has always been, the true aim of Christian missions.

Its detail varies as we learn more of what is involved in it. It means to us now, as always, saving life. It means representing to the Orient the spiritual sources of western civilization, while its other aspects, technical and material, are being represented so vigorously in other ways. It means paving the way for international friendship through a deeper understanding. It means trying more definitely to strengthen our own hold on the meaning of religion in human life. Should we try to express this conception in a more literal statement it might be this:

To seek with people of other lands a true knowledge and love of God, expressing in life and word what we have learned through Jesus Christ, and endeavoring to give effect to his spirit in the life of the world.

CHAPTER IV

THE SCOPE OF THE WORK OF MISSIONS

THERE is something about religion which has led it every-where to branch out into charitable activities, and frequently into education. Worship, the world over, is associated with giving of alms, as if it were felt incomplete without active charity; and as religion develops, this impulse creates its institutions of mercy and of aid. This has been in a striking degree the experience of Protestant missions in the East. The observer is likely to draw a contrast between the "religious" and the "philanthropic" activities of the mission: the former centering about the church and its services of preaching and prayer, the latter centering about school or hospital or social center, and undertaking simply to do good in the spirit of Christ.

This line of division, useful for descriptive purposes, evidently tells but a partial truth. The aim of missions is single: it has to do with the religious life of mankind. When the mission engages in philanthropic activity, it does so, as Jesus did, because it sees this as an integral part of its religious work. Whatever the variety of things the mission may legitimately undertake (and for this variety we may adopt the word "scope"), it is simply the variety which its spiritual purpose prescribes or permits. It is this scope which we have now to consider.

1. How Far Can Missions Engage in Humanitarian Work?

When the modern missionary movement came to birth at the end of the eighteenth century its objectives were clear and definite. It was an outflow of the widespread religious awakening which came to Europe and America near the middle of that century. This movement, commonly called the "Evangelical Awakening," put its chief emphasis on individual salvation. Under its stimulus men felt impelled to go to the ends of the earth to save souls and build them into the church. The great personalities who led this movement were primarily evangelists.

But they were more than evangelists. Their enterprise would not so profoundly have altered the course of events in the regions where they worked if they had not quickly perceived how much more than preaching was involved in their undertaking. In order to proclaim their own message they were obliged to master languages, translate the Scriptures, and produce literature in those languages. Almost from the beginning of their work in the Orient, there were missionaries who saw that a scheme of education was a necessity, if enlightened leaders and pastors were to be developed. The missionary as a man has always been sensitive to the suffering of others, and as a Christian has accepted a peculiar responsibility for relieving it. Hospitals and other medical service were natural developments. Thus there has been no time in the history of modern missions when the philanthropic objective has not had a place.

But in the course of a hundred years, this place has become a very large one, as thoughtful and forward-looking missionaries have gradually realized what is involved in their enterprise. Starting with the purpose of saving individual souls, they have been drawn on by necessity into efforts to build up the minds, and the bodies, and to improve the social life in which these souls are engaged. The educational and other associated interests have grown until in volume and variety they now outrank the parent activity. There is a visible tendency to regard them as having a value of their own, and as being legitimate functions of Christian missions apart from any explicit evangelization.* It is as if "salvation" had begun to take on a new meaning: men are to be saved, not for the next world alone, and not out of human life, but within human

* We shall use this term for lack of a better single word to cover preaching and personal persuasion, holding religious services, and giving religious instruction to converts.

life. A thoroughgoing acceptance of this view would mean a new epoch in the conception of the task of missions. This trend, however, has not had its way without serious resistance.

For the idea that the missionary's task not only begins with the proclamation of the message, but also ends there, has remained solidly entrenched in the minds of many missionaries. There are not a few who regret to see the newer objectives introduced and oppose them, either through inability to alter their perspective, or through inertia, a formidable factor in all religious institutions. One receives in some areas an impression that the missionaries as a group are but hazily aware of the extraordinary changes going on in the mental world around them, perhaps through extreme absorption, perhaps through a training which fails to engage their interest in problems of culture. It is to be expected that the positive qualities which have made the missionary, his earnestness, his certainty, his belief in his own program, will in some cases shade into self-sufficiency and limitation of outlook. The unchanging nature of religious truth is often taken to justify an equally invariable method of announcing it.

But while there is plenty of inertia in the mission field, there is here, as elsewhere, very little *mere* inertia: at the root of it there are genuine difficulties.

The needs of the Orient, like the needs of America—if one looks at them with the eyes of a philanthropist—are too vast to be taken as the burden of Christian missions or of any other one enterprise. One would know neither where to begin nor where to stop. To accept them indiscriminately as a general task would lead in many directions which have no clear relation to the religious interests of the race. One must ask the mission-philanthropist how he chooses which ones of the infinitude of human needs he desires to help.

As funds are drawn into these channels, there are those who feel that the place of the central business of missions has been usurped and its resources impoverished by something—important, indeed, but less important. And as missionaries give their energies to humanitarian tasks, there are those who feel that even the central aim of missions is being forgotten.

Philanthropy can be very silent about religious truth and doctrine: on this account it is questioned whether the drift in that direction may not indicate an enfeebled faith. There is a variety of "liberalism" which gives itself to social activity in order to compensate for a loss of clear-cut spiritual vision: the missionary who is dedicated to the work of evangelism is determined to guard against such a decline.

Further, any Christian effort toward general social uplift in the Orient is destined to merge with the similar efforts of other religions, of government, of private secular agencies, so that its very identity may be lost.

In view of these and other considerations we find in various places counter currents tending to reassert the dominance or even the sole importance of evangelism.*

In the fears thus expressed there are real dangers to be guarded against. There is a danger that diversifying the scope of effort horizontally may be at the expense of depth. Uplifters and social betterment experts easily fall into the vain supposition that by simply improving the economic basis of life or by cleverly re-shuffling human relationships they can produce the happy world of their hopes. All proposals for cure through philanthropy alone, miss the point of central importance, namely, that there must be *first of all a new kind of person as the unit of society if there is to be a new social order.* Social efforts which ignore this principle have at times brought disillusionment: impressive and stable results are difficult and rare. What count most in the progress of society are simple day by day events, such as may take place in the

---

* The so-called mass movements in India have been to a large extent of this nature. In the gospel team movement of Burma, and to a lesser extent in the Kingdom of God movement in Japan, the center of interest is in rousing individuals to the point of a "decision." In China a number of intense revival movements have been taking place. Largely outside our own group of churches, but to some extent within it, there is a current which, regarding the evils of the existing social order as too great to be cured, despairs of the course of human history and concentrates attention on preparing the souls of men for its termination.

mind of a youth here and there or in the formation of a new friendship. These tiny rootlet processes in the long run remake civilization. The main contribution of the mission has been not in devising new social programs, but in forming the men who do the devising. Nothing therefore can displace or minimize the importance of a true and well-qualified evangelism.

The point of the tendency to enlarge the scope of mission activity is not, however, one of discounting the value of evangelism: the point is, that evangelizing by itself is incomplete on its own ground of life-building, and requires to be supplemented.

It is not without importance to mention these weaknesses of evangelism taken alone, as they appeared to us.

There are still missionaries who count their task done when they have preached to the people and have thus given them a chance to "hear the Word," an attitude whose irresponsible character we need not dwell upon, since it is not prevalent. There are many others who are content with "decisions" or with "baptisms," decisions often reached in states of emotional upstir which subside without leaving enduring changes in character or habit.

Now we have had ample experience to show that unless after such a decision the mind is informed, the will fortified, the habits patiently rebuilt, there is no genuine re-formation of the inner self. But the local evangelists and "Bible workers" in Asia are seldom competent to carry out this difficult, slow, and wisdom-requiring work: they are for the most part narrowly prepared, their message is doctrinally formulated and without sufficient background of human meaning: it lacks the thought-content necessary for any profound influence over life. Such shallow extension of a nominal Christianity excites scorn on the part of thoughtful Orientals, and in the long run reacts seriously against the standing of Christianity. These negative results are seldom perceived by the evangelists: they succeed in impressing a number of individuals, collect scores or hundreds of "signatures," count baptisms as so many substantial additions to the Church of Christ; but they

neither see nor consider the other multitude, the more reflective and morally deeper spirits, who by this spectacle may be
set against the Christian movement for the rest of their lives.
It is one thing to insist upon the regeneration of the individual: it is quite another thing to conclude that types of
evangelization which have proved their weakness in America
are in the Orient the fixed and perfect methods to that end.

But apart from these, the prevalent defects of "pure evangelism," even when evangelism is at its best in spiritual depth,
in thought, in disciplinary care, it is frequently true that
preaching, or giving messages in words, is not in the first instance the right approach. The Christian way of life and its
spirit is capable of transmitting itself by quiet personal contact and by contagion: there are circumstances in which this
is the most perfect mode of speech. If the actual tasks of life
can be shared with the people of a community, whatever
power there is in the Christianity of the worker will be revealed in operation; and will do its part in transforming the
spirit of individual lives who perceive it. This also is evangelization, not by word but by deed; not as a direct aim, but as
a by-product of a life whose sources of energy make their own
report. It does not dispense with the use of verbal interpretation when a real desire is aroused to know why and how men
are led to live that way.

It is this sort of *evangelizing by living and by human service*
—not in essence a new thing, but new in importance and scope
—of which we desire now to state the principles and illustrate
the application.

2. Principles of the Scope of Mission Work

Its first principle is that the welfare of the individual's soul
or directing self cannot be secured in complete independence
of the welfare of his body, his mind, his general social context. Therefore he who would minister to this self may choose
to do so by way of ministering to health, or to the instruction
of the mind, or by improving the social medium. He may
choose this way of approach. But he may also find himself

obliged to deal with problems of hygiene or poverty or custom before he can make further progress in building individual character.

One of the pronouncements of the Jerusalem Meeting of 1928 declared that "man is a unity; and his spiritual life is indivisibly rooted in all his conditions, physical, mental and social." The conclusion was drawn that "missionary work must be sufficiently comprehensive to serve the whole man in every aspect of his life." These words and this inference seem to us thoroughly sound. The individual's spiritual health can no more come to him by some magic gift, apart from all the rest of his life, than can his physical health.

It is true that the self has a degree of free, independent activity: it may triumph in the midst of adverse circumstances. We have not to wait, before appealing to a man's will, until his health and income are satisfactory! On the contrary, a renewed spirit is a powerful factor, and an indispensable ally, in any struggle with impeding conditions. But we cannot omit to deal with those conditions. And if we are to build permanently and well, we must eventually deal with the whole cycle.

In this cycle we must include the social context. For if a man is a member of a badly ordered home or is immersed in a sordid political group or is a unit in a social order in any way diseased, he will bear in his soul the mark of these associations. In so far as the individual person is an organic part of a complex social system, a thoroughgoing reconstruction of his life will ultimately involve either some transformation of the social structure or his removal from it.

Formerly, this interlocking of religion with the rest of life was recognized in the practice already referred to of removing a beginner in the Christian life to the missionary compound, where all aspects of his environment underwent an abrupt change. The modern mission profiting by experience inclines to adopt the other alternative: leaving the individual within his accustomed context, and assuming the slow and indeed infinite labor of improving that context. This labor will require of the missionary a far more concrete, detailed and understanding mastery of the workings of that society which he has entered as a visitor than did the former method of extrication. He will be, as the spirit of the permanent mission requires, a learner and a co-worker with the non-Christians occupied with the same task; and he will certainly not wait for a change of confession before doing what physical or mental or social good is needed. To him the Kingdom of God must be quite literally "like leaven *hid* in a measure of meal."

Here we touch upon a critical point. If we approach the spiritual life through its physical and social context, shall we continue to keep in mind evangelism as the main business to which all else is subsidiary? Shall these philanthropic activities be regarded solely as means to the end of conversion?

It was natural that educational and medical work should at first have been regarded as direct auxiliaries to the evangelical work of the mission: this was the way they grew up. For the most part, they are still so regarded. And as long as this means-to-end view is maintained, it will furnish the principle of selection among the needs to be supplied, and the persons to be helped. It will tend to limit aid to those classes most readily brought into the church. When there is necessity for curtailment, those activities will tend to be sacrificed which are least profitable in terms of verifiable harvest.

There is logic in this view: nor is it intrinsically selfish. The aim to elevate spiritual life by whatever means is not a selfish aim! and whatever calculation there is in it, is calculation to do good.

Nevertheless, when medical aid or education are thus consciously subordinated to explicit evangelism, there are unfortunate effects in various directions, including the quality of the education or of the medical aid. The service remains unselfish, but it ceases to be "disinterested:" it has an "ulterior object." The philanthropic object is likely to be pursued in a manner savoring of a commercial interest in the promotion of one's own type of piety and of association. This danger is perhaps inseparable from human agency in building institutions, however glorious their purpose. But when Christian missions fall into it, they provoke resentment on the part of their very beneficiaries, who feel that advantage is being taken of needs they confess in order to promote another ministry which they have not invited nor desired.

When Orientals talk of "proselytizing," a term almost universally used in a derogatory sense, this tying of an ostensibly disinterested service to a function of preaching is likely to be taken as its main illustration. This is one of the main points in Gandhi's criticism of missions.* Such resentment is a fact to be reckoned with, if only from the psychological point of view. It is not directed against the reformation of individuals, nor against the spread of the spirit of Christ. It is directed against something which looks like adulteration of the quality of mercy.

Is there a point of principle here at stake? We believe that there is, and we desire if possible to bring it into clearer light.

The principle has been implied in what has already been said. Ministry to the secular needs of men in the spirit of Christ *is evangelism,* in the right use of the word. For to the Christian no philanthropy can be mere secular relief. With the good offered there is conveyed the temper of the offering, and only

* It may be of value to repeat here some of his often-quoted words: "If instead of confining themselves purely to humanitarian work such as education, medical service to the poor and the like, they would use these activities of theirs for the purpose of proselytizing, I would certainly like them to withdraw . . . Let me now amplify the bald statement. I hold that proselytizing under the cloak of humanitarian work is, to say the least, unhealthy. It is most certainly resented by the people here. Religion after all is a deeply personal matter, it touches the heart. Why should I change my religion because a doctor who professes Christianity as his religion has cured me of some disease, or why should the doctor expect or suggest such a change whilst I am under his influence? . . . In my opinion these practices are not uplifting and give rise to suspicion if not even to secret hostility. The methods of conversion must be like Caesar's wife, above suspicion."—Young India, April 23, 1931. Gandhi does not believe that conversion from one religion to another is desirable; yet he objects much less to the preaching of Christianity with this aim in view, than to the use of "modern methods," which he feels are indirect ways to the same goal. Unless they are pure in spirit, they are worse than the old methods, not better.

because of this does the service become wholly good. The principle stated above that the health of the soul requires the soundness of other aspects of human nature, is a principle already recognized in germ in classical antiquity. But the converse, our present principle, is peculiarly Christian: that the sound welfare of the body, of the mind, of the economic and social order, requires the welfare of the soul. In this conviction, the act of giving becomes at the same time an expression of faith.

If such an act is then made subservient to a more vocal operation of preaching or appeal—especially if undergoing such an appeal is made obligatory as a fixed condition of the service to be rendered, as it were an admission fee—the peculiar force of this silent ministry of the deed itself is destroyed.

It is worth noting that deeds of this sort are never controversial. They are the expression of a faith, but not of a sectarian view. The silent language of humane action is always simple and rests on the essentials. For this reason it invites and permits united action across denominational lines, and even across religious boundaries. It persuades by first engaging the mind within the region of agreement.

The social aspects of the mission therefore do not attract the defeatists and the spiritually dull; but they attract many who are doubtful whether the inherited divisions of the Church express the living theological issues of the present, and who desire to reach the vital issues from a ground of fundamental agreement.

But there is a special reason for regarding the ministry of deeds as a fit vehicle for a Christian message. For Christianity, in contrast to religions of illusion or of pessimism, regards the condition of the human being in human society as an express object of God's concern. Human history becomes a field in which the divine life and the divine solicitude are manifested. "Inasmuch as ye have done it unto one of the least of these my brethren ye have done it unto me." To regard social service as something more than a humanitarian act of relief, namely, as an act of union with God's will, is thus in a special sense an expression of the kernel of the Christian faith.

We believe, then, that the time has come to set the educational and other philanthropic aspects of mission work free from organized responsibility to the work of conscious and direct evangelization. We must be willing to give largely without any preaching; to cooperate with non-Christian agencies for social improvement; and to foster the initiative of the Orient in defining the ways in which we shall be invited to help.

This means that we must work with *greater faith* in invisible successes. We must count it a gain when without addition to our institutional strength the societies of the East are slowly permeated with the spirit of Christian service. This attitude will be in accord with the *greater patience* implied in the permanent mission program: the universal church is to arrive, but by its own mode of building, and in God's own time.

3. *Illustrations of the Scope*

We may now briefly illustrate various aspects of the developing scope of missions in view of these principles. A completer survey and estimate of the present situation will be found in the chapters which follow.

First, the medical work, in which, as we noted, missions were early engaged, with whatever skill and means were at hand. This is now an indispensable feature of the modern mission; and Western medicine, one of the most beneficent, is almost certainly the most welcome of all missionary contributions to the life of the East.

It was natural that to most missionaries of the earlier generations medical work in all its ramifications should be thought of as a means to an end: it offered a remarkably effective method of evangelization. The receptive attitude of the patients, the leisure of illness, the fixed association in their minds between healing and the miraculous, made the hospital, the clinic, the dispensary, so many opportunities to press for conversions. This attitude was never universal; but it is still true that evangelization in the narrow sense is generally regarded as the real justification and therefore the true objective of mission medical work.

But the perception that the relief of suffering may be of itself a genuine interpretation of the Christian spirit, never absent, now increasingly if slowly wins its way. All that is an essential part of medical mission work will eventually be regarded as an end in itself, as one of the ways of liberating and enlarging life. And when this work is done "in the name of a disciple," the hospital, quite without any pressure of preaching and prayer in the wards, may be as truly a place where human and divine love are revealed as is the most religious sanctuary.

Something similar is the history of the extensive educational work which in its full sweep is probably the major contribution which missions have made to these countries. It has profoundly touched and stimulated to higher issues almost every aspect of life among the peoples of the East.

At first, education was considered as a necessary adjunct of the work of the church, for instructing converts, for bringing their children up in the faith, for developing an intelligent leadership and ministry. It was at the same time an admirable method of bringing the Gospel to the attention of non-Christians young and old who might enter the schools. Chapel exercises, Bible classes, occasions for religious teaching, were an essential part of every mission school from the kindergarten through to the university. In the prenationalistic period, these methods of evangelization met little or no criticism and were under wise leadership often effective.

But at their best these were only partially good methods of religious penetration. They always made religion seem too much like an addendum to life rather than life itself. The truest type of education takes for granted that the spiritual quality should be interfused with every step of the educational process—interfused, not superadded. It comes into play best

when it is present as an indefinable trait of life in the teacher
and works all the time as an unconscious influence, an atmosphere which everybody breathes, a mode of interpreting that
aspect of the world with which the teacher is dealing.

Some of us found a young teacher in one of our larger
oriental universities of whom we were told that every student
who came into his classes was changed by the experience.
There was no need for his students to have special chapel
exercises or classes for religion. He did not *urge* religion: he
diffused Christianity. Under such teachers there will be no
need to worry over the effects of acts of government which
exclude required chapels or compulsory courses on religion.
The full business of education can still go on. There has not
been either in China or elsewhere in the Far East, nor is there
likely to be, any prohibition of the use of the supreme spiritual
literature of the world nor of the lessons of history nor of the
creative influence of the loftiest personalities: every teacher
might well be satisfied with the reach of these possibilities.
And this kind of work will be felt to be an end in itself, not
a means to something beyond.

Not all teachers (and not all mission boards) have yet accepted this view of education; and there are persons abroad
and at home who quickly lose interest in education if it cannot be made an agency for direct evangelization. There are
still some who make their gifts conditional on the explicit
propagation of a sectarian doctrine. But those who have seen
into what beauty young lives can be transformed under the
touch of a great teacher will be satisfied with that fruit.

There has come in the last few years an awakening of interest in the quality of life led by the people in the extensive
rural areas of the Orient. They are themselves widely restless
in the desire to attain better standards. In China there are over
a million villages, and fully eighty per cent of the immense
population of that country live in them; in India the villages
number three-quarters of a million and contain ninety per
cent of the people; in industrialized Japan, still about half of
the population is rural.

It is especially with regard to these vast peasant populations that we are compelled to recognize the interdependence of every aspect of human life. The pressure of population upon subsistence, religious beliefs which urge forward the growth of population, poverty, malnutrition, brevity of life, early maturity, the social lag of women, absence of opportunity for education of children, tenacity of custom—these constitute a typical cycle of conditions each of which confirms and is con-firmed by the others. The chief difficulty which confronts an intelligent effort to bring new life to these under-privileged millions is not their numbers but the fact that it is compara-tively useless to attempt an improvement at any one point without attacking the others also.

There have been intensified efforts to preach the Gospel to the villages, experiments to improve the productivity of agri-culture, establishment of health centers, forming of coopera-tive societies, opening of schools for children and for adults—all of these, as sporadic and separate efforts have a limited and local value; taken together they reach somewhat better results; but all told they have had until recently a very re-stricted promise. The added element of hopefulness in the present situation is that in all these countries national and provincial governments have begun to concern themselves seriously and effectively with the conditions of rural life; and at the same time are beginning to perceive that no government can do all that is needed.

No increase of economic values, no improvement in the vital statistics of villages will suffice nor even persist without a cor-responding step forward in the morale of the people. There must be a change in the spirit of village life, carefully con-serving its traditional elements of moral strength; there must come a new sense of moral responsibility and a new capacity for association across clan lines without breaking the ancient sanctity of the family; there must be a release from supersti-tion without a loss of religion. There must be better nourish-ment and better health; but there must also be better hope, both economic and spiritual, and a better spirit of brotherhood. If, in the immense rural stretches of Asia, the gradual growth of intelligence and power is to be joined with an equal growth of discontent and hatred, the newly awakened aspiration of these millions may bear bitter fruit. If on the other hand to these stirring villages can be brought the picture of a long struggle upward, in mind, in body, in property—a struggle arduous but hopeful, not against the social forces around them but aided by their determined good-will—the outlook for civilization is appreciably improved.

The crucial problem is, how to accomplish such an immense undertaking. Nothing could be a more legitimate function of the Christian mission than to have a part in this labor if it were prepared to do so. At present, in our judgment, it is not prepared. It is a tempting fallacy to argue directly from the troubles of the world to the opportunity of missions. We should be remiss in our duty if we failed to emphasize the intervening consideration—the capacity and fitness of the missions. It would be a calamity if the churches of America were to rush into this situation with the amateurish equipment, the unintelligent divisiveness of effort, and the almost total lack of statesmanly comprehension with which they now confront this great event, the rapid rise of nationalism and the attendant awakening of the masses of Asia. If the work cannot be done by a method of evangelization which begins and ends with preaching, nor by the formation of a rural church of the old type, neither can it be done by piecemeal, ill-devised starts in unrelated directions of social uplift. It must be essentially a cooperative effort in which the spirit of the mission, the inherent vigour of these ancient cultures, the specialized knowledge of experts, and the resources of government are brought into effective working union. If the American missions are to qualify for even a minor role in this great labor, they must be prepared to understand and to work with the other three factors, and they must be willing to begin with patient experimentation and with the equally patient training of persons, not at present numerous, qualified for such leadership.*

A number of experiments already made or under way

* The part the Christian Church should have in this work will be dealt with in the next following chapter, chapter V.

indicate that America has such men and women, and that the notion of their rendering aid in the improvement of village life in the Orient is not chimerical. It is true that the home-born worker in the East has an advantage over any foreigner, and that the work in its total magnitude must obviously be carried out by Orientals. But experience has proved that there are born rural leaders, having the first-hand feel of country life, knowing from the inside the problems of our own villages and the ways of meeting them, able to adjust their experience to the widely different conditions of the East, and to learn much *de novo* from local usage; and that such persons can retain a highly serviceable initiative even in countries not their own.

Growing out of these tasks there are others, relating to the wider social and political order in which village and city, industry and home are enmeshed. Until recent times, Protestant Christianity has been but dimly aware of the extent of its concern in these issues. Our own type of civilization presents its ethical problems: if we call this civilization individualistic or industrial or imperialistic, such qualities as these do not at once either praise or condemn, but they invite moral judgment and change by those human agencies which have built them up. Or consider the peasantry of the Orient of whom we have been speaking: their well-being is not separable from the entire scheme of economy and taxation into which their occupations send their products. If church or mission embarks upon the policy of social help, it cannot stop short of questions of general justice and the moral foundations of world order.* It goes without saying that the church at home or abroad moves but slowly into these wider reaches of its responsibility, and can move but slowly.

By a true instinct, missions have habitually concentrated attention upon the personal life of individuals, and have moved out gradually from that center. This has been their principle of selection in dealing with the appalling mass of

* The role of the mission in dealing with some of these is dealt with in chapter XI.

human need. Accordingly, they have first attacked the grosser evils, ignorance and disease, because these are the most direct and evident impediments to personal growth. Their activities of teaching and healing, addressed to these evils, happen to be at the same time activities in which the personal factor is a decisive element in success, and in which therefore the spirit of the action most readily transmits itself. Missions have as a matter of course always engaged in the immediate aid of distress. They have played a distinguished part in public emergency, such as famine, or the disastrous floods of central China.*

By beginning in this way at the personal center and the relief of obvious ills before developing completer social programs, the missions have followed a natural order of imperativeness and also of certainty. For such relief is always more unquestionably beneficial than positive social constructions, whose total effect may remain an unfinished problem of scientific theory. It is not surprising that the mission is at present conspicuously fitted only for the former kind of work.

Neither church nor mission, however, will be permanently content to serve solely as a general social ambulance corps, especially since this work will gradually be taken over by other agencies. If their message is positive, so will their social vision be positive. They are now entering upon the positive stage in answering the need for experiment and for pioneering. The private agency is required in many cases to prepare the way for the more general and powerful, but more conventional and impersonal, agencies of the state. Often what is needed is a preparation of the minds of the people for an innovation which in the end must be implemented by government; the mission, through its power of winning confidence, can sometimes bring to a proposed reform that essential factor of goodwill which the state alone cannot command. It goes without saying that this confidence can be had and kept only through

* Sir John Hope Simpson has paid a warm tribute to the services of missionaries in his great work of Flood Relief in China: he found their presence, with ready and intelligent cooperation, an indispensable resource.

that genuine and courageous love of the people which should be everywhere the mark of the Christian.

This intelligent love and this courage will bring the missionary ultimately into direct relation to the state; his problems may become political. Interest in the individual man may become an interest in the moral character of the state. The mission owes to the political order under which it operates its loyal obedience, and its fixed preference for orderly as distinct from violent progress. It owes to no political order the assumption that errors are impossible and all reform unnecessary. It should decline to serve under any government which requires such an assumption, or which makes impossible the natural and judicious expression of constructive criticism by its members, when that criticism is directly relevant to the aim of the mission. The mission should enter into no engagement with government which in advance hampers its members in thus expressing their considered views for the benefit of people and government alike. It is not the business of the mission to "meddle in politics," least of all in the politics of a foreign country in which it is a guest: not every political issue *is* relevant to the welfare of souls, nor does the expression of views imply alignment with political parties. But in such issues as *are* relevant, the postulate of the mission must be that no government can have an interest in defeating the personal development of its citizens, nor in suppressing any competent opinion on this subject. The Kingdom of God is the strength, not the weakness, of every righteous social order: and the mission, through well-equipped and well-balanced men and women, must be free to think, speak and work for its coming.

Whatever else the Kingdom of God may mean, in the complete significance of that great phrase, it carries with it, beside the full development of individuals and the maturing of social groups, also the spiritual unity of all men and races. This means something more than agreement in the essentials of religious faith. It means that the moral sense of mankind comes to accord on the deeper principles of right and wrong.

So C. F. Andrews establishes new common ground between India and the West. It means, too, that the powers which science has delivered into special hands become a common human heritage. So Grenfell brings to Labrador the science needed by its fishermen. It means that art and beauty, without losing their local quality, become a treasury open to all and protected by all. So in China, the mission through its universities aids in giving back to the nation the glory of its ancient architecture. The Kingdom of God has its interest in the means and tools of common life: but it has a special concern in the *values* of existence. Whatever heightens imagination, or intensifies affection and joy, enters directly into its province.

Any of these interests may therefore become relevant to the work of the modern mission. To some extent they are already recognized by it. In whatever field he works, the duty of the missionary is to live among men as an undiscouraged lover of their ideal interests, as well as of themselves: and in this way not to offer solutions, but to participate in solutions which, in the growing community of man, become increasingly cooperative tasks. In this view of its work, the mission should be able to enlist in its adventure men and women of high and varied talents, inspired by a common hope.

But let it everywhere respect the dignity of its work, and count nothing good merely because piety has entered into its fabric. As the mission faces the future, it becomes a matter of honor that its standards of teaching, or of medical service, or of art or music or literature or whatever it touches, are higher, not lower, than those of secular performance. If the future way of the mission is to be—as it can be—the exacting way of the best, its welcome abroad will be secure, its position permanent, and its command re-established over the hearts of those to whom the difficulties of great tasks are an added incentive.

PART II

ASPECTS OF MISSION WORK

CHAPTER V

THE MISSION AND THE CHURCH

Introductory. It was a perfectly natural desire on the part of the missionaries who went out to the Orient more than a century ago, and for those who followed them, to build up Christian churches as a permanent expression of their message and as the visible organ and instrument of its transmission. The Church seemed to them an essential feature of the entire Christian program. Their own spiritual lives had been nurtured by it, the vital content of their faith had been transmitted by it and they could hardly conceive of Christianity dissociated from it. The Church, furthermore, had sent them out to win new peoples to its faith, and they took it as a matter of course that some corporate body must be formed to become the visible incarnation in these eastern lands of the principles of Christian life and truth which they were imparting.

Every student of history will recognize at once how difficult was the task which confronted those pioneer missionaries who undertook to build up, under new conditions of racial culture and customs of life and thought, the church structure which was to preserve, embody and transmit in each one of these countries the truths that they were endeavoring to plant in the hearts of their converts. It need not surprise us that the Church which they builded leaves much to be desired. It should be reckoned to their credit that they contributed as much as they did that has permanent value and real significance. There has been a slow cumulative power revealed through the process of the years, and the Church in missionary lands, in spite of the weaknesses which we regret in it, has proved to be an important spiritual force. It is now carrying on—in some places without any help from missionaries—the lines of work which the missionaries began, and new lines of activity as well which it has inaugurated on its own initiative. One of the most impressive evidences of real creative work, in the sphere of the Church, is the large list of striking Christian personalities and leaders who have been nurtured in the Church and through the influences which have flowed from it. There have been persons and there still are persons whose lives are identified with the churches of these countries who in saintliness of life and prophetic quality rank in the class with those who first brought the message to them and with the leading Christians in the home churches from which the missionaries came. A sympathetic visitor in the Orient, looking for constructive influences, can hardly be oblivious of the Church as a spiritualizing and civilizing agency. It has been here, as elsewhere, both salt and light in the world where it exists.

It ought, nevertheless, to have been a far more creative, inspiring and transforming force in the world that environs it than it has been or now is. It would have risen with greater breadth and power if more time had been taken to interpret the life of Christ and the central ideas of his teaching before these people were hurried on into the construction of a permanent institution. The spirit of Christianity and its way of life have too often dropped to a place of secondary importance while the sphere and position of the Church have filled the foreground of attention in the missionary mind.

The ideal method.   The ideal method of church creation, if it could have been realized, would have been for the missionaries to present to the races among whom they came the vital principles of Christianity, those truths and ideals of life which constitute the eternal aspects of it, and to have let this direct spiritual impact upon the Oriental peoples produce, in its own fresh form, its peculiar type of organization and its unique modes of corporate development, so that the Church in these lands might have been from the first truly *indigenous.* Under this method Christianity would have come to the Orient as under St. Paul's leadership it came to the cities of the Aegean Sea in the first century, namely as a fresh inspiration, a new sense of the certainty of God, a new redemptive power, and a transforming spirit, not as a fixed and finished system of doctrine, or as an unalterable type of institution.

If that could have happened those who responded to the message which the missionaries brought and who felt the attractive power of the Christ whom these missionaries interpreted, would slowly have found their place as living members of what may be called the universal Church. Instead of a rigid institution, it would have been a group or a fellowship of believers and seekers of many names and types, all cooperating in life and spirit to interpret in fresh ways the religion of Christ in India, in Burma, in China, in Japan. Many times during the history of western Christianity men's hearts have turned from the rigidity of the ecclesiastical institution in which the spirit of Christ's religion seemed to them to be smothered, from the stiff and hardened phrases in which the living faith of the Founder seemed to be stifled, and they have longed for what a mediaeval prophet called the Eternal Gospel, expressed in free ways through a universal Church, vital, spiritual and growing and expanding with the life of man. It has, however, always been well nigh impossible in the western world to break through the folds and bands which a long historical development has woven around the spiritual faith that had its birth in Galilee. Experiments in number have been tried to effect a return to the simplicity of the Gospel, and to inaugurate a movement free enough and spiritual enough to grow into a universal Church. Every such experiment in the West, however, finds itself in rivalry with the churches of the ecclesiastical type already holding the field.

Might not a beginning, unfettered by any historical system, have been made in these missionary lands of a Church after the order of this "Eternal Gospel," which could in its unfolding processes have revealed in broad lines the nature and scope of a universal Church? It would have avoided the dangers which beset great organizations. It would have imposed no unalterable dogmas upon the minds of unborn generations. It would have trusted to the contagious power of truth and love and have left each generation to find its way into the fuller truth which might break upon the world. There are, as we shall see later, a very large number of persons today in Japan, in India and China who want to be Christians according to what they consider to be Christ's way, but who are repelled by the churches as they find them in their rigid forms. The freer type of church might well have brought over into itself the most important leaders of life and thought in all these lands and have marked the beginning of a new era in the life of Christianity. The Church has needed and still needs the unique contribution which the Orient could make to its life.

This method of procedure would have made it possible to have met the Oriental mind with the objective facts of the Gospel narratives rather than with the speculative theories of the creeds. The approach might thus have been the charm and attractive power of a great personal life rather than metaphysical statements about his essential nature. The appeal of suffering and self-giving love would have been brought to them rather than the perplexities of speculation, inherited from the third and fourth centuries.

What actually happened. These questions which we have raised are perhaps vain ones to ask as we look back over the past, for such a free church creation was in the nature of the case impossible of realization. The missionaries who went out in the early nineteenth century had grown up in the circles of the Protestantism of that period and they could hardly be expected to approach their task with their minds detached from rigid forms and molds, or with principles of truth so free and fluid that they could find and absorb new ways of expressing their truth and new forms of incarnating it. They carried out with them a set of pre-formed doctrines which seemed to them essential to Christianity and they felt at the same time that they were the bearers of a sacred church model.

The result was that they put down a foreign-made system upon the minds of their converts. They ignored in large measure the racial habits of the people among whom they worked. The long stages of the ethical and religious culture of these people, their customs of family life and clan life, their ingrained appreciations and dispositions toward art and worship and organized group effort were treated as relatively unimportant. Feeling as they did that non-Christian religions were "false" and "idolatrous," they had little appreciation even for the nobler traits of religion and worship which they found. That was an unfortunate beginning and it has meant a serious loss to the whole missionary enterprise of the century. No one can blame these men and women for the intellectual atmosphere and inherited attitudes of their time but one can only wish the Christian Church in the Orient might have come to birth under somewhat more favoring circumstances.

Still more unfortunate was it that the missionary endeavor had its birth at a time when the Church was divided, as it still is, into a large number of separate denominational church communions, with widely different conceptions of organization and government, with a variety of forms of worship and sacrament, and with varying emphasis on what were considered essential points of doctrine and belief. This situation brought and has continued to bring a large amount of confusion to the minds of the people in missionary lands, and it constitutes a major scandal of Christianity for those who look upon it from the outside. But, once more, the missionaries were not themselves to blame for the cleavages and divisive tendencies in the Church. Those things sprang out of conditions over which they had no control. Denominational mission boards expected denominational churches to be built. The defects which appear in the missionary Church can all be traced to weaknesses in the Church at home. In many respects the missionaries of the creative period rose well above the general level of the churches at home, certainly in faith, in courage and in the spirit of adventure.

Conservative aspects of the mission church. The religious situation in India and China, and, to some extent, in Japan cannot be fully comprehended unless one realizes that besides the major denominations there have been many smaller intensive sects engaged in missionary work in these countries. They have added to the confusion by having their own separate churches in which certain aspects of doctrine or practice are presented with striking vigor and are held to be essential to salvation. The views of these intenser sects are presented with a sense of infallible certainty and a directness and simplicity of statement which carry conviction to the minds of the types of people with whom they mainly work. We are referring here especially to groups of Christians who do not expect to change the intellectual currents of the age or to transform the social and economic order or to build a new civilization for children to be born into. They expect a new age which will end wickedness and inaugurate perfect conditions of peace and joy, to come by a mighty supernatural event.

It should be further recognized that very many of the churches even of the larger denominations in the Orient are strikingly conservative in thought. They were formed at a time when a precise and definite theological system of doctrine was generally stressed as vitally important, and this theological emphasis has remained up to the present time a dominant feature of these conservative churches. This excessive occupation with theological doctrine has kept such churches out of touch with trends of thought and intellectual problems in the world around them. Churches of this sort appeal only to a certain type of mind. Students in the main leave them coldly alone and are apt to be turned against Christianity if this is the only kind of Christianity which they know. It seems to them too often a complicated religion of words and phrases, dealing with the issues of a former age, not a living force for the moral transformation of the world and for the remaking of the present social order. There is, too, a pietistic tone in the Christianity of many of the churches, with a tendency to hem life about with legalistic rules and regulations, many of them negative in character.

This darker side of the picture can hardly be missed by a careful, honest observer and it impels one to conclude that the missionaries have been less successful in their creative work for the organization and guidance of the Church than in any other one of their major undertakings. The task was far more difficult than any of the others and the obstacles have not been overcome. The greatest obstacle of all has been produced by the attempt to put a foreign institution down upon the lives and minds of a people instead of having the Christian movement take on its forms of organization out of the indigenous life and culture of the people themselves. India and Burma had for centuries cultivated the mystical life and the Church of these countries should have given more place to meditation and to the appreciation of man's direct approach to God. In China the creators of the Church should have taken more account of the family life as a unit and should have given more significance to the existing community life as a factor in the life of the Church. In Japan the aesthetic appeal should have been given much greater place than it has received and the Christian movement should have ministered more completely than it has done to the moral and intellectual life of Japan.

Constructive churches in important centers.   But it would be a quite unfair consideration of the facts if this critical estimate were taken to be a full account of the Church as it really is. There are large churches in the important coast cities of China, and in the great centers of life in India and Japan which are notable for their spiritual power and impressive interpretation of Christianity. Where the congregation has been under the influence of an exceptional missionary or has had long training in the manners and customs of a typical church, and where the Sunday school has made an effective preparation, the church work and the church services compare favorably with similar ones in American cities, and there are in these churches ministers to be found who in quality of preaching and in prophetic insight compare favorably with our best at home. There is an occasional city church to be found in the greatest centers of population where there is a group of well-trained laymen who have a public influence and a range of religious and moral activity quite comparable to those in the best churches at home.

It is possible, too, to find churches where the solemnity of worship and the fortification of life which comes from genuine communion are probably as much in evidence as is the case in any part of the world. "Institutional churches," which carry on a variety of social, educational and recreational activities are not numerous, but some such churches are to be found which match in good degree the work done in similar churches in America. When we pass, however, from the outstanding churches of wide influence and constructive power and come to the ordinary churches as they are found scattered about in cities and villages throughout these thickly populated countries, the story to be told is not all that one could wish. There is a long list of weak churches and dull services to report.

Self-support. The degree of self-support attained by local churches varies widely from country to country and among the denominations. In spite of happy exceptions, the general situation is one of excessive and long-continued dependence on mission grants. The highest percentage of self-support in East Asia, if not in the world, has been attained by the Karen (Baptist) churches in Burma, but all the churches in Burma rank high, the Baptists reporting eighty per cent. and the Methodists fifty. In Japan the Kumiai (Congregational) and Churches of Christ rank highest. In India, particularly in the Telugu (Baptist) and Sialkot (United Presbyterian) areas, the proportion of self-supporting churches has greatly increased in recent years, and it is also high in the Arcot (Dutch Reformed) and Madura (Congregational) areas.

The lack of accurate financial records and the loose use of the term "self-support" make it impossible to give comprehensive figures or to make close comparisons between denominations. Many churches are "self-supporting" only because they pay nothing toward the support of cooperating missionaries and derive a considerable fraction of their receipts from mission employees.

In India, China and Japan alike, great numbers of weak rural churches are receiving grants from the missions. If self-support were defined as the proportion of the total cost of the evangelistic enterprise borne by native gifts, the showing as a whole would be very poor.

The chief remedial measures advocated by church leaders, and already being tested by them in a few areas, are to place a larger burden of church ministry on unpaid lay workers, to combine small units into larger parishes and to draw larger contributions from the members, despite their poverty. In any case the rigorous reduction of the grants by missions to churches appears to be very desirable.

Community worship. It is extremely difficult for observers from the outside, handicapped as they are by lack of language and viewing everything with foreign minds, as they must do, to gain a true estimate of what a church is really accomplishing for its members and for its larger environment. The natural impression which one gets is that the standard preaching is far too doctrinal and is a complicated system of ideas instead of being a thrilling way of life. It lacks in constructive and stabilizing power. When we turn to consider the quality of community worship in the rank and file of the churches there are some high peaks of attainment but a general level which runs fairly low. There are numerous types of worship and a great variety of orders of service with corresponding differences in quality and value. It must always be kept in mind before passing judgment in such delicate matters, that the people of these countries, before the coming of Christianity, had not been trained in community worship and consequently had few habits that fitted into the typical western community service. It should be said in general that the pastors and leaders in the countries which we have visited seemed to us too apt to pray at great length in a conventional manner. The period of prayer on many occasions seemed to be a time of formalism instead of being a time of fused and heightened group-consciousness.

In the Christian churches of all three countries the music and worship run pretty true to the western type. In India one notes a growing interest in the adaptation and use of native bhajans and other tunes. In most of the churches visited no other music was sung but these Indian tunes. They were sung with fervor and sometimes with beauty of tone. The accompaniment was with the instruments most frequently in use in India, the drum, the small stringed instrument, and the little reed organ, playing only the melody in octaves. The Indian Christian often chafes at the western type of worship. He would often prefer to sit on the floor rather than in a pew, and to prostrate himself in prayer rather than to bow or stand. But the tradition of early missions and missionaries is strong. There is large opportunity for real enrichment of the worship in ways to appeal strongly to the soul of the Indian.

In China there is even less of the influence of native customs and ways, and in Japan less still. The worship is less orderly and reverent in China than in either of the other countries. There is a noticeable tendency to move about and the habit of coming in late is disturbing. This situation is due in large measure to the fact that the Chinese are not accustomed to the forms of worship which prevail and are not prepared by previous training to enjoy them. It might be well to make experiments with other types of service and to endeavor to meet more nearly the needs and aptitudes of the Chinese mind. In Japan there is a reverential atmosphere and there are usually periods of helpful silence in the service.

Church music in both China and Japan is almost wholly western in type. There are gratifying signs in the new hymnals of an awakening of interest in the music of the land and of the people. Yet much patient work must be done by the small groups interested, if there is to be any large place for indigenous music in the churches of India, China and Japan. There is material which might be of value in Buddhist chants and popular songs, some of which is already in use. One feels sure that in no one of these three countries will the native music get very far into the life of the churches until it shall have been developed along harmonic and contrapuntal lines similar to those which mark the extraordinary development of modern western music from primitive beginnings. Such a development might greatly enrich the worship of the Church universal.

Imponderable features. No final estimate can be made of what the churches have done or are doing without more knowledge than a visitor can ever get of those imponderable and intangible changes in the moral and spiritual quality of life which have taken place in those who make up the church membership. Some of them have certainly been raised from a life of low potency to one of high moral power. When the test of persecution and endurance has come to them they have again and again met it with a firmness and fearlessness which reveal a deep-seated staying power and many of them through the years have met the still harder tests of subtle temptations, of frustrated hopes and the drift of powerful currents of life around them, and have kept their faith and vision.

We do not, furthermore, forget that the weaknesses and failure which we observe in the mission churches are to be found also in home churches as well. They are reviewed here because it is a part of our business as a Commission to see what changes are needed and to suggest lines of improvement or reconstruction where the indication of new directions can be discovered. The task of transforming the Church in the countries of the Orient from what it now is to what it ought to be in order to fulfill its purpose as a great spiritual agency can only be done by long and patient experimentation. It is from the nature of the case an undertaking which essentially belongs to the leaders of the Church itself in each of the countries, since if the Church is to be truly indigenous it must be built from within and not from without. Nothing is more patent than the need of profound transformation and an increase of efficiency and power.

Far-reaching transformation needed. There is pretty clear indication that many persons of insight and leadership in these countries deeply feel the need of help and counsel in what is bound to be one of the most difficult pieces of creative work in the world. In many respects reconstruction will be more difficult than the original construction was. It is not possible now to go back to the beginning, make a fresh start and undo what was begun on wrong lines. The Church is a

going concern, and it must continue to perform its functions
while the progress of reconstruction is under way. But however
difficult this task of the reconstruction of the Church may be,
those who share most deeply in its life and feel most profoundly the weight of responsibility for its future, are pretty
well agreed that it must undergo a far-reaching transformation. They are, too, in like manner agreed that the religious
leaders of the countries which helped to construct the original
missionary churches ought to feel a sense of obligation to render any possible assistance in their power in the no less important work of reconstruction.

But it is obvious that only persons of the wisest and best
type, persons who possess large spiritual insight and the quality of statesmen can be of real assistance in such delicate business as that, and in any case they should go only when they
are invited to come for counsel. If there is any increment
of wisdom, accumulated through the years, in the countries
that sent out the original missionaries, there should be a
quick response in those countries to any call, if such call comes,
for counsellors of insight to help in the processes of readjustment to meet the needs and demands of what is in many respects a new epoch.

Let there be an end to sectarianism. Among the changes
that are most often referred to by Christian leaders in the
several countries as urgently needed if the Church is to become an adequate organ of spiritual life, the one that would
certainly come first would be a change away from sectarianism,
and a narrow denominationalism, and in the direction of
complete Christian cooperation. Missionaries who are to go
out in the future ought to leave all their sectarian baggage
behind and go out to work for a unified Christianity and a
universal Church. But much more than that is needed. We
must discover some way by which the existing denominations
at home can rise above their separate entities and cooperate
in a world-wide expansion of Christianity as urgent and essential at home as it is abroad. The tasks which now challenge
Christianty will call for the corporate wisdom of the united

Church and for all its spiritual resources. It concerns America as much as it does mission lands. Any plan which can be devised for carrying forward toward completion the work which missionaries have begun abroad will almost certainly fail unless the churches in America can draw together for a united spiritual task.

The spirit of cooperative effort has been growing in depth and volume in recent years on all of these missionary fields in the Orient and some measure of united action is already not only in sight but in actual operation. Organic union does not seem to us necessary. It is in many ways an advantage to have in all lands varying shades of thought and interpretation and a different emphasis on significant points of organization and practice if they can be maintained without interfering with unity of spirit and without interrupting cooperative work for common ends. Conformity is by no means desirable. Differences of thought and emphasis should be welcomed. They become tragic only when each one of those who disagree claims to be infallibly right, when each excludes the other from fellowship, or when the disagreements reach the point of engendering hate and bitterness and defeat the possibility of sharing life, ideals and common purposes.

There are already some signs of growing unity. It will need to become very much stronger before it can draw together all of the hundred or more missionary societies now engaged in carrying on Christian work in these countries. Some of them will never unite with others but there are tendencies and beginnings either of union or of cooperative fellowship in each one of the countries. The divisions within the several denominations have in many cases been closed and the parts have drawn together into a whole. Some of the denominations that are similar in type have affiliated or joined together. The beginning of an ambitious movement toward a United Church of China, of India, of Japan, has been made. So far, however, the churches that have resulted are too much like another large denominational body, one among many others like it, and they give the impression of being constructed from the outside on a western model instead of being spontaneously germinated by inward processes of life. There is still much to be learned and much to be done in this task of achieving unity.

Each one of the three countries has created a National Christian Council for the mobilization of the spiritual forces of the churches for the achievement of specific aims of life, which have become urgent for awakened Christians. They are pioneering bodies for the expression of Christian ideals in the life of individuals and social groups. The National Christian Council of China has attained the largest measure of success of any one of the three, but they have so far all been hampered by the fears and the conservative tendencies of some of the Christian bodies. They have been unable to draw all the Christian forces into cooperation and they always face the danger of having some denomination withdraw from the Council whenever a bold forward step of leadership is taken. In Japan the National Christian Council has been closely identified with "The Kingdom of God Movement." This Movement was inaugurated by Dr. Toyohiko Kagawa in 1929 for a more intensive evangelization both of the rural areas and the large city centers of Japan, for the spread of co-operative methods of life and for an increase of the spirit of mutual love in human relationships.

Less emphasis on doctrine. If the need of closer cooperation takes the first place in the minds of those who are eager to see the Church transformed, the importance of a changed outlook toward the place of doctrine in Christianity seems hardly less urgent. In fact, the chief obstacle to united effort is almost always found to be grounded in fears over what may happen in reference to theological views. We have heard intense desires expressed for less emphasis on traditional theological doctrine and for more stress upon a religion of life, of inspiration, of spiritual leadership, of re-creation and of social transformation.

For years in most of these mission fields the message has been *doctrine-centered*, sometimes almost centered upon the use of phrases. The preaching, the Bible teaching and the Sunday school work with children has been to a very large extent built around theological conceptions. However effective this method may have been in the past, for the period now before us and for awakened minds, it is psychologically the wrong approach to begin with complicated abstract doctrines, dogmatically asserted. It runs counter to the well-tested methods in education now in vogue throughout the world. The Christianity which is to convince and bring spiritual content to thoughtful and serious-minded persons in any part of the world today must put the emphasis where the founder of Christianity himself put it from the first, namely, upon the realization and fulfillment of life and upon those methods and processes and energies by which life can be brought to its divine possibilities. This does not mean in any sense that the interpretation of Christianity in ways that fit the intellectual needs of man's life is unimportant. It only means that stereotyped patterns of doctrine and static phrases which have gone dead should give place to a thoroughly vital message, expressed in the living forms of thought which convince and persuade the mind today.

Those who are most eager for the Church in India and China and Japan to rise to a place of influence and leadership are convinced that it cannot do so unless it can effectively answer that ancient central question which once more confronts everybody today—how can a person attain to completeness and fulness of life? In a world confused in its thinking and caught in a drift of secularism and materialism, the most absorbing single problem now before us is how to "overcome the world" not by going away and leaving it but by a spiritual victory in it, how to rise above the things that are seen and handled and to live in the life and power of transcendent spiritual realities. If the Church in any land has no answer to that question it is doomed to be neglected. Conventional and pious answers are no answers at all. Actual springs of energy must be found, a power of life must be discovered which brings its own demonstration and which makes life a victorious and joyous business. The call which sends the interpreter of this fuller life out to those who are living without it should be and for many persons *is* in every way as great today as that which sent out missionaries a hundred years ago. This work of transforming itself is the most important task the Church in any country has on its hands. It is not an imaginary one, but a very real task in the sphere where men live. It calls for a very different preparation from what was needed for doctrine-centred preaching and in fact it demands quite a different kind of person if it is to be done with efficiency and power.

The problem of meeting the student class. Hardly less important is the necessity, plainly laid upon religious leaders of the Church, to put the message of life in such a clear and demonstrative manner that it will carry conviction and transformation to the student class of this present scientific age. The Church cannot hold its place unless it can convince and hold the loyalty of the new generation. The youth of today are to be the makers and molders of the next period and the message of life must be formulated in terms that will not leave them uninterested and untouched, as is too often the case in the churches of today. Real Christianity must redeem not only the individual soul but the structure and form of the corporate life as well. Christianity must stand forth as a power to regenerate and re-create the communities where it has its centers of activity. Students everywhere in this present time are primarily concerned with these problems of human life and human society. They have been tremendously impressed by great social experiments now being tried, and they want a Christianity that has something vital to say about how life is to be lived here and now. They can hardly be expected to turn with keen interest to a church which is busy with abstract theology concerned with another world, and which has little or nothing to say about what to them is the central business of life. And yet the number of Christian leaders in these three countries who have made any serious study of the social, industrial and economic situation is pitiably small.

Another point frequently emphasized as one talks with those who want to see the Church fit more intimately into the spiritual tasks waiting to be done in these countries of the

Orient is the importance of having a clear and convincing message of *idealism*. The excessive realism of the epoch, with its tendency to look for relief only in material changes, and with its deep tinge of pessimism and futility must not, of course, be met with a skillfully manufactured idealism, softly optimistic. Nothing less than an idealism solidly based upon the testimony of human experience and upon the eternal nature of the universe itself can meet that issue. Somehow the Church of Christ in the world of this age must answer to the yearning in the hearts of youth for a deeper significance of life and for the discovery of a genuine basis for such a deeper significance. Only persons of well-trained minds can do this work of constructive interpretation, but the leaders of the churches in the Orient will need the help of the best qualified Christian thinkers in all countries if this hope is to be realized.

The city church. There is a general feeling in all these countries on the part of those who are careful observers that the city church ought to be a more effective Christian influence in the life of the cities of the Orient. The problems of life have grown more complex with the increase of industry and with the consequent influx of population from the country, and these changes have enlarged the tasks and the responsibilities of the church in the city. The city church, it must be said, has been more successful, as one would expect would be the case, in holding its congregations together and in ministering to the needs of its members than the rural church has been. And we have noted the fact that a few of the churches are undoubtedly effective. The city pastor has usually had a longer and better preparation for his work and he has a more responsible group of lay workers to assist him. But even so, most of the city churches in the Orient have moved in too restricted a sphere of life. They have hardly had a vision of their spiritual mission and leadership, and they have too often lacked the spirit of expansion that would send them out to bring a richer life to groups of people outside their own church circle. The tendency has been for the pastors to be satisfied to do only what was required of them in order to go

through the expected round of services and activities. They
have too often lacked that expectation and conquering power
through which Christianity overcomes obstacles and pushes
out to new victories. Somehow, by better training, or through
the impact of greater inspiration, this miracle of fresh creative
life must be worked for the city churches of the Orient, if
Christianity is to become a constructive power. Almost none
of the churches is fully awake to the social message and mission
of Christianity. Problems of labor and industry remain so far
outside. It has hardly dawned upon the Christian consciousness in these countries that the conditions under which men
live and labor should concern the Christian pastor as deeply
as does the salvation of the individual soul.

In each of the great metropolitan centers, especially in those
centers where large masses of people are concentrated, such
as the cities of Calcutta, Shanghai and Tokyo for example,
provision might be made for some one outstanding interpreter
of the Christian message. What is needed is a person who pos-
sesses striking qualities of life and character joined with
prophetic insight and leadership. The person of greatest spiritual range and preaching power to be found in each one of
these countries should be brought where his prophetic voice
could carry to the whole nation and where he could present
life in its largest spiritual scope. For short periods it might
be arranged for the greatest preachers in other lands to be
set free to carry their message to these important pulpits in
the metropolitan centers of the Orient. There is no better way
to use missionary funds than to provide for the interchange of
prophets from one part of the world to another.

The rural church.   The maintenance of the rural church has
in the past been one of the most baffling of all missionary
problems. The transformation of this rural church is one of
the most urgent of all these tasks of church transformation. It
has been almost impossible to find pastors who would go to
the small country church and there has been a tendency for
them to give up and retire from the field after a brief experience of the difficult struggle. The strain of financing the tiny

isolated church has always been a serious one. It has been quite sundered from the life of the larger community of the region, engaged in its own affairs, and usually looked upon by the community as a foreign importation, bringing nothing of value or interest to anybody except to its own members and consequently often regarded with a hostile eye. The pastor of it in like manner has been thought of as a paid propagator of a foreign religion and therefore not a germane part of the community itself.

The constructive rural work of the future should not be done with the primary aim of organizing churches, but rather with the aim of penetrating country communities with ways of life that will bring enriched living to all the members of it, a truer spirit of cooperation, a more genuine interest in the education of the children, in the productivity of the soil and in methods of raising the economic level of the neighborhood as well as in the health and spiritual growth of the people. The governments and public servants in these countries have already become awake to the importance of rural betterment and of improved methods of agriculture so that all future missionary work in these fields should be done with a full understanding of government policies and in cooperation with department experts. But there is a work of guidance and leadership needed in these communities which cannot be done by governments and which will call for well prepared and devoted men and women with spiritual ideals.

Recent studies that have been made to discover what influences have been most effective in winning converts to Christianity in rural sections indicate that personal contact of a friend, or a Christian worker, or a relative, wins far more persons to Christianity than any other one method and almost as many as all other methods combined. There will no doubt always be a place for the person who knows how to present Christianity by the method of preaching, but more and more the other method of personal approach will take first place. The new type of rural worker will not *begin* his work primarily as an evangelist, and he will not necessarily be an expert agriculturalist or a doctor, but he must first of all be pro-

foundly interested in all the aspects of the life of a rural community. He must have the first-hand *feel* of rural life. He must
know it intimately from the inside and understand the farmer's
mental attitudes. He must expect to share the joys and sorrows
of the community. He must love little children and have those
qualities of personality that appeal to boys and girls. He must
at the same time have some kind of expert training which fits
him to become a genuine leader among the people with whom
he lives.

The work to be done is too extensive and too varied for any
single agency to occupy the entire field, and at the present
moment there are very few persons adequately trained to enter
it effectively. There are many aspects of this work for rural
communities which belong quite naturally in the sphere of the
Christian mission. It offers an opportunity, for those who have
the gifts and training for it, to bring a fuller and richer life
to many persons and to many homes, and it is a type of service
which peculiarly reveals, if rightly done, the creative and
constructive spirit of Christianity. It ought to be entirely
free from sectarian bias or influence and it ought to be inspired by broad and constructive aims. If it is to be effective
it must have the support and the wisdom of the united Church
both at home and abroad.

Wherever the National Christian Council of a country is
organized and equipped for undertaking such an important
task this work can probably be best directed through a department of the Council on Rural Community Work. Where
it is not possible for the Council to draw upon the united
strength both of the mission and the church in the country
these two bodies should cooperate to form a joint committee
on Rural Community Work, as an intelligent and far-seeing
agency for planning the activities, for selecting and training
the personnel and for making the necessary financial ar-
rangements.

As we have said, the primary aim of this community work
should not be the formation of a local church. It should be the
dissemination of spiritual influences in country communities.
If a church *is* formed it should be the natural outcome and

expression of the awakened religious life of the community. Its formation should not be hurried. It should slowly develop.

Experience in rural work in general has made the fact clear that it is extremely difficult for a small local church to succeed. It can very seldom become self-supporting. Standing apart as it does from the life of the community, it has little prestige and slight constructive influence. It is pretty sure to wane and die. If there is to be a continuous and impressive form of organization of Christian activity the unit should be larger than a local village church, and it should deal with all the community problems and interests. One possible plan of carrying the aims and ideals of Christian life into operation in the rural communities of the Orient would be the method which has come to be known as "the larger parish idea." It has proved to be a valuable method in the spiritual rehabilitation of sections of New England and in other parts of the United States. It has, too, proved to be effective in a number of experiments which have been made in the countries of the Orient.

Under this larger community plan a religious leader of striking personal qualities of life and character and with special expert training, who might be either a man or a woman, is given the oversight of a community which includes a number of villages grouped into a natural cooperating area. This leader has under his direction assistant workers, some of whom are women. The person in charge of the field endeavors as rapidly as possible to select and train lay-workers, in each one of the local centers to assist in all the various lines of activity. He himself visits the centers frequently, studies the community needs, organizes the forces for the transformation and elevation of the community life, starts classes for children, work for illiterates where needed, instruction to mothers in home improvement, taking the leadership, where he is prepared for it, in health work and in agricultural advancement, and with his assistants and lay-workers maintaining centers of religious life and instruction, usually in some large home of the neighborhood, or where possible, in a church building or hall, or unused temple.

Any person who sees the unique possibilities that are open

for life and service through such a field of work will feel that
this kind of a life-task is great enough for him and that it
offers scope for all his powers. It has proved fairly easy in New
England to finance such work, since it makes its appeal not
only to the little church group at the center, but to the whole
community as well. It is bound, eventually, to win its way
into self-support, as hospitals have done and as the best
Christian schools have done. The crux of the whole undertaking will lie, of course, in the problem of finding leaders and
in training them for this significant business.

Training centers. The work of transformation which we
have indicated will never be accomplished nor will the great
modern tasks which we hope to see done in the cities and in the
villages be carried forward, or even contemplated, until there
are new methods established and new ideals put into operation in the centers where men and women are being trained
for religious service.

To a student of the religious needs of the countries of the
Orient, the theological seminaries as they stand today seem
strikingly inadequate for training the type of spiritual leaders
most needed at the present time. They are reproductions on
a small scale of the American denominational seminaries of a
former generation. There are some excellent scholars at work
in the best of them, but these institutions have not been
uniquely planned to meet the peculiar problems and tasks of
the countries where they exist, nor are they well adapted to
fit the spiritual needs of the time. So long as the preaching
emphasis was expected to be doctrinal the seminary of the
present type no doubt had a well-defined function.

In the first place, there are far too many seminaries for the
needs of the situation, and the denominational emphasis revealed by the number and variety of them is quite out of date.
In countries like India and China the problems of distance and
of dialects present serious obstacles to merging the many seminaries into a very few, though even these obstacles could be
overcome if there were a determined will to overcome them.
In Japan the obstacles do not exist and the existence of twelve

seminaries in that country, besides a number of Bible training schools for women, seems to the observer inexcusable.

The moment that the message of the teacher and preacher is made to focus on a way of life instead of on abstract doctrine and the central business of the minister comes to be thought of as leadership for the enlargement of life instead of being a defender of a theological system, a markedly different preparation becomes necessary from that in vogue in former times. Preaching which consists mainly in the homiletic exposition of Scripture texts and which tends to keep the preacher in the scenes and the setting of an ancient world, remote from the one in which we must live our lives and work out our moral issues and our specific duties, seems to youthful listeners today largely artificial and quite foreign to the world in which they live. The approach of the preacher, if it is to be effective, must be a vital one and it must attach to what is primarily inherent in the issues of life itself.

It is apparent to this Commission that the training places for the spiritual leaders and Christian workers in all three of these countries should be profoundly transformed as well as reduced in number. It would be an advantage to drop out the word "theological" altogether from the name of the institutions where preparation for life-guidance is to be the central aim, unless the word "theological" can be raised to a richer significance. The study of the Bible which ought no doubt to take a prominent place in the future as in the past, should lead not so much to the acquisition of skill and ability to expound texts as to the discovery of inspiration and power for the tasks of life and leadership. The kind of study that is needed is that which produces the prophet rather than the kind that makes the scribe. Vision and deepened insight should be the aim, not the artificial interpretation of texts for homiletic purposes. To find fresh light on the eternal issues of life as it is lived here in the tangled conditions of the temporal world should dominate this period of preparation.

The unique features of the message and mission of Christianity would naturally be considered essential to any genuine leadership for one who is to become a Christian expert and

guide of life and some knowledge of the historical process of
Christianity as it has met and conquered the new issues and
problems that have confronted it in the various countries of
the world, the changes it has undergone to meet the various
needs of different times and different races, will prove to be a
vital force in any course of training for Christian service. But
throughout all the work of preparation the acquisition of
vitality, insight, spiritual quality and capacity for genuine
leadership should be the central aim—not abstract scholarship.

The students will need language tools, historical background, a central nucleus of religious and philosophical
knowledge, sound training in economic and social questions,
but almost everything else in the course of preparation ought
to be practical and experimental. The principles and methods
of religious education, not theoretically taught but for practical training in life and leadership, should have large place.
Training in child psychology, not as book learning but as a
way to the hearts and lives of children, is an essential preparation. Every religious leader should receive guidance in methods
of worship and should be helped to find his way to a divine
reality and power to live by.

Up to this point the preparation will fit for religious work
either in city or in rural districts equally well. The rest of
the training should to some extent differentiate according as
the student proposes to locate in a city field or in a rural one.
Social and economic questions, causes of poverty and political
ills, problems of city life, and practical experimental work with
a variety of social groups, will be important for those who are
preparing for work in city churches. The rural leader, especially for the larger community type of work, will likewise
need careful training in social and economic problems, especially those concerned with agricultural and neighborhood
life, but he will need to do a large part of his experimental
training in the actual country where the problems are, working under the guidance of an expert in these matters. More
and more the seminary will become an experiment station
and in many instances the student will take a year or more as
an assistant under the leadership of a person in charge of a

larger community field. Besides the institutions for the more practical type of training, there should be at least one first class institution of university grade for advanced study in Christian fundamentals and for the training of Christian scholars, such as already exists for China in Yenching University.

It will almost certainly be found eventually that a large part of the rural work of China, India and Japan can best be done by lay-persons rather than by professional or ordained persons. Wherever some one can be found who has the training and ability for such work and who at the same time has an occupation of such a sort that his religious work can be a by-product of his every day life, the spiritual effect is greater and the elimination of the financial inducement at once puts the entire undertaking on a different level. Much of the work under the larger community leader can probably be done on such a voluntary basis. The experiment in lay-leadership has been successfully tried in North China and in Korea. These experiments have shown through a series of years that the method will succeed, if sufficient provision is made for leaders of vision and technique to guide, inspire and direct the work.

If this general line of training leaders were introduced it would tend at once to sink theological differences into insignificance. It would make it possible for a number of existing denominational seminaries to combine. It would give a young person a thrilling task full of adventure and human interest. It would be possible to raise money for such training work, because the practical demonstration of its effect on life would immediately make a powerful appeal. It would be easy to find experts in these lines of training and experiment who would go out from America or England for short terms of service.

Some one outstanding seminary could be equipped and prepared to take the lead in creating such a training place, and it would soon set the pace for the new order of events. In every way possible the inducement to a young man for entering upon this great business of life should be the extraordinary opportunity it offers for life and service, and as far as it can be done the financial inducement as an appeal should drop into the background. There have been serious results attaching to the custom of giving free education, with the inducement of an expected income for life, to prospective ministers. It has frequently injured the man himself and it has given him an unfortunate status in the minds of his countrymen. It may be impossible to eliminate the financial factor entirely, but everything should be done that can be done to put this noble service on the plane on which it belongs.

The indigenous church and the mission.   More and more in the future the church in missionary lands will become indigenous in the proper sense of the word, as it certainly should be, and that will mean that it will not be financed with foreign money, or conducted by foreign workers, or projected and patterned on a foreign-made ecclesiastical system. It must become a living organism rather than the copy of a structural pattern. It must express in its own life-forms the free functioning of the Christian spirit. That means that it must not be afraid to change its temporal form or to outgrow the peculiar features stamped upon it by the dominant personalities who nurtured it. It should become in the truest sense the living expression of the ideals and principles of Christ and these ideals and principles should control its entire life.

No sudden, revolutionary change, however, can produce forthwith the self-dependent indigenous church. The work of past years must not go for nought, nor should the relations between the mission-built churches and their friends at home and on the field be severed at a stroke. There are deep mutual obligations and interrelationships which cannot easily be dropped. The mission group must cease to be an authoritative body, and in many instances it has already done so, though the way of authority yields only slowly to the way of love and cooperation. At the same time the mission group must in friendly ways give these younger Christians the advantage of the mature wisdom, spiritual insight and trained leadership which its members possess, wherever and whenever this counsel is desired. The problem of creating a wholly independent indigenous church is peculiarly difficult in India in parts of the country where there is a preponderance of depressed class people forming the membership of the church. So long as a church is composed of members of that class it is extremely difficult to induce members of higher castes to join it, and there is, too, the further difficulty that the depressed class members themselves do not welcome additions to their membership from the castes. No quick and hurried solution of the problem can be made. The mission must go as far as it can go in wisdom toward meeting the aspiration of the members of the church for independent control and it should in every possible way prepare the church members for the leadership which they desire.

There are many possible ways of working out the plan of relationship between the mission and the church on the field. It is perhaps too soon to settle down to any one final solution of that problem. The process of experimentation will still go on. The most advisable relation between them is the one that gives the church the largest freedom to develop its own autonomous life unhampered by external authority and at the same time gives the leaders of the church the largest opportunity to draw upon the accumulated wisdom and intelligent guidance of Christians from abroad.

One plan, which in some places successfully meets the conditions of the situation, is the organization of the mission group in a particular country as a council of advisers on the field, and as a liaison body, linking the church abroad with the church at home. This plan, however, has not everywhere given satisfaction, and it will not work well anywhere unless the council of advisers is made up of wise members of broad sympathies, of generous cooperating spirits, and willing to take a subordinate position. Under this plan there will be certain types of work which can be managed and carried on by joint committees, composed of members of the church on the field and of the mission council. In every case the mission council should be thought of as a temporary expedient and as a preparatory stage. It is extremely important that the mission group, however named or organized, should be a spiritual band of friends and helpers, not an instrument of authority or of foreign control. Where missionaries on the field are ill-qualified for the broad constructive work now needed they should be withdrawn and only persons of the highest type and quality should be sent out for the future, as they are called for from the fields where they are needed.

Subsidies. It is doubtful whether any single thing has brought weakness in life and morale to the missionary church to the same extent that the payment of foreign subsidies has done. It has introduced an element of commercialism into the very inner courts of the church. It has tended to produce para-sites, it has cut the nerve of forward-moving adventure on the part of those who should have been the leaders of the indige-nous church, and it has often given an undue influence to the missionaries who dispensed it. There are naturally solitary cases where subsidies have been a blessing and where they have not had such serious consequences. And there are churches in India which cannot well be expected to finance themselves completely under present economic conditions. But no church in any land will be robust and virile until it supports itself out of its own resources through its own endeavors. All new churches should, so far as is humanly possible, be indigenous and self-supporting from the start. The new Christian groups will of course need an early period of nurture by leaders from nearby churches and they must have visits from the officials or laymen who live within reach of their area, but when commu-nity groups begin life as organized churches they should ex-pect to stand on their own feet.

Should the creation of a church be the primary aim? But there is a somewhat more fundamental question to be faced than any we have yet asked in this chapter: Should the creation and development of the church on the mission field be a primary or should it be a secondary aim in the new era of missions? It ought to be the primary business of an interpreter of the Christian religion in the future to permeate the per-sonal life of the individual and the fabric of human society with creative ideals and energies which will renew and revitalize both the single units and the group rather than to build a church as an institution to stand out as an entity in itself apart from the larger whole of society. The organization of churches and the zeal to proselytize into them members who could be counted in statistics and reported to boards at home have in many cases defeated the central business of missionary purpose. The convert has been prematurely hurried into a church as though it were a terminus and an end in itself, when what he rather needed was an enlarged view and outlook of life and friendly help and guidance to take the slow steps which would lead on into a more robust moral and spiritual life.

The answer to such fundamental problems as these will be determined very largely by the nature and character of the Church which is to emerge from the work of the future. If it is to be thought of, as it has too often been thought of in the past, as a kind of magical institution, which confers certain mysterious gifts and graces upon its members and which becomes an ark of safety for those who through it hope to secure thereby their eternal salvation in another world than this, then it will almost certainly stand in the way of the profounder missionary aim and it will be likely to defeat the main missionary purpose. If, however, on the other hand, the Church is to be thought of as a spiritual fellowship and communion of those who have found a new spring of life and power by the impact of the Christian message, who are eager to join together as a living growing body of believers through whom the ideals and the spirit of Christ can be transmitted and his principles of life promoted, then that type of church will always have a function in the work of building the Kingdom of God, whether on the mission field or at home.

The church of this order will not be a substitute for life; it will rather be a spiritual organism which can further the true ends of life. With that purpose in view, modes of baptism will take a place of lesser importance; forms of ecclesiastical organization will fall into the background; the exact formulation of doctrinal phrases will have less significance; statistics as a measure of success will drop out of focus; and all the great lines of missionary activity will converge on the primary business of raising as many persons as possible into their full measure of life and preparing them to make their contribution to the world.

The need of a wider Christian fellowship. Meantime the spiritual seeker for a larger and fuller life often fails to find in his region a church which seems to him to be free of superstitions, to be thoroughly spiritual in its aims and methods, to be a fearless interpreter of truth and ready for the creative tasks of this age. The church which he finds is often going in quite a different direction from that in which his own awakened spirit is travelling. It will apparently be a long time before the Church will be able to draw into its fold all those who share in the deeper life of the Spirit. In fact, it will never draw them until it itself is profoundly transformed. While we are waiting for the necessary transformation to take place, may it not be possible to bring these seekers for larger life and light into some closer fellowship with one another?

No one can study the religious life of the countries of the Orient without being impressed with the fact that Christianity in these lands is something very much larger than the roll of church membership would indicate. Christianity has plainly out-stripped the Church. It is notable how many persons there are who have felt the attraction of the ideals and personality and teachings of Christ and who are not enrolled as actual members of the Church. They have never been counted nor can they ever be counted, but no one can fully estimate the effect of the missionary impact until he takes into account the fact that there are great numbers of persons who have felt the unimaginable touch and drawing power of the life of Christ and who are quietly living on a higher level because of it. Persons of this type are in the cabinets and councils of all these countries. They are leaders in education, in agricultural development, in social endeavors, in the work of city planning, in prominent business houses, in Y. M. C. A. and Y. W. C. A. work and in most of the good adventures which give promise for the future. The reasons for their failure to ally themselves with the Church are many and varied, some of which have been alluded to in the course of this chapter. There is a similar situation in our own country and to some extent in every country on the globe where Christianity has been disseminated.

The intellectual horizon has widened out for those whose minds have been trained in scientific and historical research, while the Church too often has been busy with ideas and issues out of line with the dominant thought of the period. This has produced an *impasse* for many persons. It is a situation which ought to receive the profound consideration of every church in every country, but for the moment we are concerned here only with the problem on the mission field. The returned students of China, India and Japan, after their period of study in the West, and to almost an equal extent the graduates of the higher institutions of learning in these countries, have become accustomed to a type of teaching and to a method of interpretation that are quite different from those that prevail in ordinary church services. The whole drift of the mental processes of these students is likely to make them impatient with views of life that are out of adjustment with scientific thought and that are promulgated by mere assertion of opinion.

The total effect has been a slowing down of the Christian movement within intellectual circles. It has become more difficult to bring students to a decision to adopt the Christian faith and to identify themselves with the Christian Church, and a far larger proportion than formerly go out of Christian institutions without making any positive committal of themselves. They have, however, in a multitude of cases felt the breath of a higher spirit of life. They have caught a glimpse at least of a great Person whose life and teaching has through the centuries shifted the level of the western world and whose way of life has challenged and transformed the best and noblest leaders of humanity. They are perhaps not ready yet to go the whole way on the road which Christ travelled but they acknowledge his attraction and they recognize the supremacy of his life and spirit.

There are, too, many adherents of other religious faiths who feel their spiritual aspirations unsatisfied in their own religious circles and who desire a fulfillment of life which transcends the capacity of the leaders of their own religious faith to supply. They welcome the glimpses they have caught of a larger spiritual life and they would enjoy the companionship and inspiration of large-minded Christian persons, ready to appreciate their own background of life, and their hopes and aspirations.

There are many persons who, in desperation over social injustices and over the evils of the present social order, feel driven to adopt radical panaceas, who would gladly accept the idealism of the Kingdom of God if they saw Christians seriously engaged in the practical task of following the obvious teachings of Christ and undertaking the actual experiment of life that would make the Kingdom of God a reality. There are many others who would join the church without hesitation if they could be convinced that the church in their community was a genuine incarnation of the ideas and ideals for which Christ lived and died and if they could feel at home in its atmosphere.

In a number of instances, notably among students, fellowship groups have spontaneously formed and are exerting a profound influence on the life and the thought of those who have joined them. Some of them have adopted simple forms of community worship. In every one of these oriental countries there are larger or smaller spiritual movements under way outside the church, but in warm sympathy with Christian life and ideals. This tendency, strongly in evidence, for such individuals to draw together for mutual fellowship and for the cultivation of common aims of life should be in every way encouraged. There is hardly a city in the Orient which does not have a large number of persons who have spiritual aspirations and who would welcome intercourse and cooperation with kindred spirits if it could be on a free and friendly basis, and not one of organization and system. Such a fellowship as that, already begun in many places, if it were guided by persons who have no selfish or conventional ends to serve, would

almost certainly spread and grow in normal ways, by contagion, by inspiration, by personal contacts and through the
influence of great literature. Under a quiet, unhurried leadership and with the right encouragement, it might eventually
grow into a World Fellowship and become one of the greatest
spiritual forces of our time.

There are missionary leaders of the ambassador type in all
these countries who have the right vision and true spirit to
be the promoters of such a wider fellowship, and there are also
outstanding persons who belong by birth and race to those
countries who are nobly endowed to take a formative part in
such a movement. A few persons of kindling faith, with a vital
message for the time and with those qualities of personality
that arouse complete confidence, would by natural process
carry the movement forward. An interchange of visits on the
part of the most impressive spiritual leaders of the Orient with
occasional visits of the best interpreters of life and thought in
Europe and America, would help the movement to grow.

Hardly less important for the progress of this movement
would be the creation of types of literature designed to express
in vivid and vital ways the spirit, aims, ideals and social program of Christianity in the world of today. For this purpose
the foremost writers of our time should be drawn upon for
the production of literature of interpretation, and those who
constitute this group of seekers should themselves be stimulated to produce in their own languages books and articles
that express in impressive ways the spiritual hopes and aspirations of the leaders of thought in these countries. Cooperative
efforts for the relief of human suffering in emergency situations, such as famine or flood-relief or for the care of refugees,
have drawn Christians and non-Christian fellow-laborers into
very close relationships of life, and that will always be a
vital way of creating fellowship. The moment men and women
join together to conquer some hard and stubborn situation
that confronts them they find themselves thrown back upon
the deeper spiritual forces of the world for support, and they
are drawn nearer to that life which has revealed in such remarkable measure the redemptive power of love and service.

If, as we believe, the Church is to be thought of as a means for the fulfillment of life rather than as an end in itself, then the enlargement of this group of men and women who have caught the vision of international fellowship and cooperation, who are kindled with love and admiration for Christ, and who are eager to make their lives count for a world-wide kingdom of peace and brotherhood, will in the long run promote in genuine fashion the ends for which the Church is established.

Conclusions and Recommendations

1. The most important single conclusion of this sub-committee is that a profound transformation of the Church in the mission field of the Orient is needed. The lines of the transformation are indicated in this chapter. The main direction indicated is away from sectarianism toward unity and cooperation, and away from a religion focussed upon doctrine toward a religion focussed upon the vital issues of life for the individual and for the social environment in which the individual lives.

2. We are convinced that the time has come for a thoroughgoing coordination of activities on the mission field and for putting an end to sectarianism and denominational rivalry. We believe that the Church should eliminate the complexities and irrelevancies which have crept into it through the controversies of the past, and that it should move steadily toward complete cooperation in the interpretation of its message and in all moral and spiritual tasks. In view of the urgency of united action particularly in the newly inaugurated fields of endeavor, where the mistakes of the past may be avoided, we recommend that the work of betterment to be undertaken in rural communities, since it concerns all branches of the Church, be carried on in each of the countries under a single committee, either as a Department of the National Christian Council, or, where that is not feasible, under a committee appointed jointly by the churches and the missions of cooperating denominations.

3. We recommend that the number of theological seminaries in China, Japan and India be greatly reduced and that the type of training be profoundly transformed, so that the emphasis may be put upon preparation for the practical, social and human tasks which confront a spiritual leader in the actual world of the present time, both in the city and in the rural community. More effort should be made to develop and deepen the inner life of those who are to be the spiritual leaders in these countries. The aim of the seminary in training its workers should be to discover and present the universal and essential features of Christian life and thought and service, and the denominational aspect of the training should take a subordinate place.

4. We recommend that the churches in India, China and Japan be put on an independent and self-supporting basis as rapidly as the necessary adjustment for it can be made. In preparation for the emergence of a truly indigenous church in each country, we recommend that mission boards specify a short period of annually decreasing subsidies for most of the churches now receiving them and that at the end of the specified period foreign subsidies shall cease altogether as a method of supporting churches or church personnel.

5. We recommend that the initiative for calling missionaries for work within the sphere of the Church shall in the future be the right and privilege of the churches on the mission field and that they shall indicate through the proper channels the type of person needed for the specific task in sight as well as the length of the expected service, whether for a short term of years, or for a life engagement. It is our judgment that only persons of the highest quality, fitness and tested ability should receive the approval of the sending boards.

CHAPTER VI

EDUCATION: PRIMARY AND SECONDARY

Mission Education in the Far East

EDUCATION has three tasks. It must inform. It must prepare for the business of living. It must find the springs of personality and release them. Secular education in the West has been inclined to count its work done with the first two of these. Education as conducted by missions has never forgotten the third.

This is not to say that it has always achieved this great aim: the art of education is still in its infancy. In attempting to reach and speak to the soul of the Orient, our missions have commonly imparted religion as if it were information. They have not always considered that the soul has a history.

But the soul of the East has a long history, which now, in the midst of change, maintains the distinctive quality of the Orient. Its old civilizations had their own modes of education, not more through their schools than through family life and through personal centers of prestige. Its arts, technical and fine, were handed down by apprenticeship as well as by schools. Its philosophy and science, accessible to a few in written characters, were open to many more in oral tradition passed on through ample memories. Cultivation in these lands has always been more extensive than literacy. This older education, though its scientific side was arrested in growth shortly after giving to the West many early impulses in arithmetic, astronomy, logic, had its elements of strength and adequacy. The enduring spirit of the East is sufficient proof. The old techniques of teaching are gone, except for a few traces still to be found in China and India; but through a hundred channels of giving and listening, the Orient still transmits itself.

The new systems of education, brought in through contact with the West, have in the main supplanted rather than utilized the older cultures, and their arts of teaching and learning. With western methods there came also western curricula. Let us glance briefly at the beginnings of this process.

Early western schools. In India, western education was introduced by government, by Indian reformers, and by Protestant missions at about the same time (1810-1830). Parliament in 1813 directed the East India Company to devote a sum of money to "the revival and improvement of literature, the encouragement of the learned people of India, and the introduction and promotion of a knowledge of the sciences." It was a matter of warm debate for a time whether Oriental or western learning was here intended. William Carey and Alexander Duff, founders of the earliest missionary colleges, threw their influence on the side of western learning. This was done in the sincere belief that since India was worthy of the best the West could give, all the channels of training should be western. This coincided with a growing interest of government in fitting Indians for civil and professional service under British authority. The Macaulay Minute of 1835 directs that "all funds be henceforth employed in imparting a knowledge of English literature and science through the medium of the English language." As the mission schools became associated with, or parts of, the government system they have for the most part continued to reproduce in India the content as well as the language of English high schools. This constitutes one of the chief problems of education in India, a problem which we must face.

In China, mission schools from 1839 onward were long the only schools giving western education. This education was desired on its own account by many forward-looking Chinese, who saw in it necessary elements of a new era for their nation. These schools remained in clear antithesis to the system of classical training, culminating in the famous literary examinations for the mandarinate, until the abolition of that system in 1905. Since that time, and especially since the Revolution of

118 RE-THINKING MISSIONS

1911, the Chinese Government has developed schools along lines strongly influenced by mission and other western patterns, but with attention to Chinese history and literature, and taught in the Chinese language.

In Japan, as in India, the Protestant mission school arrived at nearly the same moment with the modern development of government schools (1872). But in this case, as in China the nation was turning of its own accord toward the West; and the language as well as much of the content of instruction, remained Japanese. The Meiji Government adopted French methods in education. The mission schools brought chiefly the American and British patterns of their day.

Aims and achievements of mission schools. The aims of the mission schools and colleges in all countries were essentially the same. They were regarded primarily as means of evangelizing, and of training leaders for the church. The missions desired at the same time to spread the western conception of life, of which they were, for some time, the chief interpreters in the Orient: they assumed that even secular subjects taught from western books by western teachers would convey the Christian view. Enlightenment and Christianity were considered inseparable if not synonymous. The higher schools were especially necessary to recommend Christian culture to the lettered classes. Hence it is that in all these countries, Christian higher schools and colleges were started very early, sometimes before interest in primary education had taken shape. But it was soon found desirable to develop a complete series of schools from the elementary grades to the training schools for religious workers and the colleges. The primary school had the added advantage of reaching the impressionable years, and of affording access to the homes.

The general history of these schools, until the last few years, has been one of steady growth. They now use approximately one-half of the money and occupy one-half of the personnel of the entire mission enterprise, as well as of that portion carried out by the seven boards engaged in this survey.

The secondary schools may be considered as at present the

most vital element in the educational system. Of 11,338 middle
and high schools in India and Burma (1926-27), 937 were mission schools. Of 1,339 schools of corresponding grade in China,
196 were mission schools (1930-31). Of 1,471 in Japan, 54
were mission schools (1931). These 1,187 mission schools constitute roughly nine per cent of the total number of secondary
schools here listed. Their 236,000 pupils are approximately
eight and one-half per cent of the total number enrolled in
all these schools. It is evident that Christian secondary education occupies a very substantial place in the educational system
of each of these countries. It is also clear to us that in each
of these countries, mission education has had a much greater
influence than the mere number of schools and pupils can
indicate.

These schools, even when growing up together with government schools, as in India and Japan, did a great pioneer
work. They formed the characters as well as the minds of many
leaders in these countries, not alone in the church but in all
walks of life. They gave a strong impulse to renewed thought
on problems of religion and ethics. They brought new horizons
to their students, whose knowledge of other lands was, as a
rule, exceedingly limited. They brought all the stimulus of a
foreign civilization, which enjoyed at first both novelty and
prestige. For this knowledge and stimulus, Japan was never
so much dependent upon the mission school as China and
India. From the Restoration of 1868, Japanese have been
active travelers and inquirers; the Emperor Meiji, in 1871,
advised the nobility who went abroad to take with them their
wives and daughters so that they would "see for themselves
how, in the lands they visit, women receive their education,
and would also learn the way to bring up their children."* But
in Japan also, mission schools and colleges have done an indispensable work: they have so interpreted the confused fabric
of modern life that the central and silent influence of religion
has been made visible. This has been a contribution of the
highest and of undiminishing importance.

* M. D. Kennedy: The Changing Fabric of Japan, 136 f.

Problems of the future place of mission education. It is clear however, that the striking developments in national education in the Far East must tend in some respects to diminish the relative importance of mission institutions, an expected change which is in no small degree a measure of their own success.

Likewise with the changes, slow or rapid, that are occurring in the social fabric of Oriental states, and which will amount in the end to revolution. The outcome will be neither the ancient order nor a reduplication of western culture. The types of education which have hitherto suited western states can hardly be presumed of final value for the coming Orient. It is not clear, therefore, that in this period of groping for new adjustments, the mission schools and colleges, whose methods and outlook are still, in the main, distinctively western, will be able without change to contribute largely to the needed leadership. We have found these peoples seeking guidance, not always, but chiefly, elsewhere.*

There are other problems, relating to the quality of educational work, to organization, to the teaching of religion and the religious liberty of students, which will bear upon the future place of mission schools as these lands develop their own latent powers. We shall examine the situation in each country, first as it relates to primary and secondary schools.

* In educational matters, for example, from secular colleges of education in the United States and Europe, from individual educators, from a Commission of the League of Nations.

EDUCATION: PRIMARY AND SECONDARY

India

The energies of India are for the moment absorbed in working out a complex political problem in which, because of their position as guests, American missions can take no part. They may, however, contribute to the future of India, whatever its destiny, by considering anew its educational need, and the possible place of the mission schools in meeting it. The relation of these schools to the government system will necessarily enter largely into the view of any serious appraisal.

Present background of the mission school. The laws which resulted from the Macaulay Minute of 1835 were framed in a wholly unprecedented situation. India was the first, and until 1882 the only, great Oriental civilization to come under the control of a western power. These educational laws, therefore, were a first experiment: though well-intended, they were not the laws of a normal country. Yet in substance, they are still in force after a hundred years of experience.

The content as well as the language used in carrying on high school education is still English.* In the interests of government service, higher education for the few is still stressed, and the village population of India, ninety per cent of the country, is still for the most part neglected. Even for those who receive the education, the process entails, with all its marked value and practical advantage, a heavy educational

---

* In the first four years of school life, the vernacular is used. The second four or six are weighted, for those who expect to go on to the high schools, with the acquiring of sufficient English so that when the high school is reached, all subjects may be both of English content and taught in English.

loss.* For such complete displacement of one's own educational content and habit by the tradition of another race cannot fail to result in much formalism and externality, in overemphasis on memory, imitativeness and routine. The alienation of their youth from their own culture is the result most deeply resented by cultivated Indians. Yet "all the efforts made in the last hundred years to correct the initial bias away from Indian culture, away from mass education, away from a reasonable primary school system, have never been able to restore the balance. Indian education still remains a top-heavy inverted pyramid."**

Indigenous schools. India herself is making efforts in various directions to round out her education. Thirty-eight thousand religious schools—Hindu, Moslem, and Sikh—schools of many years' standing, were listed in the last quinquennial report; the ashrams and attendant colleges, whether of the type of Gandhi's, attempting social reform together with vocational education, or Tagore's, creating an education where Indian art is genuinely a part of life; Fergusson College and Thackersey College at Poona, the latter founded to give girls a higher education in their own language, and resulting in a superb training in progressive education; the Dayanand Anglo-Vedic College at Lahore, which stresses, beside Indian language and culture, the need of technical education in arts and industries, and the bridging of the gulf between the educated classes and the masses:—the country is dotted with such efforts. One can hardly form an idea of the courage and sacrifice required in a land of such widespread poverty as India to conduct these independent ventures in education, especially those of collegiate scale. The general impression they gave, except in a few internationally known cases, was one of finan-

* "Our education has done far less for Indian culture than for the material and political progress of India. She looks to our schools for equipment in the struggle for existence; for the secret of happy living, *vivendi causa*, she looks elsewhere."—The Education of India, Arthur Mayhew, p. 4.
** E. Oaten, Professor in Presidency College, Calcutta, in Annals of American Academy of Political and Social Science, 1929.

cial struggle and of educational isolation. Their existence, however, and their numbers indicate pressing educational needs not otherwise met.

Mission schools. Mission schools, primary and secondary (including Catholic schools) are six per cent of the registered schools of India. Pupils in mission schools number nearly 600,000. The following table will indicate the variety as well as the astonishing magnitude of these undertakings:

291	English high schools	with	92,031	pupils
339	English middle schools	"	43,828	"
82	vernacular middle schools	"	9,617	"
11,158	primary schools	"	421,182	"
100	teachers' training schools	"	4,104	"
257	other schools	"	8,945	"
12,227	schools all told	"	579,707	"

Beside the Roman Catholic, there are represented here some one hundred Protestant sects. Of their 5,000 missionaries and 49,600 Indian workers, 1,100 missionaries and 26,000 Indian workers are engaged in educational work. The six boards co-operating in this Inquiry conduct 4,000 schools with 160,000 pupils. These statistics give a suggestion of how much these schools are contributing to Indian education, and how serious an impoverishment it would be if they were to draw out.

The work of these many schools is hard to draw into a single picture. Nor is it possible in a brief space to be just to its many aspects, if only because its quality is so uneven. Often the best schools in a city are mission schools, and also the worst. As other schools of good rank grow up around them, mission schools will more and more be judged by the people of India on the ground of their comparative general educational worth. We must accordingly consider them by this standard as well as by their contribution to character. Indeed, it is not possible to dissociate these two standards; for it is becoming, and should become, more and more difficult to influence character unless the educational standard commands respect on its own ground.

When we turn to education for women, we find that in all

of the registered schools in India, only 35,000 girls per annum go beyond the primary schools; and that of these the mission schools provide for nearly half, a pioneering and invaluable work. Taking the Catholic and Protestant missions together,

the 13 Christian women's colleges are 50% of the registered women's colleges of India,
the 67 teachers' training schools are 50% of the training schools of India,
the 101 girls' high schools are 45% of the girls' high schools of India,
the 197 girls' middle schools are 30% of the girls' middle schools of India.

This work is even more significant than its numbers would indicate.

Grants-in-aid and registration. Before describing the different types of mission school, it would be well to consider the present system of grants-in-aid and government recognition and their effect on mission schools.

In 1854 there was a new start in Indian education. Sir Charles Woods' despatch among other important things initiated the system of grants-in-aid which meant that instead of carrying on schools itself, Government would give grants of money to already organized schools or schools about to be started, be they municipal, district, private, or religious—the proportion to be based on the salaries already paid in these schools. In these grants no preference was to be shown to one religion over another. They were to be given only to schools that conformed to government regulations in material things like buildings, equipment, finance, etc., and in educational matters such as examinations, appointment and dismissal of teachers, choice of textbooks, and curriculum. Such schools are "Recognized Schools," and besides financial help they secure advantages for their pupils in easing the way to higher schools, and later on to government positions. Government positions and some others are open only to those who have matriculated in recognized *English* high schools. This more than anything else prevents the provincial governments (Indian staffed) from making the vernacular rather than English the medium of instruction in middle and higher schools.

The government control over recognized schools has had great advantages: the improvement of the equipment, the limitation of the size of classes and of the number of holidays (a thing much needed in this land of many religions), the exercising of a healthy supervision, and the making it possible for schools to expand.

But there are also disadvantages. This very expansion has had much to do with turning the mission schools from comparatively small schools, with a chance for personal acquaintance and quality of teaching, into large institutions similar to any other pre-progressive government city school, in India or America. Having to hold to the government curriculum and textbooks, little experimentation is possible, and rigid insistence on rules and regulations is obstructive to natural growth, making "cramming" and sticking closely to the textbook the general habit, putting dread into the heart of teachers and children, and killing joyousness and wider freedom of investigation. Real teaching is, after all, a fine art—not a standardized product.

The question is still an open one—as to whether grants-in-aid and recognition have been a greater harm or good to Indian mission schools. One missionary commented: "If we refused government grants we should have to close most of our institutions, and many of our buildings (having been hypothecated to Government in order to secure building grants) would be lost to us. We should be compelled to devise our own curricula, provide our own inspection and auditing agencies, and it is doubtful if the graduates would have any standing. I am in favor of working with Government, even though the method and system as a whole is out of date and badly needs revising." This is a policy of patient resignation. There is little of contagion or leadership in the lines.

A second way of meeting the changed situation is that of the Marathi Mission. They surveyed their entire field in 1930, reevaluated their work, and decided that part of it was duplicating government work, and was no longer necessary. "Twenty-five years ago," said their report, "our mission schools led Government. Today they follow. In twelve city primary schools the mission is spending Rs. 9,380 annually to educate fifteen Christian and 905 non-Christian children through the second standard, in widespread competition with government schools." Their decision was that "at the end of the current year, all the city schools of the mission, save primary departments of the high schools, be closed." This frees both personnel and money for pioneering work elsewhere which in their case is social work in the crowded districts of Bombay.

The best of all the alternatives was that of the Presbyterian school at Moga under the leadership of W. J. McKee (1920-1924). He, too, realized that the system needed revising; but his decision was—not to conform, not to transfer—but to stay within the government system and take part in that revising; to which work he brought rare educational insight and power to break new paths, and to fit education more closely to the life of the Indian people.

It would be a matter of real moment to India if a body of schools as significant as these four thousand could follow the lead of the Marathi Mission in undertaking a serious re-appraisal of its work, and then, in the spirit of Moga, could make each school in its own way what every living school should be, an experiment in taking part in the total life of the human beings it touches. We desire to indicate here a few ways in which such a constructive change might take place.

English high schools. There are 291 English high schools conducted by missions, 101 for girls and 190 for boys—92,031 pupils in all. With few exceptions, girls' schools are in a class by themselves. Their standard is on the average far better than the standards of boys' schools. The expenditure per pupil is twice as large. The percentage of trained teachers and of Christian teachers is greater. Sixty-nine per cent of the pupils themselves are Christian. Being more often boarding schools, sometimes in the country (vernacular middle schools), teaching the children of village Christians, sometimes in beautiful buildings in the city (English middle and high schools), teaching not only the children of the middle class but also those of wealthier Indian families; the teachers living on the compounds with the girls and devoting full time to their work—the atmosphere of those schools is more personal and the whole undertaking more satisfactory.

One would wish to say the same of the 190 English high schools for boys. They are not without their occasional great teachers. There are some very noble school plants; and there are among them schools which are preferred for their children by cultivated Indians, both for their spirit and for their excellence in education. As a whole, however, the city schools for boys conducted by the missions are now lagging behind the government schools, and are often duplicating their work. Too often the Indian teachers are ill prepared (the fact that a majority of Indian Christians are from the depressed classes is a disadvantage when an educated class of Christian teachers is required); too often the principal himself has had training in theology, not in education, and has been pressed into the service by a board in need of filling a vacancy. How can a man so unprepared teach his Indian teachers better methods?*

Many of the cultivated non-Christian Indians we met were graduates of mission schools. They spoke in the main with affection and gratitude of their schools. At one point the gratitude of the graduate commonly ceased. That related to the enforced attendance at daily chapel and the daily Bible study classes. This element of necessity, even though it was a well-understood and accepted condition of membership in the school, usually left a note of resentment, especially when the teaching was joined with disparagement or ignoring of the religions of their homes. The time for this type of requirement has passed. Though class-room instruction has its place

---

* We were told by a government Director of Public Instruction of one of the Provinces, a distinguished third generation Christian, that there were two types of school he had to threaten with removal of government grants: a certain very orthodox system of Arya Somaj schools, managed and financed by an Indian philanthropist, and *the Christian schools.* This was because our missions were disposed to appoint as principals of city boys' schools, men who were not trained teachers at all, but theologians, or men who undertook to carry on the principalship of such schools while also conducting other professions for part of the day.

in training religious intelligence, Christian character cannot be imparted as an item in a school curriculum. In practice, the daily period of Bible study, left in the hands of class-room teachers, even less well prepared as a rule than the average in American public schools, is seldom the ennobling influence we assume it to be. It should be in the hands of specially trained persons, and of the finest characters in the schools. The religious life of the school should be a privilege offered, not a duty required.

Middle schools. Of the middle schools, missions are responsible for 421 schools, with 53,445 pupils. Middle schools of India cover the four to six years between the primary and the high schools. For the greater number of its graduates, the middle school is the final period of education.

These middle schools are of two types, the English (language) middle school and the vernacular middle school. It is as if two paths diverged at this point in education. The first leads to the English high school and college: it opens the path to the culture of the West, and covers the ground of a formal and literary training. Much of the pupils' time must necessarily be spent in mastering the vehicle of future education, the English language.

Should students choose the other path, they know the language of instruction before they come, and time is saved in reaching the subject matter itself. They cannot go on to the high schools; but on the other hand they are free from the weary load of matriculation examinations and of thinking in a foreign language. It is possible for the school to experiment and to add practical knowledge to the formal textbook work.

There will always be a place for the more academic and literary training. But if we think in terms of the broad educational need which India shares with the Orient generally, that of bringing its life of thought into more direct relation to the conditions of daily activity, we feel justified in dwelling on the importance of a type of school which—avoiding a common error of American vocational schools, in which practical training tends to sacrifice the educational ideal—unites vocational with intellectual training to the advantage of both.

We call attention, then, to the fact that there are unrealized opportunities for the missions in the development of vernacular schools. For boys there are 200 English middle schools and but 24 vernacular middle schools. For girls there are 139 English middle schools and only 58 vernacular middle schools. This means that although the Christian population of India is drawn chiefly from working people and tradespeople, our middle and high schools are giving chief attention to those who are taking the line of academic and professional studies.

The Report of Village Education in India (1919-1920) realized the need for such schools, and made the vernacular middle school the "keystone of the arch of educational reform." Its suggestions have been carried out in the Punjab; but have been given little attention in other provinces, save in the indigenous schools supported privately by Indians and in a few promising Christian experimental schools. The great Presbyterian school at Moga, already mentioned, the description of which lies between the covers of W. J. McKee's "New Schools for Young India," amounts to a convincing argument for the possibilities of such schools (Community Village Schools and Community Normal Schools, Mr. McKee prefers to call them: at Moga both types are found). All over India and even farther afield one hears of the quickening power of this village-minded experiment.

In the Annual Report of the Department of Public Instruction of Burma, 1929-1930, we find these words: "In India, and especially in the Punjab, Christian missions have conducted valuable experiments in the training of village teachers, and have established institutions which have served as models. It is hoped that they will perform the same service here." Moga succeeded in making the environment of the pupils actually a part of the curriculum: one class would have as the center of its year's study the building and furnishing of a village house; another would choose the health of its community, visiting hospitals and studying the types of prevalent diseases, their cause and cure, and finally founding and carrying on a school dispensary, which was open the first half hour of the school day. Much of the subject matter required by Government was used in carrying on these projects. In every way this school made the dignity of labor and the principles of self-support and thrift things of actual practice; the boys knew that what one does, one learns. It was an epitome of community life, not only utilizing India's wealth of stories, music, art, and games, but cooperating wherever possible with outside agencies for sanitation, medicine, agriculture, economy. Above all, these boys saw in practice an example of what the real mission of a man's life might be, the lifting of the whole of life about him.*

Primary schools. Ten thousand and sixty-one boys' primary schools and 1,097 for girls, undertaking to educate 421,182 pupils: this is the mission contribution to this type of school— an immense number of children met by mission work in a land where the provision of schools for children has hardly begun. One could wish that the records of quality could loom as high.

City primary schools are usually attached to middle and high schools. One does not often find the several kinds of schools detached in India, save in the villages, where few schools rise above the primary level. In cities, primary schools generally hold the level of quality of the higher schools with which they are associated.

Village schools. And now for a glimpse of the village schools as they exist today. Alan Fraser wrote:** "We have just visited nine far-out schools. It is about the most discouraging thing a mortal man can do. The records were fine, attendance perfect for weeks at a time, including Saturdays and Sundays. There was no mistake in these, for were they not all newly written up in fresh ink, especially for our visit? Nearly all the

---

* Two memorable descriptions of the work of Moga, written by Mrs. Irene Mason Harper, can be found in Miss Van Doren's books, "Fourteen Experiments in Rural Education," and "Projects in Indian Education." Mr. and Mrs. Harper are both strong educators. They unite in the principalship of Moga.

** Village Education in India, 1920.

teachers were low-grade workers. It was unusual to find any pupil beyond the first pages of the primer; most seemed to be learning the alphabet 'forever.' Arithmetic occasionally reached multiplication by four, although addition was very uncertain. Bible stories and singing reached a higher level, but altogether the village school seemed only a name."

These are *mission* schools which he is describing. These are nine out of 15,000 we listed at the beginning of our statistics.

You go to a village, a little huddle of brown adobe huts,* sometimes inside a wall of the same color and material. You ask for the outcaste section (for most Indian Christians are from the depressed classes) and there you easily find the Christian school, a single-roomed structure usually with an open front, a teacher's desk, and a blackboard. The children sit on mats on the clean, hard, dirt floor. Usually there are gaily cut papers fluttering from strings drawn across the ceiling, for the roof is lifted above the wall a foot or more, making a long opening through which the air blows pleasantly. One could think well of these simple school buildings, with their fresh air; one could not help loving the dark, sensitive little faces of the well-mannered children; but the teachers and the teaching were, in the main, deplorable.

These teachers are Indian: a few are graduates of vernacular normal schools; others are graduates of mission schools for training evangelists; and some are simply old men or women for whom the mission feels some responsibility. They receive from $1.25 a month to $7 a month salary. Some eighty per cent of the children never get beyond the first grade, even though they may stay several years at school. The Hartog Commission estimated that no child who has failed to reach and pass the fourth standard will become permanently literate. The primary school records of these village schools show that

* The schools in 173 villages were studied by our Fact-finders. The health conditions in these villages are indicated by the following statement: Only 14 of the villages had latrines; 80-90 per cent of the people of South India have hookworm; 73 villages reported epidemics and serious diseases, including cholera, smallpox, measles, malaria, dysentery and plague, which accounted for 7,200 deaths during that year, an average of 98 deaths per village.

for four million children in the first grade, only four hundred thousand reach the fourth grade. Missionaries say, "Our first obstacle is the indifference, if not opposition, of the villager to the education of his children." But the opposition has something to do with the villager's doubt of the worth of the kind of education offered: as the education improves, opposition diminishes. "Such schools are practically worthless," "drab and colorless schools not longer to be tolerated,"—such were the comments of our Fact-finders.

A survey made by Dr. Mason Olcott of 161 villages in the Arcot Mission showed that in 22 out of the 161 villages not a single man or woman could be found who was literate, and that in spite of the fact that several of these villages had had mission schools for 35, 25 and 15 years. The result drawn from his survey was that many of our schools leave no permanent educational result. The money expended on them is largely wasted.

Some of the questionnaires sent out to experienced missionaries brought suggestive answers: "We would get farther in the end," wrote one, "if we closed one-half our village schools, and spent the money on training teachers who could teach the other half." Another wrote—"The most significant thing you can say about the village schools of our mission as a whole is that they are run as a means to help pay the cost of evangelism, not for education. For some of them the actual practice is to keep the school up enough to draw the government grant and so help to pay the expenses of the man who is first a catechist and second a teacher."* Three other answers reported that their missions were not putting any money into the schools, but that the schools were being run on government grants largely if not entirely. When one recalls that this was not the intention of the grants-in-aid; that these grants were carefully

* India Fact-finders' Report, *in loco.* Whether there should be anything incompatible between evangelism as an objective and the best educational procedure remains to be proved. What our visits and interviews, and those of the Fact-finders, confirm is the fact of a conflict. One of the Fact-finders, Mr. Leslie Sipple, thinks this conflict unnecessary: "Missions," he writes, "should cease to appoint any except trained educators to take charge of schools. A poor school is a poor evangelizing agency."

designated so that the amount of the grant was to be proportioned to salaries already provided by these schools themselves, one shrinks.

Such situations present a sharp example, fortunately unusual, of the way in which a desire to increase the numbers in our churches may not alone subordinate a real interest in education, but lead to practices one must characterize as shabby.

Vernacular normal schools. There are only two avenues through which it is at all likely that efficient teachers will ever reach the village schools—the vernacular middle schools and the vernacular normal schools.*

What we need for village teachers are not foreigners nor even the urban, English-trained Indians of the city schools. The one has never had and the other has lost "the ability to think along the furrows cut by Indian tradition." The need is for young men and women who, having grown up in a village, are used to its ways of living; and who have been given the education of teachers rather than that of evangelists, an education that opens their eyes to village and agricultural problems and gives the means of dealing with them. It is here that foreign missions can especially help at this juncture. These schools, not wholly neglected by government or missions, have as yet hardly realized their possibilities. They seem to us to hold the major opportunity of service to India. They are the narrow neck of the bottle, the avenue through which alone a necessary aid can come to one-sixth of the population of the world. They are free from the necessity of following educational conventions that hamper other parts of the school system

* For a description of a noble example of vernacular normal teaching to girls as carried out by the Baptist Mission at Ongole, see appendix to Regional Report. For boys, see an account of the government schools of the Punjab in the same place.

In some large cities one found mission schools of several hundred children whose teachers had had no other education than that of a vernacular middle school. One may become a village teacher with only this equipment, but one or two years of vernacular normal training (with what India begins to speak of as "an agricultural bias") is the proper equipment for village teaching.

of India. They have unlimited leeway for experiment. If we could help to multiply the number of these schools, if we could enrich the education that is given in them, as we in America with our newly awakened progressive education may be able to do (Moga is witness for us there), the service that we could give at this time would be of incalculable value. We would still be within the government system, and yet have found the little door that leads to India's need.

Conclusions

I. There are certain types of mission work that might be more adequately supported:

a. Since the chief educational need of India is the need of her villages, and since this can be met only as teachers can be trained who are familiar with village life and ready to meet its problems, it is recommended that each of the mission boards cooperating in this Inquiry study its own field, considering in what ways it can aid in developing vernacular middle and normal schools, so that they may truly become "the keystone of the arch of educational reform."

b. Girls' schools, particularly girls' boarding schools: such excellent work as this should not be curtailed until the general provision of Indian education for women has moved nearer to its standard.

II. There are types of mission work that might be diminished:

a. City schools for boys, in places where government schools are plentiful, strong and adequate. Mission city day schools which cannot provide a full-time person as principal would better turn their pupils over to government schools.

b. Village schools for which proper training and supervision of teachers cannot be carried out. Unless a mission school conducting education in country districts has sufficient money for the supervision of its village teachers, it has not sufficient money to provide village education.

III. It is recommended that mission schools in India make more use of the customs and riches of the local traditions. By westernizing the clothes and daily habits of the pupils they are alienating them from the environment of their own families.

IV. There is a need to find better ways whereby qualified teachers and the vacancies on the field can be fitted together. We suggest that an agency or agencies be established for registering qualified Indian Christian teachers, without regard to denominational divisions, to which schools throughout India in need of Indian teachers could turn: there would naturally be sub-offices for each major language area. This would aid in the due Indianization of mission schools.

V. The salaries of Indian teachers in city mission schools should approximate more nearly the salaries of their American colleagues whose responsibilities are equivalent.

VI. Additional ways should be devised for spreading from school to school the knowledge of successful educational methods and experiments.*

* One admirable idea which we hope will be continued is a series of books edited by Miss Alice Van Doren. It might easily, as it grows, amount to a traveling normal school built without bricks and mortar. It provides at one rupee each such books as "Fourteen Experiments in Rural Education." These books describe various experiments in teaching, told by persons who have carried them out. Mr. Olcott has added to the series "How We Learn" by Professor William Kilpatrick.

EDUCATION: PRIMARY AND SECONDARY

Burma

Lower Burma came under British control in 1852 and central and upper Burma as late as 1885. The population is about fifteen million, of whom some 260,000 are listed as Christian.* It consists of hill tribes of various racial inheritances surrounding a central core of Burmans. The statistics list 70% Burmese, 9% Karen, 7.5% Indian, 1% Chinese. The country is richer than much of India.

The Burmans are a gay, hospitable, amusement-loving people, without caste distinctions, more generous than persevering, willing to let others, such as the Indians and Karens, do the hard work of the land. The women are particularly fastidious and charming. They have entire social equality with men, sometimes their leadership makes one think them the superior sex.

The Karens (a race of different stock which poured down from the hills and occupied areas chiefly in the South) are Puritans by disposition, legalistic, stolid, cautious. They lack Burmese gayety, but they have some of the solid qualities of the Puritan, their instinct for cooperation, their respect for education, and (aided by mission training) their expectation of *paying for things themselves.*

Buddhist schools. Buddhism is almost universally the religion of the Burmese. In nearly every house there is a little shrine with a quiet figure of Buddha. The pagodas are lighted up at night and gleam golden in the city of Rangoon, and they are dotted also over the mountains throughout the country. Buddhism is responsible for many festivals, religious plays

* The Census of India, 1921, Vol. X, Part 1, p. 209.

in the villages ("whole families pack up and go to these performances"), "duty days" in the temples four times a month, "Sabbaths which bring groups to the monasteries where they spend the morning in religious discussion, hear sermons or recite holies. The quiet devotion of a layman and the dignified demeanor of some priest have their unobtrusive influence. After a picnic lunch at noontime the adults sit around and talk while the children play."

The 18,000 Buddhist temple schools,* conducted by yellow-robed Buddhist priests, are today diminishing in prestige and are being supplanted by more modern Buddhist educational institutions (called National Schools) with well-trained teachers, good equipment and noble buildings. These National Schools, some fifty in number, were established as one outcome of a nation-wide strike of students, 1920-1921, due in large part to their resentment against required attendance on Bible classes in Christian schools. The old-fashioned schools, poor as they are, and the Buddhist custom of requiring boys to go to the temple for a time and to attend temple schools, have contributed to the comparatively high literacy of the country, 34.7 per cent. Nearly all of the unrecognized vernacular schools are controlled by monks.

The school curriculum, like that of India, is the usual literary one. The Annual Report on Public Instruction, 1929-1930, sounds like an echo—"educational system top-heavy," "money spent on primary schools wasted," "teaching remote from the needs of modern life." Seventy per cent of the pupils of Burmese schools fail in examinations for the tenth standard.** This undoubtedly means poor teaching, but also a maladjustment of curriculum to the minds of the pupils. Thirty per cent of the pupils are served, but the education in some way is a misfit for seventy per cent.

Missions. Protestant missions came into this land, the Baptists in 1813, the Methodists in 1879. The two sects today con-

* Quinquennial Report on Public Instruction in Burma, 1928, p. 25.
** Data from Government Report.

trast in size: 160,655 Baptist Christians, and 1,424 Methodists.
Of the Baptist converts, 134,924 are Karens and only 7,263
Burmans. Only 1 in 600 Buddhist Burmans have become
Christian.*

Before the coming of the missionaries, the Karens were a
subordinate hill tribe, animists by faith. The missionaries gave
them education and, through the translation of the Bible, a
written language. This remarkable achievement—the giving of
a nationality to a people—has resulted in one embarrassment:
missionaries are held responsible for slowing up the Burmani-
zation of the Karens and they are denounced by the Burmese
nationalists for breaking apart this important minority group.
Karens have today a strong National Society, which has sent a
delegation to London to plead for a Karen nation (of 1,300,000
souls). They have collected much money for educating Karen
children. Their missionary zeal is in part the result of this
nationalistic movement.**

Statistics for 1930:

	Baptist Mission***		Methodist Mission****	
	Schools	Pupils	Schools	Pupils
High	20	4,632	4	395
Middle	83	8,720	5	1,044
Primary	763	32,816	18	2,316
Teacher Training	3	40		
Agriculture	1	75		
	870	46,283	27	3,755

These missions operate 900 schools, with 50,000 pupils.*****
As in other countries of the East, a good part of the burden of
girls' education rests on them. Nine high school girls out of
ten are in mission institutions, and it can be said that it is to

* Fact-finders' Report, India and Burma, *in loco*.
** *Ibid*.
*** Data furnished by Rev. W. E. Wiatt, Field Secretary of Baptist
Mission, Rangoon.
**** Data furnished by Rev. B. M. Jones, District Superintendent Metho-
dist Episcopal Church, Rangoon.
***** *Ibid*.

missions that Burma owes the insistence on the need of equal educational opportunities for girls and boys.

City schools and rural field. One could not but be impressed by the number and imposing quality of the missionary schools in Burma, particularly those of the Baptist missions. Divisions between Karens, Burmans, Anglo-Indians, and Indians —boys' schools and girls' schools—make it necessary sometimes to have a multiplicity of school systems in a city instead of one system, efficient, economical, and well-run. This also makes for duplication and overlapping. There is often great contrast in the buildings, a Karen school or a girls' school being a beautiful school while in the same town the Burmese school or the boys' school may be very inferior, sometimes a group of wooden shacks.

One finds in these large day schools of several hundred a single missionary as principal, generally a woman of fine educational training. If her teachers are men and nationals, she must do her best to humanize the rigid and doctrinal-minded puritanism of their Christianity. In the very beautiful girls' boarding schools this formalism of religion and of teaching has melted away.

Education in Burma is centered in the cities; and attention is only now beginning to turn, as in India, to the needs of the rural population. Improvement in government schools begins to raise the question of the continued necessity for so many city schools, with their large numbers, and the difficulty of making personal qualities count. In five cases we found well-trained teachers, in charge of large city schools, wishing to turn their lives toward the needs of the villages. One of the ablest of these has given in her resignation, and after a furlough spent in studying village work in some of the smaller countries of Europe, Czechoslovakia or Roumania, hopes to return to a Burmese village and build up a type of education which can spread from village to village. One agricultural school, at Pyinmana (the only Baptist school that is breaking away from the literary type of education), will be of great help to these pioneers in village work. It has two hundred acres under cultivation, though only two stalwart agricultural missionaries are in charge. If this school, while still letting its agricultural work lead, would build up the intellectual side of its program, it could go far to strike out a new type of education for Burma.

Conscience Clause. With the growth of national feeling in Burma, the Buddhist majority has felt increasing objection to the requirement in Christian schools that all students, about two-thirds of whom, in secondary schools, are non-Christian, shall receive Christian religious instruction. Some feel that "to be a good Burman one must be a Buddhist." But the legislation on this subject does not exceed the point of neutrality. It provides that "it shall not be required of any pupil that he shall attend any religious observance or instruction": this applies to both Buddhist and Christian schools. At the same time, in order that Buddhist schools might not fail to do their part in giving religious instruction to Buddhist pupils, it was also ordered that all schools under Buddhist lay management must provide religious instruction of this voluntary nature. The law is thus equable in its provision.

The attitude and practice of the Christian schools in Burma are in general hostile to this legislation: the prevalent feeling is that since "evangelization is the keynote and the main objective of our whole mission," Christian teaching for all students must in some way be maintained. As a result, the spirit of the legislation is not generally observed in the Christian schools;* and a certain tension exists between Christian and Buddhist in education, which tends to array the Christians against those nationalist aspirations which would vest power in the large Buddhist majority.

Among some very fine members of the younger missionary generation, there is a different spirit, ready to accept and cooperate with the principle of the conscience clause. This gives hope that the element of strain now in evidence may be allayed. In Burma, with its inter-racial, inter-communal and

---

* Twenty of the twenty-five secondary schools make attendance on Bible teaching compulsory. The percentage of Christians enrolled has, however, not increased during the last few years.

inter-religious strife, "it is a ministry of reconciliation that is needed."

Gospel Teams. One unusual element of the school life in the Christian schools of Burma deserves special mention, namely, the bazaar preaching and Gospel Team work which so often make a part of the program of the high schools. Boys and girls, twenty-five strong, with an older evangelist and several Bible women, drive in ox carts to a village, let us say, in the heart of the jungle, its bamboo houses, finely woven, lifted high on stilts in anticipation of the winter's rains. To this far-off little spot the boys bring entertainment during the day—games, sports, songs, band music; and in the evening a religious meeting is held, in which the spirit of gayety is continued, with secular songs and vaudeville acts, as a frame for the serious part of the program, "bearing witness" and personal appeal, usually under emotional stress, with much emphasis on the fear of hell, and with little reference to the social aspects of the Christian life.

It hardly needs to be pointed out that, however valuable the element of emotional fervor in the work of evangelism, such activity on the part of adolescent students, especially when often repeated, raises grave questions. Buddhist observers are often offended by the union of religious appeal and vaudeville play. Some Christians believe that the repetition over and again of the same testimony places a strain on sincerity. Serious also is the probable effect on village life when interpretations of Christianity by immature minds, tending to sharpen the cleavage between Christian and non-Christian, leave a legacy of division in the community. The stirring of emotion by persons who cannot be responsible for the needed subsequent nurture of character and habit in the villages visited is especially to be questioned. The educational influence of this practice is also to be considered. It cannot but interfere with the steady discipline of the class-room; and must therefore tend to bring both Christian education and Christianity itself into disrepute among thoughtful people.

These Gospel Teams from the high schools are derived by

imitation from Gospel Teams among college students, which are financed by special gifts from America; and which have made tours in India and Siam.*

Self-support. One of the highest rates of mission self-support to be found in the world is that of the Baptist work in Burma. Among the Karens, 98 per cent of the 977 churches and 700 of the 870 Baptist schools are entirely self-supporting. In the largest Karen district they have built all their own chapels and all their school buildings. The total value of the school buildings on the Bassein Sgaw Karen compound (exclusive of three owned and used by the missionaries) is well over a million rupees. These have been paid for by the Karens. One group of Karens raised over $200,000 in five years for buildings. In many cases America gave the land and the nationals paid for the buildings. Such instances could be multiplied.

Yet, in spite of this sturdy independence on the part of the Karens, the old custom of early mission days holds over: to a very large extent the legal ownership of these properties, given by the Karens, rests with the American Baptist Foreign Mission Society. There can be no doubt that the trusteeship of these properties is fairly exercised, yet the wisdom of this prolonged paternalism cannot fail to be questioned. There begins to be a sense of insecurity on the part of the nationals. "The Pwos and the Sgaws think they own it, and the mission legally owns it." A few years ago one group complained that the mission had taken away its property. "Many dissensions about property have come about in Thonze, Mandalay and Pegu. This gave rise to an independent church." In brief, much Karen and mission property are so far entangled that there is real danger that with growing nationalism this question may breed trouble in the future.

The American Baptist Foreign Mission Society has begun in general to think of "a holding body representing the indigenous Christian community, competent to take title for the property in accordance with any specific agreement that may

* In Christmas week in 1930, 188 young men and women formed themselves into 17 Gospel Teams for "campaigns" in 53 villages.

be entered into at the time of transfer." Without passing on the problem of the rate at which actual devolution of control is possible, a rate which varies with different sections, it would seem that action looking toward the ultimate transfer should, in the interest of future amity, no longer be deferred.

Recommendations

1. That the ultimate transfer of school property to the nationals be now provided for, so that the spirit of cooperation on the part of the nationals shall not be forfeited by delay.

2. That the devolution of key positions such as the principalship of schools proceed as rapidly as may be consistent with efficiency. Complete devolution in some places seems only to await authoritative action; in others it is important that nationals be selected and trained with care for the assumption of responsibility and that the missionaries provide them with advice and assistance until their capacity is demonstrated.

3. That the impulse toward village work on the part of well-trained teachers and other missionaries be welcomed, and that opportunities for specialized training in rural education and industrial and vocational education be furthered wherever possible.

4. That mission schools cooperate cordially and in good faith with the Government in respect to the rules regarding the teaching of religion.

5. That mission schools, through sport and teachers' associations, cultivate cooperation with the other schools of the country.

6. That the practice of using high school students in evangelistic campaigns be carefully reconsidered, with a view to its effects both on the students and on the villages visited.

7. That the question of bringing a vocational, and especially an agricultural, element into the curricula of certain schools (as in the Pyinmana Agricultural School) be carefully considered.

8. That a program of reduction of numbers and raising of quality of urban schools be worked out.

EDUCATION: PRIMARY AND SECONDARY

*Japan**

Historical background. Protestant education in Japan begins with the Meiji Restoration. It was not till 1868 that the edicts against Christian teaching were relaxed, and it was in 1870 (62 years ago) that the first mission girls' school was opened.

Missions were permitted to come into Japan by its own Government, not, as in the case of India and China, introduced under the protection of outside powers. This has made for a different temper throughout their stay.

Japan's extraordinary system of public schools must be the background of any picture of mission work. Japan has

  44,000 schools of all grades
  25,000 primary schools (compulsory, age 6 to 12 years)
 260,000 teachers, 200,000 of whom are primary
     857 schools for girls
     797 vocational schools (technical, agricultural, commercial, merchant marine, aquatic products, industrial crafts)
      16 Christian middle schools for boys
      38 Christian high schools for girls
       2 Peers' and Peeresses' schools
       3 experimental normal schools.

The registered schools of Japan, admirable in their thoroughness, are under the most rigid regulation we have yet encountered: rules as to the hours of teaching each subject, requirements on the use of every building, on the preparation of every teacher, and even on the tuition that can be charged.

* For the sake of the development of the argument, the order of discussion here deviates from our usual order: consideration of education in China will follow that of Japan.

Only the last five schools on the list are omitted from this iron formula, the Peers' and Peeresses' schools, which are given a curriculum of their own, and the three normal schools, which are given full freedom to experiment for the benefit of the whole nation.*

Christian girls' schools.** In earlier days, mission schools were usually small. Intimate touch of character on character was possible.

Not so the large present-day mission institutions, with their frequently imposing buildings, their government-managed curricula, and pupils who come as second choice, preferring (even though they are of Christian families) to go to government schools, such is the prestige of government schools both in education and in the securing of positions later on. The comparative scantiness of government higher schools for girls still gives girls' mission schools an advantage over boys' schools, as to quality of membership, though probably a temporary one. Educationally the Christian schools tend to consider their work done if they conform to government regulations and meet examinations. Too much of their effort has gone into buildings, too little into the quality of teaching. Their work usually resembles that of an average high school in America.

Occasionally one finds an unusual spirit in the school, the quiet friendliness of the Quaker School for girls at Tokyo, or the dedicated devotion of one woman, who transmuted a personal grief into the founding of a School for the Deaf, or the Tokyo Episcopal School, where the girls slip into chapel as individuals, no one counting them, with perfect freedom to stay away if they wish. As they come from the bustle of their

* For a description of this system and its results, refer to Regional Report on Japan.
**   38 girls' high schools
      23 of these add 2 junior college years
       2 of these add 4 senior college years
   13,695 girls educated
      223 girls receive education in religious work
   $223,500 cost of all these schools to the American mission boards.

school work, entering what is truly a chapel, noble music lifts them into another mood—no wonder no girl misses it! Such things are far above creed or controversy; they are the heart of peace in a day's activity, a little avenue to God. And all this is because two women, the present teachers, have built their own love of music and art into that chapel. That is what makes a school, that and nothing else—the quality and insight of the people who teach in it.

We agree with the lately published report on Christian Education in Japan that these girls' schools should be coordinated in a single plan; for the divisiveness of Christianity is a distinct weakness. It is not only that it has made each different sect forge ahead on its own, the great buildings of one fortunate denomination only making the other sects more discontented with their smaller buildings (though in America the smaller buildings themselves would be considered a very fine private school plant). There are places (as at Yokohama and Sendai) where schools are duplicating each other's work. These are problems requiring consideration working toward either coordination or unification. In places where the buildings are too old for effective use, the question of discontinuing the school should be considered. In cities like Tokyo, the *teaching* might be coordinated by having each school emphasize a different field of study—

College entrance	English language
Physical education	Japanese language
Primary education	Household economics
Commercial education	Music.

This would make it possible for a girl to select her school according to the profession she hoped to follow, instead of having all the schools specialize as at present on the teaching of English and home economics (the usual mission specializations).

*Christian boys' schools.** But these problems in regard to girls' schools are comparatively slight. One can look at these

* 16 boys' middle schools
9,802 boys educated each year

schools with satisfaction. It is in boys' schools especially that a clear judgment and power to act are needed. These schools also are filled with students for whom they are the second choice. Those who succeed in the government examinations are not found here. Those who fail frequently fall back on mission education.

In the mission schools for boys there is one central defect, namely, that their imitation of the government schools is carried out to the point of losing their Christian character. Their excessive size is an added cause of this defect. On account of being limited by government regulation to a charge of $20 gold a year for tuition, the missions' alternative is to take on numbers far beyond the possibility of filling them with spirit.

One sits on the platform of one of these schools for the morning exercises, looking into a sea of boys' faces, 900 boys, in a huge assembly hall, with no atmosphere, spiritual or material, to quicken it. Men walk up and down the aisles occasionally to keep order (happily not a usual thing). "How many of these boys are Christian?" one asks a teacher. "About fifty," he answers. Fifty out of 900—not an overwhelmingly Christian student body. Every registered school must have military training.

Some of these schools, as at Aoyama, have a noble equipment; some, like Kwansei, have new buildings of good quality; but the impression left by many of these boys' schools was that the equipment was ill-kept, the numbers overwhelming, the quality of the students poor, and little human material on the faculty strong enough to stem the tide and make a Christian atmosphere. It is generally agreed that the average educational standard is low: "Their standards must be raised if they are to compete."* These sixteen boys' schools, according to the Report on Christian Education in Japan, need at present $2,230,000 gold for endowment to maintain them at their

---

$311,387 yielded by tuition
$250,000 from American boards for missionary teacher salaries and deficits; $93,129 for deficits alone
$39,683 from Japanese gifts.
* Report on Christian Education in Japan, p. 49.

present standard of efficiency. In our judgment, that standard is not sufficient to justify their continued support: such justification would call for both a higher educational level and a more distinctive religious spirit.

Need of expert and unified management. It is clear that there are problems here demanding firm and thoroughgoing handling. There can be no satisfaction in merely palliative treatment, nor yet in piecemeal treatment. There must be such a reorganization as will require united action at home, studying the group of fifty-four secondary schools as a whole and planning for their future. The question of finance will be one of the first concerns of such a study.

Among the financial problems demanding attention is that of the low tuition charges (made obligatory by the government) paid by pupils from well-to-do families, throwing the burden of support back upon the American churches. There are doubtless reasons for this anomaly which require careful weighing. We feel it our duty simply to call attention to the situation.

At a very fine girls' school, an addition to which was built three years ago with American money, and provided with gymnasium, outdoor tennis courts, laboratories, home economics rooms for cooking and housekeeping—an equipment such as few American private schools possess—the tuition charges were sixty yen per year. Of the five hundred students, many were from well-to-do families, of the professional or official classes. The mission boards pay for this school an annual deficit of $7000 gold and the salaries of four American teachers.

This situation is the rule rather than the exception. The American contribution to these schools, including deficits and teachers' salaries, is 680,220 yen per annum.

The tuition rate is not unalterable. There are modes of registration which allow some latitude in the scale of charges. It is possible to carry on without entering the government system of control if the school is willing to forego certain advantages. Acceptance of governmental regulation is not considered a duty to the public authority, as in China: it is an official relation which may or may not be adopted. It carries with it certain privileges such as the ready admission of graduates to higher schools and the consequent advantages to these students of later employment and position. The price that has to be paid is acceptance of the government curricula, inspection, restriction of religious teaching (now considerately interpreted), and limitation of tuition fees with resulting pressure toward numbers.* The leading private schools in Japan guard their freedom in this way. But the mission schools are hesitant about such risks. They have in mind the competition of excellent public schools with low tuitions. And they fear that numbers would fall off if there were any jeopardy of their keeping in step with government requirements, a fear that seems hardly justified in view of the large number of candidates for the government schools for whom there is no place.

In Japan, more than in any other country, one realizes that the quality of the teacher makes the school. Here is a government system of spacious outline, with room not only for the usual school studies but for music, drawing, Japanese flower arrangement, out-of-door study of nature and historic places (school trips of ten days' duration). There, in each public school, one found not only a modern gymnasium, but a traditional Japanese room (with sliding panels) reserved for lessons in tea ceremony and "Japanese customs." Within the system home industries are taught—sewing, cooking, table service. The cooking in the hands of one scholarly little Japanese teacher—at St. Agnes', Kyoto—had merged into the work of the chemical laboratory and had resulted in original experiments on the chemical changes that come about during the

---

* The following official statement may indicate the different statuses recognized as legitimate:

"Religion is entirely eliminated in schools erected by central and local governments. In middle schools and girls' high schools where curriculums are determined according to government regulations, religion is also not taught. Religion is free to be taught, however, in private institutions, universities and technical colleges, and other miscellaneous schools, whose curriculums are not controlled by the governmental regulations." (Kinichi Takebe, Director of the Bureau of General Education, Tokyo, May, 1932.)

processes of boiling, baking, and frying. These experiments had been printed and sent to a chemical society.

We do not advise leaving the government system, in the belief that if that came about all would be solved. We urge, rather, that teachers be more ingenious in using to the maximum the chances within the government system. This quality we found more often in the girls' schools than in the boys' schools. It is only a few exceptional schools that can wisely cut adrift from the central system in Japan, and it is important to observe that there are such schools: we shall mention two outstanding ones.

Schools that train for leadership. There are in Japan two deservedly well-known bits of education, standing outside both the government system and the mission system. Mr. Obara and Mrs. Hani, founders and principals of these two creative schools, are Christians though not connected with missions. They have no lack of students, for they are giving educational riches that far outweigh the advantage of getting into government colleges without severe extra examinations. Mr. Obara's school, whose faculty is wholly Japanese, is based upon old Japanese methods of school life and of teaching.

It is precisely on the side of the truly religious spirit and of uplift to character that we feel the strength of these schools. In simple devotion and reverence it would be hard to find mission schools whose chapel services could compare with these. At Tamagawa (Mr. Obara's school) a service is held, as in Gandhi's ashram, out of doors, whether in winter or summer, at 5:30 in the morning; the school meets on a noble hill-top behind the little chapel, and with a circle of mountains about them and a beautiful foreground of valley and farm below, they say their morning prayers.

If you are absorbed in bringing to earth ideas great enough to use all your power, then you look upward and can safely forget the "competition" of other schools, or the recognition of Government. Nor do you need to spend time crying out for leadership. These great teachers, themselves natural leaders, by their simple absorption in bringing wider lives to their students, are eliciting leadership in a direct and un-self-conscious way.

Conclusions and Recommendations

The impression becomes clear in respect to Japanese schools, that as a country reaches the stage in which Christianity is simply accepted as one of its own religions, the mission school is less and less the primary source of Christian teaching and thought. Her own Christian sons and daughters, carrying on their own schools or leading their lives within their own professions and callings, become the chief interpreters, unembarrassed by the sense of special position and office. In respect to primary and secondary education, Japan has reached this point in its history. Hence the mission school authorities seem somewhat on the defensive, and are driven to the belief that the essential trouble is in a deficiency of financial support. The signs seem to us to call, on the whole, not for more expenditure in these schools, but for the beginnings of a prudent and considerate withdrawal of our participation in them.

In certain of them our participation should continue. There will be a permanent place for some few schools of marked excellence, especially for girls' schools, in which the presence of American teachers will make for a welcome liaison between the cultures of America and Japan. To raise a few such schools to a level of educational dignity would greatly contribute to the meaning of the Christian view of life in a land quick to detect every note of cultural and spiritual distinction.

With regard to the secondary schools as a whole, in view of the more pressing need for mission funds elsewhere, we recommend:

I. That a general policy be adopted of reducing and ultimately discontinuing financial grants from mission funds to schools in Japan on somewhat the following lines:

That at the end of a specified period, longer for girls' schools than for boys' schools, these schools should be prepared to meet their own operating expenses;

That during this period, grants should be gradually reduced;

That the continuance of grants during this period should be conditioned on making the changes necessary to bring these schools into a state to fulfill their purpose.

II. That we endorse the findings of the lately published Report on Christian Education in Japan, in urging the reorganization of this group of schools with the aim of improving their quality: consolidating schools on a union basis where necessary to avoid duplication; freeing them to do specialized work where it is needed; closing such schools as it may be necessary to close to accomplish the highest purposes of the group of schools. Action to this end should be in accord with, and may form a part of, the administrative plans urged in chapter XIV of this Report.

It is recognized that the missions have a responsibility to effect these changes before turning the schools over to Japanese responsibility and control.

EDUCATION: PRIMARY AND SECONDARY

China

The present task of education in China is more formidable than that of any western nation. For no western state is attempting to bring children into adjustment to a world widely different from the world of their parents, and to develop for that purpose widely different habits if not a different character. Not only is the nation itself in the aftermath of a great revolution, but it is a great social revolution as well as a political one. China has relied more than any other great civilization on the immense educational force of the family: it now finds itself impeded by that force. It has to analyze its whole cultural inheritance into those parts which must be discarded and those which must be kept. For many years China's educational advisers have tried to meet this situation by imitating western models. She now begins to realize that there are in the world no models which she can safely copy; because no educational scheme has been devised to meet a problem as deep-reaching as hers.

In dealing with it, the training of character occupies a central place. The National Government recognizes this necessity to some extent. In inculcating the "Three Principles of the People" of Sun Yat Sen, it is facing the need of education at once political, social and moral.

In this matter of character training Christian schools should have a notable part; their contribution has been highly valued and some of China's greatest leaders have been trained in Christian schools. There is reason to fear, however, that these schools are at present less effective in this way than formerly. Some of the factors bearing on this point we have now to examine.

*A glimpse of mission history in China.** It would be interesting to make a chart of the growth of the mission schools
and to suggest the psychological causes for their rise and their
present decline. In 1807, Robert Morrison came to a very conservative China. In twenty years he had made only five converts. In 1877 there were 6,000 pupils in Protestant mission
schools. It was in this era that Japan and China were becoming
acutely aware of the fact of their great difference from the
rest of the world. The result of this psychology was a growing
desire for foreign schools.

In 1899 there were   7,000 pupils in mission middle schools
" 1911   "   "   102,000   "   "   "   "   "
" 1915   "   "   170,000   "   "   "   "   "

By 1920 it had become "almost the fashion to become a Christian"; since 1922 the tide has turned.

This was caused partly by the disillusionment of the World
War and the widespread impression it left that the West did
not really believe the Christianity it taught, partly by continued resentment over treaties requiring the grants of special
privileges to religious bodies, as well as to economic interests,
partly by the Communist influence which painted Christianity
as an unscientific superstition, an ally of capitalism and im-
perialism, and partly by two incidents, which shocked China
throughout its length—the first Shanghai Incident (1925) and
the Canton Incident of a month later.** Then came the inter-

---

* Population: 400,000,000.
  Protestant church members: 400,000.
  Cooperating Boards:

Baptist	11,164	Presbyterian U. S. A.	3,518
Congregational	21,851	Episcopal	9,007
Methodist	46,214	Dutch Reformed	3,418

  Missionaries:

America	3,052	Cooperating Boards	1,368

  Schools:
  Primary: Some thousand.
  Middle: 196. About 30,000 pupils.
  (The decreased Presbyterian members are due to the fact that many of
them have fused with the Church of Christ in China.)
  ** As in all such events, versions vary, and an exact statement of fact
may be impossible. It is possible, however, to say how they appeared
to the Chinese. For the first Shanghai Incident it was held that unarmed

nal disturbances in China, including anti-foreign agitation, during 1925-1927, which compelled many schools to close, especially those in country districts.

The following statistics show the results of these feelings and events:

In 1915 216 Christian middle schools
" 1919 265 " " "
" 1924 339 " " "
" 1927 100 " " "
" 1928 172 " " "
" 1932 196 " " "

As a leading Chinese Christian summarized the history: "Once we looked up to the missionaries as if their very shadows were holy. Then we saw the kind of things which Christianity allowed, and there was a sharp reaction. Now we have begun again as equals."

Regulations regarding religious teaching. In 1916, the Government of China began establishing rules regarding religious teaching.* In that year a regulation was passed: "No religious teaching or ceremony shall be *required* in Primary Schools." In 1921, came a decree making attendance on religious education voluntary in the middle schools. Our Fact-finders report to us: "No indication was found that these regulations were observed by the mission schools." The natural result of this failure followed in due time.

In 1929, the regulations grew more severe. The president, principal or dean of every school in China must be Chinese,

---

students who had marched to a police station to protest the arrest of fellow students were fired upon by an over-fearful English police guard. In Canton, a month later, a students' parade marching along the water side opposite the foreign settlement on Shameen Island was exposed to a broadside of foreign shot, and many were killed and wounded. European fear of Communist influence in China may have played a part in both incidents.

* China differs from India in that it gives no financial grants-in-aid to mission schools. The enforcing power of Government rests on registration. If a school desires to be registered, it must obey government regulations, otherwise Government may refuse the school its permission to open the following year.

and religion must not be given as a required subject, nor religious promotion carried on through class instruction. Pupils must not be *compelled* to attend religious exercises. The curriculum was to be according to government code.*

The passing of a regulation as definite as this broke the Christian community into two camps, according to their interpretation of the rightful function of a school. To those who believed that a school was a chance to share life, this rule brought no consternation. They noted that the regulation was not directed against Christians alone, but against the use of the schools for propaganda by *all* religions; that voluntary courses in religion were permitted outside of the school buildings, or sometimes in the school buildings but outside the school hours; that the course on Great Men of History, which was listed under Ethics for the junior middle work, included the life of Christ; that the Government permitted courses in philosophy and ethics and an introduction to civilization, which recorded the contribution of Christianity to the world. There was here an ample channel for giving one's best, and the required passing of headship to Chinese principals was but hastening a transfer toward which the missions aim.**

But there are other groups of educators who still hold with

* An interesting bit of investigation and reflection made two years after the cataclysm by Professor Timothy Lew of Yenching is recorded in the Christian Education Review of January, 1931. It describes a test given to 1000 students who had attended middle schools. He asked them to note what had most influenced them in their religious life as they had encountered it in the schools. Here in part is the tabulation:

       1st Personality of the teacher (90%)
       2nd Christian literature
       3rd Personal devotions
       4th Religious worship
       7th Religious instruction.

"It indicates," said one of our Fact-finders, "that the agencies prohibited by the government regulations are those which from the standpoint of effectiveness could most easily be spared."

** It has been a common thing and a glorious one to hear from missionary headmasters and mistresses who were succeeded by Chinese officers, "If we could only have foreseen how much better it is now, we would have done it ten years ago," or "One hundred and sixty girls who *want* to come to chapel mean so much more than three times that number who don't!"

the aims of education as formulated by Dr. Mateer in 1877, according to which the school's essential service to China should come through the doors of the Church; to those the ruling was an obstacle in the way of duty. They have closed their schools rather than submit, and they have returned to their homes. The missionaries who remain and continue their work are perhaps the ones better fitted to help China at this moment in her history.

Educational changes in process. There are at present 1,339 middle schools in China, 196 of which are Christian. These schools are not, as with us, usually separately housed in primary, grammar and high school buildings. An upper middle (or high school) usually has in the same compound, if not in the same building, all the lower grades, down to the very earliest primary class; so when one isolates the members of the upper grades, one gets an imperfect picture of the large size of government and Christian city schools. The easiest way of managing crowded classes, as is well known, is to hold strictly to the system of lectures and textbooks, and this is done.*

In the South and in the larger cities of the North our mission schools are largely what we would call in America private schools, nobly built architecturally, and teaching the wealthier girls and boys of China. To them this informational type of work serves the ends in view. They are bound for college, some with hopes of study abroad, and in these schools they are well prepared for this; their education is entirely western. They learn English and they live a happy, normal boarding school life, often with European clothes and furniture, western

---

* "A large part of the work in Christian schools," wrote one of our Fact-finders, "appears to be confined to the memorizing of facts—terms, words, and definitions of words. But Christian and Government middle schools alike have not broken away from the traditional practice. To do so would be very difficult. Many of the American and Chinese teachers in these schools know only the old methods. They teach with little originality and almost no opportunity for free self-expression on the part of the children. Both sets of schools are influenced by the same inertia."

sports, and delightful gardens and buildings, many of which are given to the missions by wealthy Chinese parents.

But it is in the smaller cities, in Hangchow, Nanking, Taianfu and other cities of Shantung province, that the question becomes serious; for there mission schools teach the children of artisans, townspeople and farmers, and this formal type of education unfits them for their future life. Mission schools seem to know but one objective for education, *college entrance*, and the boys they are teaching in these central and northern schools are better fitted for other aims than college.*·

This has come about through China's having imitated the West rather than having studied her own needs. Today she begins to realize this and she is seething with educational experiments, hunting for better ways before her educational system crystallizes, as has Japan's. She knows that she has not at present an industrial and factory system such as ours, which can absorb the partially educated products of her school system. She begins to know from experience how serious it is to give a merely academic education to the children of artisans and farmers.** The province of Shantung has taken the initiative in this matter. It has made a law that no more schools will be hereafter registered unless they offer a vocational education in connection with their literary one. This movement will probably soon spread further, for on every hand we found reflective Chinese educators, filled with anxiety about the maladjustment between the school curriculum and the children's future.

Protestant middle schools are numbered at present at 196,

* "We are," writes a prominent Christian missionary, "actually in danger of rendering a disservice to China by adding to the number of college graduates unfitted for useful careers, or in excess of the capacity of the country to absorb them, as is already so disastrously the case in India, Japan and the Philippines." The schools are supplying to some extent only what students demand. Nevertheless, they have a certain responsibility for stimulating and directing the demand.

** "My observation is," said the Chinese Principal of one of the largest Christian middle schools in Nanking, "that the reason so many of the student class join the Communists is because they are without a sense of security in having an interesting craft that will furnish a living wage."

or about one-half their maximum total number in 1924. The present number of pupils would exceed 20,000 and may approach 30,000. If a block of schools as important as this should seriously dedicate itself to the reforming of education on modern and more living lines, it would mean a gain for China quite out of proportion to its numerical strength.

The phrase "vocational training" has in America taken on a meaning so utilitarian in character that one hesitates to use the term. The schools which China needs are better illustrated for us at Berea, or in General Armstrong's work at Hampton, or in the ideas of Saunderson of Oundel—schools that train both head and hand and yet whose intellectual content is so good that it leaves a student able to push on, if he wishes, to higher studies.

The Report of the Commission on Christian Education in China of ten years ago, under the chairmanship of Dr. E. D. Burton, has this proposal: "The grade of education should not only be related to life, but each course should also be occupational in character, and at the same time prepare students for higher education."

This recommendation is carried out in its entirety in but few mission schools.*

But could our more formal mission schools change their staid buildings in such fashion as to take part in living work like this? It would mean a pioneering work as great as that of

* Outside Nanking, the Seventh Day Adventists have established one, modelled after the work of General Armstrong. Mechanic arts, farming, and fruit-canning are being taught to about two hundred boys. The academic program is not lessened by a jot. It was more far-reaching than the average middle school curriculum, yet these boys are left after six years of training with a thorough mastery of metal work, and the knowledge that during the process their work had paid the greater part of their school expenses. Five hundred dollars (Mex.) over expenses was cleared this year by the steel furniture made in this school, and sold in the open market.

Mr. Sam Dean, of the Presbyterian Mission of Peiping, has not only created a self-supporting school for machinists, but has, with forty boys, created an Institute of Architecture and Engineering that is a perfectly original variant of this idea. Even the few independent ventures which stand out among the 196 middle schools that we direct win China's appreciation.

the first missionaries. It would also be as difficult. It might mean registering these schools as Institutes, studying the old apprenticeship method of education to see what it had to teach us at the present day, selecting one craft, or two, such as the school's equipment would permit, finding and employing artisans who could teach that craft, and working these men into the teaching staff, while not diminishing the strength of the intellectual education which would make the other significant. It would mean cutting down that excess of numbers which at present are necessary to meet expenses. It would mean meeting those expenses in other ways: some schools have done this by selling the results of the student's craftsmanship. It would mean keeping close to the life of China, through watching its own notable experiments in the work of such educators as C. H. Chuang, P. C. Chang, Po Ling Chang, W. T. Tao, Y. C. James Yen, not to imitate them for evangelizing purposes, but realizing that they are nearer the heart of their people, to learn much from that genius which promises important contributions to the future educational wisdom of the world.

It was chiefly in the schools of the Mass Education Movement that we felt the spirit of sacrifice and of a warm human devotion touched with a patriotic vision actually quickening the consciousness of young people. Whether carried on by Confucian or Christian, this movement spread abroad that quality which we have come to think of as the spirit of Christ. All told we have seen nothing in the Orient more wisely and honorably planned and nothing promising so much for the equipment of China in mind and character.

Conclusions and Recommendations

It is evident that the mission schools, while adapting themselves slowly to the new situation created by the Chinese Revolution, are doing comparatively little to respond to the new tasks which China as a whole is undertaking. It is an unparalleled opportunity to aid in a vast and critical national transformation.

What is it, beside the natural momentum of the system, that stands in the way of a more adequate response?

One part of the difficulty is the lack of new thinking about the relation of Christianity to the special problems set by Chinese life. The doctrinal formulae of a past generation are not related by any living spirit to the needs of pupils.

Another part is our disunity. The 30,000 pupils of Christian mission schools in China are divided among scores of denominations, each school managed by its own mission. Further, that mission is not made up of teachers and educational experts: "it actually consists of evangelists, doctors, teachers, usually a majority of women—wives of missionaries, and single women. They are supposed to pass judgment as a body, and that body is not qualified to deal with matters of education. Their thinking is in terms of the activities of their own mission."

Any one who has been the principal of a school will realize the impossibility of allowing an outside committee of untrained people, no matter how good they may otherwise be, to dictate the policy of educational detail and management. There is no surer way of dooming your school to mediocrity— yet that is the custom among mission schools.

Denominational divisions, stagnant thinking, lack of expert direction—these are the chief causes of our relative ineffectiveness. None of the obstacles mentioned are necessary: the way can be opened to a far greater service. The contribution and the welcome of mission schools to China continues. They give a substantial education, of conventional patterns; their academic standards are in general as high as those of the public schools; their instructors are less hampered by student democracy (even to the extent of being felt in tenser moments cold to the national interest); their work is less liable to interruption; and their income, until recently, has been more reliable. They have resources which should be mobilized to a much greater advantage.

1. We recommend that the curricula of the middle schools under the societies represented by this Commission be radically re-examined and revised, with the end—not of forfeiting

their cultural value—but of offering direct aid to students in such callings as will render them most serviceable to China.

Some middle schools will remain primarily preparatory schools, though even they should have some definite path whereby each student participates in, and so understands, the types of activity which will so largely make the careers of his fellows.* A considerable number should turn their energies into vocational channels.

2. The general policy of financing Christian schools in China is to do so entirely from tuition except for American missionary salaries paid by the mission boards. Schools in India have government grants. Schools in Japan have alumni who are better able to assist them financially than have many of the schools in China. The middle schools of China are worthy of better financial support than they are getting from the mission boards.

3. We recommend that as the missionary personnel is gradually withdrawn from assignment to individual schools the funds represented by missionary salaries and allowances be continued to the schools whether for the employment of Chinese teachers or for other uses.

4. Since the proper place for Christian schools is that of a component part of a nation-wide educational system, we recommend that teachers in these schools cultivate professional relations with other Chinese schools, as by joining teachers' associations open to general membership.

General Recommendations for Mission Schools in the Far East

I. That where missions are conducting schools, the aim of these schools should be primarily education, not evangelization, and that teachers and administrators should be chosen with this standard in view.

* In the school of Mr. P. C. Chang in Tientsin one sees the work of a great educator who in the daily school life, through investigation and use of afternoon hours, brings his students into direct relation with the physical and economic conditions of human existence.

II. That mission schools in all Oriental countries cooperate in good faith with the governments in their efforts, through conscience clauses or through agreements in registration, to protect the religious liberty of the citizens; and to this end

That non-Christian students be not required to attend Christian services of worship nor Bible classes. This does not mean that religious services or classes for all students need be omitted, but that they should be carried out in a tolerant and sympathetic spirit.

III. That religious education and worship in the schools be reorganized under expert guidance to the end that they may have vital relationship with the problems and lives of the pupils, and that only teachers specially qualified for this work be responsible for this part of the school program.

IV. That a Board of Specialists be established at home, maintained by united action among denominations, advising a united enterprise in Christian education abroad, and keeping in mind the special and changing needs of the Oriental peoples (a phase of the reorganization proposed in chapter XIV).

A large responsibility for the future of Christian education in the East rests upon the mission boards and agencies at home. Only by the most genuine cooperation at home can these problems abroad be met, and the strongest teachers be enabled to serve as Christians would wish to serve.

CHAPTER VII

EDUCATION: HIGHER

1. *The Purpose of the Christian Colleges: Changing Emphasis*

IN ALL of the three countries we have visited various motives conspired, as we have noted, to the founding of Christian colleges and universities. (For convenience we shall refer to them collectively as colleges.) The purpose of these institutions has been two-fold: To propagate the Christian religion, and to aid in the higher education of youth.

In earlier days the purpose of propagating the Christian religion clearly predominated. Moreover this purpose was conceived of chiefly in terms of the nurture of Christian youth, the development of enlightened Christian leadership and the conversion of young men and women from other faiths. There has been, however, a gradual shift of emphasis. The missionary teachers and executives, partly because of the disappointing number of formal conversions resulting from their efforts, and partly because of a broadening vision, have come to think of the religious purpose of the college largely in terms of the permeation of their students, and through the students the community, with Christian ideals and principles. And what is even more significant, there has been a growing recognition of the importance of the second objective, a growing tendency to stress the opportunity and privilege of the Christians of America, in the spirit of Jesus, to express their friendship and good will by stimulating and aiding the people of the Orient to provide for the higher education of their youth.*

* In the Bulletin of Ginling College (Nanking, 1931) we read: "The founding of the College and its continued support have been inspired by the spirit of international good will and the desire of Christian people to share their best with China, looking for the day when East and West shall be united in closer understanding, and work together for the good of the whole world."

This shift of emphasis has been more pronounced in some institutions than in others, and there are doubtless many missionaries in the colleges who are little affected by it. But it is safe to say that the more thoughtful and open-minded leaders in the field have become increasingly concerned with the development of the colleges along lines which will make them, first of all, excellent instrumentalities for the study of national problems, the perpetuation of the best in national cultures, the demonstration of the best that the West can offer to the Orient, and the training of young men and women for useful service among their own people.

This connotes not a diminished zeal for the Christian cause but a broader conception of Christian service, not a slackening interest in the spiritual welfare of the students but a realization that religious influence is vitiated by second-rate instruction in secular fields and that the process of regenerating the spirit must go hand in hand with the cultivation and discipline of intellectual powers. Religious instruction is everywhere maintained; the endeavor by precept and example to instil the teachings of Jesus has nowhere diminished; but the fundamental importance of high educational standards, while too often disregarded, is receiving encouraging recognition.

2. *The Christian Colleges in India and Burma*

Great Britain has naturally played a larger part than America in the establishment and maintenance of Christian colleges in India. Of thirty-eight colleges, however, nine receive their foreign support from the United States and three others are maintained by the cooperation of British and American societies. The American colleges are Judson in Rangoon (Burma), Voorhees in Vellore, the American College in Madura, Andhra in Guntur, Ewing in Allahabad, Lucknow and Isabella Thoburn (for women) in Lucknow, Forman in Lahore, and Gordon in Rawalpindi. Those which are maintained by British and American cooperation are the Women's Christian College of Madras, Kinnaird College (for women) in Lahore, and St. Christopher's Training College (for women) in Madras. In addition, two of the leading British colleges, Wilson in Bombay and Madras College, receive a measure of assistance from America.

The staffs of the nine American colleges aggregate over 300, all but about sixty of whom are Indians. Of the Indian teachers approximately 40 per cent are Christians. The total enrolment of students is in the neighborhood of 4,500, of which number about one-seventh are Christians. The proportion of Christian students varies widely and is governed largely by the proportion of Christians in the vicinity of the institution. The proportion of Christians is much higher in the colleges for women than in those for men.*

The situation of the Christian colleges in India is peculiar in that they are related, by incorporation or affiliation, to an elaborate government system of universities. Nearly all receive recurring grants from the government toward their support, and all are subject to detailed government and university regulation. While this connection with the government system has doubtless served in many instances to maintain scholastic standards, it has just as certainly and very seriously hampered the colleges in initiative and experimentation. Furthermore, the standing of some of the Christian institutions has been unfavorably affected by the rise of government colleges, whose larger resources have enabled them to surpass some of the Christian colleges in equipment and teaching staff.

The stronger colleges still maintain a high position. Some of these, we are glad to report, are American colleges which have on their faculties a number of thoroughly competent scholars and scientists interested in the problems of India and contributing toward their solution. But there are a few which are discouragingly weak and as a group they have lost the leadership which they once enjoyed. There is reason for serious concern as to their future. At a conference of missionary and Indian Christian educators held at Agra in 1929, resolutions were adopted which declared that because of increasing competition, increasing costs and the increasing stringency of

* The figures in these paragraphs are drawn from the Report of the Commission on Christian Higher Education in India, 1931.

government and university control the situation of the colleges was critical and called for drastic measures of concentration and coordination.

As a result of the resolutions to which reference has just been made, the International Missionary Council constituted a Commission on Christian Higher Education in India, consisting of educators from Great Britain, India and the United States, under the chairmanship of Dr. A. D. Lindsay, Master of Balliol College, to make a study of the colleges and to report measures for the solution of their difficulties and the strengthening of their position.

The recommendations of the Commission which in our judgment are of the greatest importance may be summarized as follows:

1. All the Christian colleges should be regarded as cooperating in a common enterprise. To this end there should be created in India a Central Committee representing all the colleges with the functions of coordinating educational programs, distributing information as to available men for teaching positions, and formulating needs to be met through the cooperation of home authorities.

2. The government of the colleges should be transferred from mission boards and missions to governing bodies functioning in India and consisting largely of Indian Christians.

3. To the teaching function of the colleges there should be added those of research and extension, with the particular purpose of supplying the community and the Christian church with the knowledge they need for the solution of their problems.

The first and second of these recommendations seem to us both wise and feasible. They are in substantial harmony with the general policies advocated in our own report, and call for no supporting argument at this point. We earnestly hope they will be promptly adopted.

The third recommendation is sound in principle and of the greatest ultimate importance. There is no doubt that a carefully formulated and adequately supported program of research and extension, such as the Commission on Christian

Higher Education outlined in its report, would bring fresh stimulation to the faculties of the colleges and increase their usefulness both to the Christian community and to India. We hope that as rapidly as funds for the purpose become available the recommendation will be carried into effect. But it is obvious, as the Commission on Christian Higher Education recognized, that the support of a comprehensive program, in which all or most of the colleges should in a helpful degree participate, would require very large sums of money. We gravely doubt if the American colleges are justified in asking for such additional support under the conditions which prevail in them today. In our judgment, the support which they now receive should first be brought under such united control and direction as to assure its more economical and effective use. The primary importance of such concentration, since it bears upon mission policy in China and Japan, as well as in India, will be considered at a later point in our discussion.

The practice of many of the Christian schools and colleges of India in requiring their students, non-Christian as well as Christian, to attend religious exercises and instruction in the Christian religion, has in recent years aroused a good deal of criticism and resentment. In some provinces the agitation against it has crystallized in prohibitive or restrictive legisla-tion. We think it deeply regrettable that the authorities of some of the colleges have not been more sensitive to sound public opinion on this question. Complete adherence to the principle of religious liberty, in spirit as well as in letter, should be rigidly insisted upon. Indeed, a Christian college should be the last institution in the world to encroach upon a right so fundamental to the welfare of humanity. Further-more, we believe that the religious purpose of the colleges will be more effectively accomplished if attendance at religious exercises and instruction is placed on a voluntary basis. It puts religious instruction in fair and wholesome competition with the other courses in the curriculum; it liberates religious dis-cussion from the chilling suspicion of insincerity; it makes for a more genuine interest in religious questions and a finer quality of religious life.

The subject of devolution, which raises so many problems throughout the missionary enterprise in the Orient, presents unusual difficulties in India. The greatest success of the missionaries, at least in winning open adherents to Christianity, has been among the depressed classes, and there is not yet an adequate number of Christian Indians well qualified for leadership by capacity and education. Yet nowhere is there a more insistent demand by Christian nationals for the transfer of authority to their hands. Sensitiveness on this point, which is due in large measure to political conditions, is readily understandable, and there is no doubt that devolution must proceed without unnecessary delay even at the risk of some mistakes and some temporary loss. This is eminently true of the Christian colleges. Instances were observed by us in which the failure to appreciate the importance of this policy has resulted in bitterness which must be seriously harmful to the institution concerned and to the Christian cause.

3. *The Christian Colleges in China*

There are thirteen Christian colleges in China, all of which are supported in part by contributions from America. Two, Yenching and Cheeloo, are in the North; six, Nanking, Ginling, St. John's, Soochow, Shanghai and Hangchow, are in the East; three, Fukien, Hwa Nan, and Lingnan, in the South; one, Hua Chung, in Central China; and one, West China Union, in the West. Seven of these colleges are union institutions, five are denominational and one, Lingnan, is non-denominational. All are coeducational except St. John's which is exclusively for men, and Ginling and Hwa Nan which are exclusively for women.

The total number of teachers in the colleges exceeds 700, of which number about two-thirds are Chinese and one-third foreigners. Two-thirds of all faculty members and more than half of the Chinese teachers are reported to be Christians.

The enrollment of college students approaches four thousand, of which perhaps one-quarter are women. The proportion of Christians among the women is substantially higher than among the men. Possibly half of all the students are Christians.

There is no doubt that in the field of collegiate education the Christians of America have been privileged to render a greater service in China than in either India or Japan. The Christian colleges have not only attracted to their lecture halls and laboratories a large number of the finest type of Chinese youth but count among their graduates many Chinese who are leaders of thought and action; they have not only endeavored to inculcate the Christian religion and to express the good will of American Christians but have participated effectively—some of them conspicuously—in the establishment of modern educational standards and methods and in the study of national problems.

Although they have passed through trying experiences and at times have been regarded with profound distrust, the colleges appear at present to enjoy a gratifying measure of public confidence. In general the morale of the faculties is excellent and the relation between foreigners and nationals on the staffs, while not everywhere free from jealousy and friction, is marked on the whole by mutual respect and friendliness. Wholesome relations with indigenous educational institutions are also maintained.

In view of the rise, in recent years, of a large number of government and of privately endowed institutions of higher learning, many of them splendidly equipped and liberally supported, the question may be asked: Have the Christian colleges still an important function to perform? Both Christian and non-Christian educational leaders in China answer the question in the affirmative. Christian leaders, in support of their opinion, are inclined to lay particular emphasis on the success of the colleges in character building or the transformation of personalities through creative Christian influence and religious instruction on a voluntary basis. Non-Christians are more likely to stress the relative stability of the Christian colleges as compared especially with government institutions, under existing conditions, and the more effective intellectual discipline which prevails in both faculties and student bodies.

And to this one thoughtful Chinese educational leader added that the habit of organization which the western teachers have brought to the Christian colleges is something the exemplification of which China greatly needs.

There is one grave difficulty in the Chinese situation, the prompt solution of which is imperative. We refer to the deplorable lack of unity and coordination.

More than ten years ago the Educational Commission which under the chairmanship of Dr. Ernest D. Burton made a study of Christian education in China for the mission boards pointed out in its admirable report that the number of Christian colleges in China, while not large in proportion to the population, was quite unjustifiable economically in view of the available resources for their support. It therefore urgently recommended consolidations which would reduce the number of colleges to six, and a program of correlation which would diminish costly and wasteful duplication of work. Only one of the consolidations recommended has actually been accomplished and the correlated program, while it has been the subject of endless discussion, is far from realization. Here again the futility of recommending concentration without conferring upon some competent and disinterested person or group of persons the actual authority to carry it out is painfully apparent. We shall deal further with the subject at the conclusion of our discussion.

The Government of China has adopted a system of registration and regulation of schools and colleges. It ostensibly refuses to accept the registration of a college which has for its purpose the propagation of religion, it requires that the executives of registered colleges be Chinese, and it prohibits colleges from requiring the attendance of students at religious exercises and instruction. These regulations have generally been interpreted by government officials with considerable liberality, but they nevertheless have presented serious problems of policy to the Christian colleges. The authorities of one of the oldest and best known of the colleges have thus far refused to register, chiefly on the ground that by the regulations "the liberty of Christian worship and instruction is seriously curtailed." Consequently neither the institution nor its degree is recognized by the Government. In various ways this is a handicap to its students and graduates, and unless the Government's policy is changed must in the long run diminish its prestige and its usefulness. All of the other colleges have registered or are in the course of registration. So far as we could learn their officers agree that registration is essential to the maintenance of harmonious relations with the Government, to the cultivation of the confidence and good will of the Chinese people and to their own permanent success. Furthermore, they have not found that registration interferes with the accomplishment of their Christian purpose, for while an aggressive effort to change the religious faith of their students would violate the spirit of the Government's policy, there is no objection to the exercise of the influence of Christian teachers and the maintenance of voluntary religious exercises and instruction.

4. *The Christian Colleges in Japan*

There are in Japan eight Christian colleges for men, as follows: Rikkyo (St. Paul's), Meiji and Aoyama in Tokyo; Kwanto in Yokohama; Tohaku in Sendai; Doshisha in Kyoto; Kwansai in Kobe; Seinan in Fukuoka. The faculties of these colleges aggregate more than 450 teachers, of which number about six-sevenths are Japanese. Many of the Japanese are part-time men. Of the full-time teachers, seventy-one per cent are reported as Christians; of the part-time teachers, thirty-one per cent. The total enrollment of students is about 6,400, and it is reported that in recent years about twenty-seven per cent of the graduating classes have been professed Christians.*

With three exceptions these institutions are not colleges in the sense in which we commonly use the term in America. They compare more closely with our junior colleges, though chiefly vocational rather than academic in character. In

---

* The figures in this and the following paragraphs are drawn from the Report of the Commission on Christian Education in Japan, 1932.

Doshisha, Rikkyo and Kwansai, however, the provision of more advanced work in certain departments has led to their recognition by the government as universities. The recognition of Kwansai is very recent. In Doshisha and Rikkyo, the departments which have university status employ the services of about two hundred teachers, nearly all Japanese and many of them part-time men. Of the full-time teachers, about one-half are Christian; of the part-time teachers, not more than one-third. The total enrollment of the students in the university departments of the two institutions is about twelve hundred.

Since the Japanese Government has only recently begun to provide for the higher education of women, it is not surprising that a number of higher Christian institutions for women have been established. They vary widely, however, in character and in the extent of their curricula. Many are in reality only what may be called post-graduate additions to high schools, offering special or supplementary courses, chiefly vocational. Others may fairly be called junior colleges. Two—Kobe Women's College and the Women's Christian College in Tokyo—are colleges in the full sense of the term.

Altogether there are twenty-three institutions for women offering some instruction above the high school level. They engage the services, full-time or part-time, of more than four hundred Japanese and somewhat less than one hundred foreign teachers and have a total enrollment of about 4,500 students. Of full-time teachers, eighty-one per cent are reported as Christians, of part-time teachers, fifty-six per cent. In recent years the reported percentage of confessed Christians in the graduating classes has fluctuated between sixty-five per cent and seventy-three per cent.

The Christian colleges in Japan—especially those for men—are maintained under conditions of singular difficulty. For the Japanese Government, with a thoroughness which commands our admiration, has built up an extraordinarily comprehensive system of public education extending from the kindergarten to the great imperial universities and including almost everything from an Aquatic Products School to an Academy of

Music. The system is in many important respects different from our own. We may find much to criticize in it—as the Japanese may find much to criticize in ours. But it has given Japan a high literacy rate, it enjoys the confidence of the people, and on the whole it presents an impressive demonstration of the ability of the Japanese themselves to provide for their educational needs at every level.

There is no doubt that in earlier days the Christian colleges rendered a valuable service in Japan. There appears to be little reason for continuing the service unless they can make a contribution either of helpful experimentation or of stimulating excellence. We have been reluctantly forced to the conclusion that, taken as a whole, they are not making such a contribution today. It is true that they are endeavoring, with devotion and a measure of success, to nurture Christian youth and to inculcate Christian ideals in all their students. But their religious instruction, for the most part, is of a conventional and uninspiring type, and the accomplishment of their religious purpose is in large degree defeated by the mediocrity of their educational service.

This mediocrity is easily explained. In the first place, the strength and prestige of the government institutions are such that they command the services, with rare exceptions, of the most talented scholars, scientists and teachers, not excepting those who are Christians. Secondly, the government colleges offer such superior attractions to students that even Christian young men generally prefer them, with the result that the students in the Christian colleges are in general of inferior quality. Thirdly, the Christian colleges, chiefly because of inadequate financial resources, offer an extremely narrow range of instruction, the institutions for men specializing in training for business at a rather low level and those for women in the education of teachers of English. In none of them is there a first rate curriculum in the social sciences, and, what is worse, practically no instruction whatever is offered by any of them in either the physical or the biological sciences.

The two Christian colleges for women in Japan enjoy a prestige higher than those of corresponding grade for men and are rendering a distinctly greater service. The Government has been tardy in entering this field and the Christian colleges have consequently enjoyed a larger opportunity. In a sense they are still pioneering institutions. It must be expected, however, that the Government will soon be aroused to the importance of providing for the collegiate education of women and will take adequate measures to that end. The time is likely to come, therefore, when the Christian colleges for women will find themselves in a situation as critical as that which confronts the colleges for men today.

Is there still an opportunity for the Christian colleges as a group to render a service of great and lasting value to Japan? This question cannot be answered satisfactorily until the possibilities of drastic reorganization, redirection and concentration under unitary control have been thoroughly explored. But it seems not improbable that if the resources of all the existing colleges were brought to the support of two or three institutions and placed under the executive direction of men thoroughly equipped for educational leadership and familiar not only with the needs of Japan but with the current movement for the improvement of education, including religious education, in the West, demonstration centers of the highest value might be built up.

Many of the Christian leaders in Japan have long advocated the establishment, with the assistance of funds from America, of a Christian university of high grade. Such an institution, they contend, is needed for the education of Christian teachers for the colleges and lower schools and for the training of leaders of thought who may become the spiritual prophets of Japan. The Commission on Christian Education, while it did not endorse the proposal for a new institution of the unitary type, recommended the organization, upon the foundation of the existing colleges, of a federated university.

It must be remembered in this connection that the studies of the Commission on Christian Education had no bearing on the relative values or needs of other enterprises; according to its terms of reference the primary problem was the declining prestige of Christian institutions. The federated university was proposed as a solution in the hope that it would eliminate the duplication and competition of Christian colleges aspiring to become separate universities, and strengthen the program in higher education as a whole through the specialization of individual colleges constituent in the university and through centralization of control.*

Considering the problem in relation to the entire missionary enterprise, we are satisfied that the time is far from ripe for an attempt to set up a Christian university, either federated or unitary, in Japan. In the first place, the colleges which would be the feeders of the university must be reorganized and greatly strengthened before they can supply students of requisite capacity and training for university work. Secondly, we believe that it would be impossible, under the conditions which exist today and are likely to exist for some time to come, to collect a Christian faculty composed predominently of first rate Japanese scholars and scientists. And thirdly, in view of the more urgent educational needs of other parts of the world we do not believe that the Christians of America should now be called upon to provide the whole or any considerable part of the large endowment which would be required to put the university on a sound financial basis.

We cannot conclude our consideration of higher education in Japan without a brief reference to the excellent work that is being done by a few well qualified missionaries who have established personal contacts with groups of students in non-Christian universities. This type of service might well be extended to the stronger government colleges and especially to the Imperial universities where superior students in large numbers are to be found. If missionaries of the right type were selected for the work and if the sympathy and cooperation of the Christian professors in the respective institutions were enlisted, a leavening influence of incalculable value might be exerted.

* There are at present three nominal universities in this group empowered to grant degrees. The establishment of a federated university would imply their surrender of the coveted university name and function. It is one of the major obstacles to the plan that such surrender is improbable.

5. *In General*

There are four points we wish to make which have a bearing
upon the situation of the Christian colleges in all three of the
countries covered by our study.

1. A grave danger inherent in the attempt to maintain
Christian colleges and universities in the Orient is that of sub-
ordinating the educational to the religious objective, particularly in appointments to the faculties. The importance of
giving first consideration to the intellectual qualifications of
a candidate is generally recognized in theory, but there is no
doubt that in many instances men of inferior capacity, training
or teaching ability have been appointed to college faculties
because of undue emphasis on religious and even on denominational affiliations. This is one reason, though by no means
the only one, for the mediocrity of many of the Christian
institutions.

We feel that we cannot overemphasize the importance of
being constantly on guard against this danger. The Christians
of America will render no real service either to the Orient
or to Christianity by maintaining or assisting to maintain colleges which do not command the respect and confidence of
educated nationals, and if the Christian character of an institution cannot be maintained without the sacrifice of educational standards, it should be closed.

2. Another danger that calls for vigilance is the persistence
of "foreignness." In the nature of the case the Christian colleges began as foreign institutions and it is only by a gradual
process that they can become Indian, or Chinese, or Japanese,
as the case may be. But it is only by becoming thoroughly
naturalized that they can hope ultimately to be supported by
the nationals, and to realize their potentialities for service to
the Orient. This involves not only the gradual and whole-
hearted devolution of authority but increasing cooperation
with indigenous institutions, increasing devotion to the study
of national genius and culture, and increasing concern with
the problems of their environment.

3. It is the common practice of mission boards in America to select and appoint those western members of the faculties of the Christian colleges whose salaries are paid from mission funds. In most cases, probably, the officers of the colleges are consulted and an endeavor is made to make appointments satisfactory to them. The fact remains that their freedom of choice is often seriously restricted.

This seems to us extremely unfortunate. It is the invariable practice of American colleges that appointments to the faculty are made by the college authorities themselves. No respectable American college would accept an arrangement by which the power to select some of its teachers was delegated to an outside body, however friendly and intelligent that body might be. It is our judgment that the time has come for the adoption of this American practice in the administration of the Christian colleges in the Orient. Their officers are assumed to be competent to appoint nationals to their staffs. Why are they not competent to appoint foreign members as well? It may be argued that they are too far away to make wise selections, but if there were a central bureau of information in America this difficulty would in large measure be obviated. Furthermore, the officers in the Orient would undoubtedly seek the assistance and advice of their supporting boards at home. We see no objection to the formal ratification of appointments by the home boards. The point is that the officers of a college, who are familiar with its conditions and its needs, should not be handicapped in the attempt to build up and maintain a strong faculty by the dominant authority of a mission board across the sea. We therefore recommend that the mission boards hereafter make their contribution to the colleges exclusively in the form of money grants, standing ready to assist in the selection of western teachers but leaving the ultimate choice without restriction to the college authorities.

4. Unquestionably the most serious weakness of the missionary enterprise in the field of higher education is the lack of unity of administration. In all of the three countries we have visited there is a discouraging diffusion of energy and resources. The number of colleges is disproportionate to the

funds available or likely to become available for their adequate support and in many instances they compete wastefully with each other. Many of them have lost or are in serious danger of losing the reputation for excellence which they once enjoyed. Some of them are not a credit to the Christian cause. Yet every attempt by voluntary agreement and persuasion to bring about the adoption of a comprehensive program of union and coordination has failed.

We are convinced that the only remedy for this condition is the establishment of centralized authority. From the point of view of American contributors the Christian colleges in the Orient should constitute a single enterprise; the control of all missionary funds for their support should be placed in the hands of a single competent board; and the board should be vested with ample authority to deal drastically with the stituation.

This proposal is identical in principle with that which this Commission is making in Chapter XIV for the reorganization of the administration of missions. Perhaps there is no field in which the need of such reorganization is more urgent than in that of higher education. In our judgment the Christians of America still have a great opportunity in this field not only to express their friendship and good will toward the people of the Orient but to render a service of inestimable value to the world. It would be a calamity if through the persistence of denominational divisiveness, parochial interests and institutional pride, this great opportunity should be lost.

CHAPTER VIII

CHRISTIAN LITERATURE

A STUDY of the activities of Christian missions would be incomplete without considering their use of books, newspapers, illustrations and other ways of delivering their message besides the spoken word. The number and variety of means of dissemination of ideas related to commerce, science, politics and general news is of frequent observation. To what extent and with what effect have Christian missions used books, periodicals, newspapers, the radio and moving pictures? Do these constitute a practical and appropriate means of telling the gospel story and of communicating that which is inherently bound up with it? Let us consider what has been, and is being done.

Earliest publications. Missionaries to remote and backward communities have found themselves face to face with the urgent problem of perpetuating the content of their instruction. It is surprising how many races and tribes have managed to get along without a written language. A missionary, resident among such people, has almost invariably found it necessary to reduce the spoken language to writing. Fortunately there have been, and still are, missionaries with the capacity and willingness to render such service. We have seen several men still actively engaged in that elementary task. A lasting contribution has been made by missionaries who have performed that service. The resources available for the work have been slender indeed. It has usually been overtime work on the part of the missionary. The spare time of many years has been consumed in composing a dictionary and translating the Bible or parts of it. The New Testament has recently been put into Romanized text for Chinese readers. The plates for the Old Testament in that text went up in flames in the destruction of the Commercial Press in Shanghai.

A difficulty early encountered and never entirely overcome has arisen out of the fact that in many of the Oriental languages there are no words to express important concepts in the message the missionary desires to deliver. Such words as God, Holy Spirit, sin, have been most difficult to translate. The missionary dictionary makers, in many instances, have made useful contributions not only in preparing the original dictionaries for primitive people but in making the earliest translating dictionaries for such great languages as Chinese and Japanese. Robert Morrison's Chinese-English dictionary was a case in point. Dr. J. C. Hepburn's Japanese-English dictionary compiled in the early days of the missionary enterprise set an example for future lexicographers. It still has great value for students of the Japanese language. A scholarly Assamese dictionary compiled by a missionary many years ago is considered to be the best Assamese dictionary ever published. A request has recently been made of the mission by a private publisher for permission to reprint it.

Subject Matter

For the missions. Next to the compilation of the dictionary and the translation of the Bible has usually come the preparation of elementary school books. These have been composed and published in great variety by missionaries in many lands. As the body of believers has increased, religious tracts have been written and still are produced in large numbers in all the countries visited. Missionary journals have been found to be a convenience for the interchange of mission news, mutual assistance and information. After the early training of pastors, evangelists and school teachers, has come the problem of their continuing education and stimulation. Many books, generally translations, and periodicals have been published for this purpose.

The need and the apparent practicability of providing circulating library service to pastors and other workers has been called to our attention, but as far as we know, nothing of a comprehensive nature has been attempted. In India, where mail service is reliable and economical, such an enterprise is especially worthy of consideration. The establishment of one or more such libraries would be well worth while.

For the general public. To a greater extent in some countries than in others, there has grown up within and without the circle of mission influence a general reading public interested in Christ and his message. Missionaries and their associates have been responsible for the translation of large numbers of religious and other books, for the use of the general public. The choice of books to be translated has depended on the judgment of the individual translator. Along with useful service has gone a good deal of wasted time and money on account of bad judgment in the choice of books to be translated. In addition to translations there have come, to a lesser extent, however, original compositions by missionaries and nationals. We have been unable to discover in the fields studied any effective plan to translate or produce a wide variety of well chosen books.

Independent Christian periodicals edited by gifted Japanese played in earlier decades a more influential role than they play today. A few of the denominational weeklies, however, edited and financed by Japanese, have long maintained a fairly high level. Among the promising newer Christian periodicals is "Shinko Kiristokyo," a liberal monthly. Notable among women's magazines is "Fujin no Tomo," which reflects the Christian character of its editor, Mrs. Hani.

In Japan, newspapers have been used for about 25 years for the reproduction of sermons, dissemination of study courses and other means of spreading Christian ideas. In 1930 there were twenty-five centers for newspaper evangelism. Personal correspondence follows between those who have been interested by newspaper evangelism and those who conduct it. In this way the message reaches isolated individuals and communities out of touch with the other operations of the church.

In one prefecture in which there are 240 towns and villages, only fifteen of which have Christian churches, replies to newspaper evangelism have come from every one of the towns and villages. At one center, in 1930, three per cent of the inquirers enrolled in correspondence courses, and twelve per cent of them called for library service.

Pictures, wall posters and illustrations have been sparingly used. In a limited number of schools and hospitals there are attractive and appropriate pictures, but generally this method of instruction and appeal has not been used to good advantage. The pictures have been too distinctively Western or Palestinian in conception. Recent efforts have been made by some publishing agents, such as the Religious Tract Society in China, to give local color to their pictures and posters, yet even in these instances the subject matter has been so out of touch with Chinese thought and ways as to need explanation. Hence it makes little real appeal. When one compares with the best of such efforts the beautiful and artistic pictures put out by some of the Buddhist organizations, appealing as they do directly to the Chinese mind and needing no explanatory letter-press, one wonders if Christian publishing agencies might not well learn from their methods. Certainly there should be a much larger and better supply of picture material than is now available.

In China the Mass Education Movement has stimulated the production of printed and illustrative material by Christian organizations. The National Christian Council states that there is now being prepared a course of study in religious education based on the "thousand characters" and that a course covering women's particular interests will soon be published. Devotional literature, books for family prayers and Sunday School material are in preparation. A life of Christ has already appeared and two others are expected, for the use of those whose knowledge of Chinese is limited to the "thousand characters." Other books for newly literate people are on agriculture, health and citizenship.

One of the fields which receives less attention than it deserves is that of interpreting Christ and his way of life to students. The Young Men's Christian Association and Young Women's Christian Association have issued some books for this general purpose. The supply, however, in all countries visited has been quite insufficient. Moreover, the Christian Association type of book only covers a portion of the field. The university student, with a more mature and critical mind, must be considered. While much, and perhaps from the educational point of view, too much, has been supplied to students in the way of translations of foreign textbooks, particularly in social sciences, there remains a very large place which possibly one or more university presses might supply. This would include primarily original compositions in the language of the country. There is also room for translations of great biographies, books giving the Christian interpretation of social and economic history and for the best new books from England and America on all phases of life.

Christian Literature Societies

An effort to bring the publication of Christian books into coordination is seen in the establishment of Christian Literature Societies in India, China and Japan. There are more of these than one would expect to find, both "union" and denominational. There are forty-five societies and individuals issuing Christian publications in China. There are also six universities publishing books. There are eighteen or more Christian publishing societies in India and Burma, and several in Japan and Korea. Many of these are small and have a narrow range of interest but others have had a long history and have made notable achievements. The Judson Press in Burma is an outstanding example of success.

There is no Christian Literature Society attempting to serve the needs of all the missions in India. The Christian Literature Society of Madras publishes books for the Arcot, Madura and Telugu mission fields. For the year 1929-1930 this Society published in the Telugu language, nine new books, and one reprint, 17,000 copies in all. It published twelve new books and sixteen reprints in Tamil, aggregating 75,000 copies. The "village series of pamphlets, concerned with sanitation and other subjects of interest to villagers, has been valuable. In the Telugu area there are also a number of monthly and weekly periodicals of which "The Telugu Baptist" circulates the most widely. The circulation of books on general subjects and on non-Christian religious topics has been described as a "regular stream" of publications, compared to which the circulation of Christian books is small indeed. It is noteworthy also that two British commercial publishers are among those who are competing with local agencies in the production in Tamil of general literature.

The Methodist Episcopal Publishing House in Lucknow issues annually a large amount of vernacular literature. It also prints and finances several periodicals in Urdu and English. It supplies annually about six hundred thousand tracts in Hindi and three hundred thousand in Urdu.

The North India Tract Society which serves the North India and Punjab mission areas produced eleven new books and twenty-five reprints of books and tracts in 1929 and 1930.

The Christian Literature Society for China did an outstanding piece of work a generation ago by producing literature for the so-called *literati*. Missionaries of far-seeing vision, with an ability to sense the intellectual tastes of the educated classes, would transmit orally to Chinese writers of recognized literary ability their thoughts, gleaned from wide reading, on such subjects as the history of civilization, modern science, western culture, and the significance of Christianity. These writers would in turn reproduce the ideas thus assimilated in forms of their own choosing. Thus there were produced books which were no mere translation but were thoroughly Chinese in style and flavor. Such books had a wide and influential circulation. Large credit for this unique service is due to the leadership of a Welsh Baptist, Dr. Timothy Richard, and an American Methodist, Dr. Young J. Allen.

The Christian Literature Society for China is still doing good work in some lines but it seems deficient both in winning the respect of the better educated readers and in meeting the needs of the rural classes. The work of this Society has, however, grown in value during the past three years, under improved leadership. An interesting feature of its activities is a membership provision whereby a contribution of $5.00 (Chinese currency) annually entitles one to receive all the books issued by the Society during the year. During the past few years its membership has grown from 260 to 1,800, with promise of further steady increase. Fifty-eight books were published and sent to the members during the past year. A necessarily limited examination showed that at least a dozen of these books were of real value. Doubtless others were also.

The Christian Literature Society of Japan was formed through the merger of the Methodist Publishing House and the Literature Society of the Federation of Christian Missions in 1926. It is now the official Christian literary agency of the Federation of Christian Missions and of the National Christian Council. Its board of directors is composed of twelve missionaries elected by the Federation of Christian Missions and twelve Japanese elected by the National Christian Council. In theory the Society is thus controlled equally by foreigners and Japanese. The latter, however, are considered somewhat as consulting members with no responsibility for the financial side of the work. We were informed that the members appointed by the National Christian Council (Japanese) feel that they do not have any real part in the work, that they seldom attend the board meetings, and are not much interested in the work of the Society. The Society publishes very few books either as translations or in original titles which are calculated to produce understanding or appreciation of the contribution of modern constructive scholarship in Bible study and theology. The operations of the Society include the conduct of a central book store and two branches, the publication of books and pamphlets in Japanese and the publication of books and periodicals in English, the importation of books, periodicals, typewriters and book store supplies. The annual sales of the Society amount to about one hundred and fifty thousand dollars (gold). In 1930 it published a total of seventy-two thousand volumes, twenty-five thousand tracts and sixty-six thousand cards and folders.

An impressive amount of capital is invested in Christian Literature Societies in Shanghai, Seoul and Tokyo. Apparently there have been generous personal contributions and mission appropriations to these societies for a long period of time. The Christian Literature Societies of both China and Japan have recently realized substantial sums from the sale of real estate. These sums, supplemented by borrowed funds, are being reinvested in new buildings on Museum Road in Shanghai and on the Ginza in Tokyo.

Certain characteristics are common to these Christian Literature Societies. They have had a comparatively long history and have accumulated substantial capital funds. They own and occupy valuable buildings. Their working capital is, however, insufficient for the prompt publication of many of the manuscripts that have been approved for publication. Their business is conducted at an operating loss which is met by annual grants from mission boards, and from rents and interest on invested funds. The missionary editors, writers and executives are appointed to their positions directly or indirectly by the controlling missions.

The policy of assignment of staff by missionary organizations fails to secure editorial or administrative efficiency. It restricts the usefulness of the Society by tending to emphasize the finding of a job for a man rather than the finding of a man for the job. It should be said, of course, that the range of choice is limited. Only a few missionaries and Christians of the several countries have the literary scholarship and administrative ability to supply expert guidance to such ventures.

The evident need is for open-mindedness, originality and freedom in the publication of Christian literature. Missionaries, no matter what their qualifications of character, experience or scholarship, are seriously handicapped because of the foreignness in their attempts to supply this need. No satisfactory explanation has come to our attention as to why the control of these societies by missionaries to the exclusion of the nationals should be perpetuated. We are convinced that the Christian movement in the several countries is being retarded by such a policy.

Other Publishers

The Library of Christian Thought and Life in Japan is a Committee of five Japanese and one American—alert, capable men. Their organization resulted from the fact that the work of the Christian Literature Society of Japan was not producing books to meet the needs of thoughtful and scholarly Christians. By the use of a small revolving fund and a still smaller annual grant from interested individuals in America, the Library of Christian Thought and Life has published a number of books by Japanese writers and several valuable translations. The books have been successful—some have been very popular. They are addressed to the educated constituency, both Christian and non-Christian. A number of these books have sold widely through secular book shops. The method of procedure of this Society is to assist and stimulate independent writers to produce books to supply a definite need.

We are informed of the prospect of the establishment of a Christian Literature Fund in China, organized to operate on simple, inexpensive lines, looking to Chinese leadership after a brief period of guidance by well qualified Americans. This fund is to be directly controlled by a body of trustees, wholly Chinese, men of broad knowledge, good judgment, administrative experience and general competence to guide the literary expression of Christianity in China, particularly in the fields most inadequately provided for by existing agencies, namely, books for students and educated persons, Christian and non-Christian. Doubtless such a flexible and apparently successful plan of stimulating production as has been followed by the Library of Christian Thought and Life in Japan will receive its careful attention.

Dr. Toyohiko Kagawa deserves especial mention as an author of Christian books, as well as of popular fiction written from a Christian point of view and as a contributor to and publisher of periodical literature. His influence in Japan is widespread, and writings from his pen are eagerly received.

The Problems of Distribution and of Production

Distribution. Of course these problems vary with the different countries. Japan, with its high general level of literacy, does not present serious distribution problems. Good books sell in Japan in much the same way as they do in America. Every city has book shops and plenty of them. Christian books sell side by side with others, in proportion to the public demand.

In China the publication of books is a small enterprise indeed compared to Japan. The reading public in China is increasing but it is still relatively small. Moreover, there is comparatively little interest on the part of the general public in religious subjects. Christians are not numerous and are widely scattered. Therefore, the distribution of distinctively Christian books through the ordinary channels of trade is not practical. The Southern Baptist Publication Society has maintained a retail book store in Canton for a number of years, with only moderate success. Its sale of Christian books and periodicals at retail is small in volume. Most of the distribution is obtained by colporteurs. The principal business of the retail store is in office supplies and other merchandise. Other attempts of Christian publication organizations to conduct retail stores have been even less successful.

In China we were impressed with the sales methods of the Adventist Mission. While we do not pass on the value of their publications, it is noteworthy that this denomination, with approximately ten thousand church members, is able to obtain a distribution of each issue of its official periodical of about eighty thousand copies. This is done through a thoroughly organized "house to house" sales department. Its business methods contain possibilities that other Christian publishing societies might profitably emulate.

Diversity of language and the poverty of the Christian community present most serious obstacles to the general distribution of Christian books in India. There are said to be more ethnic groups and more languages and dialects in India than there are in all of Europe. In India as in China publishers are compelled to depend in the main upon direct retail selling in order to get distribution of books and periodicals. Missionaries, churches, schools and colleges constitute the principal channels of distribution.

Production. That the problems are not all on the distribution side is illustrated by the fact that in Japan where there is no serious distribution problem, production of Christian books of the best quality is far less than it should be.

The object, of course, is not merely to get books but to get books that are worth while and appropriate. In any of these countries the number of persons qualified to write such books is limited. Moreover, writers who can produce a type of literature that sells well are reluctant to write distinctively Christian books for the narrow market that exists. Christians with sufficient literary qualifications being so few, they almost inevitably are out of touch with each other and with any considerable number of editors and publishers. It therefore is necessary that some agencies study the needs of the field and assist writers to contribute to it.

Bible Societies

Both British and American Bible Societies have confined their activities to the translation, publication and distribution of the Bible and parts of the Bible. They distribute millions of copies each year, most of them at very low prices, often as low as the mere cost of the paper on which they are printed. As the work of these Societies is outside the sphere of our Inquiry, we have made no investigation of them.

Radios and Moving Pictures

It is frequently observed that the radio and moving pictures are almost exclusively used for purposes unrelated to religion and that in some respects their influence is distinctly antagonistic to the ideals for which Christianity and the other great religions stand. We have been able to discover little effective use of either instrumentality in the interest of religion on the mission field up to this time. It is recognized that both the radio and the moving pictures have peculiar possibilities of usefulness in the spread of Christian ideas in mission lands. Some slight beginning has been made. While it is questionable whether funds should be diverted from the publication of books for this purpose, experimentation in the use of both the radio and the moving pictures should be encouraged.

Summary

The missionary contribution to the spread of knowledge and of ideas in each of these countries has been of long duration and of immense direct and indirect benefit. The patience, industry and scholarship represented by their labors are praiseworthy. A new day has come, however. Perhaps in no other field of endeavor has the success of missionaries in making themselves dispensable been so complete. There is no permanent place for many missionaries in writing, translating or editing the literature of Christian thought in India, Burma, China and Japan. A continuing service of great value can still be rendered by men in mission service who have organizing and business experience in connection with publishing. Experience in many situations has demonstrated that one wise foreigner can exert an influence upon a group of Chinese or other national Christians that will make their work far more effective. He must be a wise, humble and resourceful man, however.

There are, of course, serious problems confronting the Christian Literature Societies. Some of them inhere in the charters under which they operate and in the conditions attached to their endowment funds. The reluctance to turn over valuable properties and the responsibility of continuing a missionary activity of such long standing, is natural. The literature societies are not only inter-denominational but international in their composition and financial support. Their officers are responsible to a widely scattered constituency. A proper sense of trusteeship suggests caution in turning over their complete control to nationals who as yet have had but limited experience in managing important business affairs. Nevertheless, the need for the transfer of editorial responsibility is clearly indicated.

In none of the countries visited is the work of its Christian Literature Society receiving anything like general approval of either missionaries or of the Christian leaders of the country. The effort to maintain a theological middle ground has not produced good Christian literature. The endeavor to please everybody has resulted in pleasing very few. It would be better far to publish books for those near each theological extreme, impartially, than to continue a foreign theological censorship. The function of a Christian Literature Society is not that of a "protector of the faith" but of an agency of the Christian people of its country to produce the Christian books they want. Language difficulties, serious enough in conversation, teaching and preaching, are well nigh impossible for any considerable number of missionaries to overcome in literature that is intended to interpret the application of the principles of Christ and the experience of his followers to the awakened and critical mind of the Orient.

What is suggested is a procedure that will make the Christian Literature Societies completely indigenous as rapidly as properly qualified national leaders can be enlisted and can gain experience in the conduct of the enterprise. Steps to achieve this are

1. To strengthen the boards of trustees by including in their membership leaders who have been successful in as wide a range of activities as possible. As boards of trustees and directors of schools, hospitals, Young Men's Christian Associations and other corporations have been able to call to their membership business executives, lawyers, doctors, educational administrators and others whose experience has been outside of the Church, as well as within, so Christian Literature Societies should broaden the representation of their governing boards. Missions should be careful to nominate either from their own ranks, or better still, from among nationals in the respective

countries, men of administrative capacity as their representatives on these boards.

2. To have the executive force of the Christian Literature Societies appointed by and responsible to the boards of governors, not to the respective missions. On no account should an aging missionary be appointed to an editorial position in one of these Societies for the purpose of continuing his service until his retirement age is reached.

3. To make every effort to simplify the operations of the Christian Literature Societies, to obtain manuscripts from persons outside their own personnel, to reduce as far as possible the number of writers on regular salary and to encourage the production of manuscripts from as many sources as possible.

The manifold service of Christian missions, through church, hospital, school and other lines of work, has deeply penetrated the thought life of all these countries. There is great interest in Christ and in what his followers can contribute from their experience to the needs and problems of their respective countries. There is interest also in what Christians in England and America are writing on religious subjects. Faithful, skillful translations of great western books will continue in demand.

In the new day of the awakened Orient, with increasing general literacy, with better acquaintance of the masses of people in each country with the life and problems of the others, surely the printed word, the broadcast message and effective illustration will play a larger part than ever before. Competition for attention will be keener. Forces of disorder and degradation will not be inactive. Christians face a great opportunity and a great responsibility to interpret Christ and his way of life not only by their "walk and conversation" but by what they write and print.

CHAPTER IX

MEDICAL WORK OF MISSIONS

1. *Backgrounds*

India. Mission hospitals were pioneers in medical service in
India, but the Government has gradually developed what is
today a comprehensive and admirable hospital system. Large
and efficient government hospitals were established in the great
cities, smaller ones in lesser places, dispensaries in out-lying
regions; medical schools and colleges were organized. The
plan in its entirety contemplates a complete system of hospitals, medical education and public health for British India.

The number of hospital beds per unit of population is less
than a sixth of those available in progressive regions of the
West, but however great the need may be, the actual demand—
judged by the empty beds in the wards we visited—is apparently being met. A body of well-trained Indian practitioners
scattered throughout India is growing up, although practically all are located in the cities and larger towns. Many of
the government hospitals are excellently equipped and staffed;
their physicians and nurses are giving skillful and sympathetic
service. These institutions are hampered, however, by limitations inherent in complex governmental machinery. Continuity
of staff is impossible because of frequent shifting and re-assign-
ments; appropriations are subject to political influences; the
necessity of maintaining a neutral position among hostile religious groups, and of yielding to the pressure of certain social
usages, tend generally to undermine morale. From certain of
these difficulties mission hospitals, in the main, are free; caste
antagonism, among a non-Christian staff—doctors, nurses, and
employees; jealousies due to religious and communal rivalries;
family pressure upon hospital officials to work their relatives

into jobs; bribery to the extent that even the patient who occupies a free bed may find that to secure medicine or have his simplest needs met he must bribe an employee—sometimes the doctor as well.

Other hardships are faced by government hospitals. The transfer of medicine in 1923 from central to provincial control and rapid devolutional changes under pressure have tended to depress the high standards long maintained by the Indian Medical Service, and to dilute its influence and the quality of its personnel. Hospitals are now coming into a phase of political administration likely to vitiate their efficiency for a long time.

Types of non-mission hospitals, other than governmental, have been multiplying in recent years:

1. Private Christian medical enterprises, such as the Lady Hardinge Hospital and Medical College for Women at Delhi, and similar institutions.

2. Private non-Christian hospitals and welfare centers, emerging from the humanitarian urge of other faiths, such as the Wadia (Parsee) Hospital of Bombay, and others.

3. Hospitals of large industrial corporations, which, while intended primarily for their own employees, are open to the general public.

4. Institutions of indigenous medicine—Ayurvedic and Unani.

Certain inferences from the general background seem justified. In spite of the imperfections noted above, the Government of India has done much in the creation of hospitals and medical colleges that is praiseworthy, and has given Indians of all classes a widening appreciation of scientific medicine. The intelligent and educated are beginning indeed to note the decreasing efficiency of mission hospitals inadequately equipped and financed to meet the demands of advancing medicine and the failure of their staffs to keep abreast of the progress of medical science.

In view of the grave difficulties faced by the government work in medicine, Christian missions, we believe, should continue to share proportionately in the relief of suffering and the care of the needy in India. A careful reconsideration by the sending churches of their entire medical program, however, is called for, in the light of the successes as well as the inadequacies of the Government's program, and of the emergence of new agencies of medical relief. Such a reconsideration will doubtless eventuate in the abandonment of feebler mission hospitals, and the strengthening of the better ones by redistribution of funds.

Burma. In Burma, medical missions have never been emphasized in the Christian enterprise, and their development has been insignificant. Now, at a time when the Burmans, Buddhists in religion, who represent ninety per cent of the population of Burma yet only seven per cent of her Christians, are threatening greatly to hamper the mission schools, the expansion of a hospital program suggests itself, since hospitals are usually the last of mission enterprises to be seriously disturbed by hostile political groups and might serve as a sheet anchor to the Christian cause in that country.

China. The contrasts between India and China as far as they affect medicine may be summarized as follows:

a. The contacts of China with the West have been more recent and far less intimate than those of India. There has been no Occidental overlordship to introduce a foreign educational system, to control legislation, or to determine national policies. The reception of western ideas has been slow, adherence to an ancient and static culture has been tenacious, and until recent years there has been a national conviction of self-sufficiency which tended to insulate the country from international cultural exchanges. It is only in the past quarter of a century that this situation has markedly altered.

b. Since 1910, or even earlier, however, transition has been going on abruptly, and with internal disruption to the point of governmental and economic chaos. Political and social changes have been not only sudden but often violent, and the outcome of the flux is unforeseeable.

c. The Chinese as a race are extraordinarily sturdy, industrious and fertile. Their population has been balanced in the past (at a high rate per square mile of all arable land) largely by famine, flood and pestilence. With the appearance of stable government, of transportation and distribution facilities, of modern curative and preventive medicine, the population problem is likely to be acute.

d. The Chinese people are singularly free from the religious inhibitions which have affected social life in India so disastrously.

e. The benefits of scientific medicine are available to one or two per cent of the Chinese population; the remainder must, and most of them would by choice, depend upon native methods of treatment. In illness, the people turn either to some form of cult practice, with necromancy and sacrifices, or to practitioners of old-style Chinese medicine.

The former is medicine by magic, mingled with religious elements; the latter, an empirical system with no claim to genuine scientific worth; the hold of both upon popular confidence is very great.

Comparisons with the indigenous medical systems of India suggest that in China native medicine has continued to flourish largely because of the lack of well-organized state medical aid. The pragmatic disposition of the Chinese, and their freedom from religious bias in such matters, make them readily accessible, once the ties of tradition have been loosened, to new and workable methods. In India, on the other hand, in spite of the abundance of modern hospitals, intense nationalist reactions and deeply rooted religious elements in the Ayurvedic and Unani systems have tended to perpetuate them in favor and to stimulate their growth.

If its resources had not been dissipated and its continuity disturbed by twenty years of internal warfare, the Chinese Government might have made great progress in medical education, the organization of hospitals and the establishment of public health services. In spite of these severe handicaps, a ministry of health was created in 1928, a thorough survey of medical education was made, and plans were developed for the improvement of the four national university colleges of medicine. Much of this work has had paper existence, rather than reality, but some solid advances have been made. The Central Hospital and Public Health Institute in Nanking and the Government School for Midwives at Peiping are examples of genuinely high class medicine, well conceived and managed, although crippled by lack of regular and sufficient appropriations.

Apart from enterprises of the national Government, there are numerous municipal and private benevolent hospitals appearing in larger centers all through those parts of China which have been exposed markedly to western influences. Most of these are meagerly equipped and badly handled, but there are heartening exceptions.

In summary it may be said that the influence of western medicine, slowly widening for sixty or seventy years, has spread rapidly during the past two decades in all of the city centers of China. For its inception, for the pioneering in hospital work and medical and nursing education, missionary effort has been largely responsible. Devolutional changes, the growth of nationalist sentiment, pressure of Government in some places, and the lawlessness of anarchy in other places, are altering many phases of the Christian program, but there is still important work to be done by mission hospitals. They hold a high place, usually, in the esteem of the people whom they serve, and in spite of the overshadowing excellence of a very few private and governmental institutions, still represent in general the best demonstrations of professional skill and human sympathy for the ailing poor of China.

Japan. In Japan, modern medicine, on German models, has been thoroughly established, and is evolving in a rather rigid fashion under close supervision by the Imperial Government. Whatever defects it has are those of its pattern, plus some difficulties of adaptation, but it is comprehensive and stable. Mission boards have long since—with one exception—abandoned medical work in Japan. With a Government so progressive, and so intent on making the best of western science its own, there has seemed to other boards little need of embarking upon a costly program of medical relief.

One notable mission hospital only has survived in Japan, St. Luke's International Medical Center of Tokyo, with its small branch institution in Osaka. Its place among mission hospitals is unique, and the scope and nature of its work differ so widely from that of medical missions in the other countries that it is reported upon separately.

2. *The Problems of Medical Missions*

This study of medical missions has been confined to those problems which seem fundamental to the enterprise as a whole, in an endeavor to relate them to principles which should underlie sound administrative and professional procedures. No attempt is made to describe in comprehensive fashion the wide range of medical work being carried on by missions, nor to deal either with individual hospitals or local situations.

(A) *Objectives.* Ministry in a Christ-like spirit to the physical ills of needy people has been from the first a challenge to adventurous service, and has found a response in the interest and support of people within and without the organized church. Medical missions have long been looked upon mainly as auxiliaries to evangelism, but the question is now widely being raised to what extent the work of healing is justified for its own sake. The answer must take account of the fact that in addition to the operation of hospitals and dispensaries, the Christian program in medicine now includes preventive medicine, nursing and medical education and various forms of welfare work.

It is our conviction that medical missions represent, in themselves, the essentials of the Christian enterprise. The use of medical skill for ulterior ends has been rightly challenged, in our judgment, by social and religious leaders in India and China, and a statement of objectives should meet this challenge fairly. The general aims of Christian medical work should include:

1. The care of the sick at a high level of professional excellence, in the spirit of disinterested services.

2. A demonstration of compassionate and equal consideration for all creeds and classes, and of the dignity of lowly tasks.

3. The stimulation of the establishment of similar institutions under local auspices, and cooperation with them.

4. The training whenever possible of internes, nurses, hospital workers and midwives.

5. The creation of, or participation in, agencies for popular medical education, social service, and of health and welfare centers.

It may not be possible, of course, for every mission hospital to undertake all of these activities, but they represent objectives now being achieved by successful mission hospitals and constitute the distinctive features of a Christian medical program. There is nothing, it will be noted, in these aims which may not properly be sought by an indigenous enterprise, whether private or governmental, but careful comparisons indicate that Christian hospitals at their best come nearer fulfilling them than others.

The place of evangelism in the mission hospital is a basic issue. Hospitals have been used from the first frankly as a means to that end, and even now—although changes are observable—there is a conscious dependence upon medical work to secure a hearing, and obtain converts. By many missionaries the use of medical service as an evangelizing device is earnestly defended. They point out that the sick are peculiarly accessible to spiritual comfort, and often seem eager to hear the message. Instances in abundance are brought forward to indicate the spiritual fruits of preaching in Christian hospitals. On the other hand, enlightened non-Christians frequently express their scorn of institutions which proselytize the sick and helpless, who are least able to resist.

It is not easy to find ground unassailable by those on the one side who charge that hospitals are being conducted for propagandist ends, and those on the other who are convinced that any mission institution in which the spoken message is not given has degenerated to the level of a devitalized humanitarianism. A gradual shift of attitude, however, on the part of many missionary doctors away from the use of the hospital for public and direct evangelism is apparent.

The following principles are offered as a basis of religious activities in mission hospitals:

1. Service rendered in love, responding to conscious need, given without inducement, offering disinterested relief of suffering, fulfills with nobility the obligations of a Christian physician to those whom he serves.

2. The spoken word may have its appropriate place in the hospital. It is not possible always to dissociate bodily from spiritual requirements; the wise physician, responsive to the unspoken needs of his patients, is often able through intimate conversation to enlarge and enrich the professional service he has given, and to convey hope and assurance to troubled minds.

3. But the use of medical or other professional service as a direct means of making converts, or public services in wards and dispensaries from which patients cannot escape, is subtly coercive, and improper.

4. Clear-minded experimentation in the religious phases of hospital work is urgently needed. Much evangelistic work is casual and perfunctory; some of it is stupid and unworthy.

(B) *Clinical work.* The impression gained from our study of the clinical work of American missions in the Orient was in general one of disappointment. The days of the pioneer are past and the professional work of the modern mission medical centers is too often inferior to the nearby government and other non-missionary hospitals whose creation their example inspired. Such service tends in time to become a liability rather than an asset to the Christian cause, no matter how earnest the evangelistic efforts may be. It cannot but suggest also that other mission enterprises, less readily evaluated, are likewise inferior. The Christian forces should hasten to improve the professional quality of their medical institutions, even though to do this many must be closed, in order that those that remain shall not only serve their communities well but also add strength to the mission cause in general.

Quality in medicine and surgery depends little on the size of a hospital's buildings, on the completeness of its scientific equipment, or on the evangelical spirit with which its work is done. It is to be judged according to professional standards. These, of course, cannot be the same for the medical pioneer in the jungle and the university professor of medicine, but the work of the medical missionary in the jungle should be the best available in that jungle. If professional work is well done, then the Christian qualities of personal interest, sympathy, equal and tender consideration for all patients, regardless of money, religion or social status, will glorify it and make it distinctive. These same qualities, however, when attached to inferior medical work not only fail to atone for its deficiencies but bring themselves into disrepute.

The story of a typical American mission hospital will illustrate how quality in medical work is easily lost.

The young missionary, single-handed, first opened a small dispensary. Having won the confidence of the people, he soon was enabled to build and organize a hospital with nurses, laboratory technician, and helpers. He, as surgeon, internist, obstetrician, took personal care of all the in-patients, was the hospital's superintendent and business manager, and preached a brief sermon daily to his patients. His wards soon were full; he was very busy, very happy, and much revered in the community. Since he tried to handle everything that came, he unconsciously developed stereotyped routine methods of professional practice which soon became the fixed habit of his lifetime. He had no time for study or meditation. As time passed, he employed one or two nationals, graduates of good medical schools, as assistants; their help increased the volume, but did not improve the quality of his work.

Daily now in his out-patient department he "does something" for every one of those who flock to the clinic. With a smile and a cheerful message he can easily handle fifty an hour. During the busy seasons, aided by his assistants, head nurse, and even his evangelist, he may prescribe for five hundred, or even a thousand, out-patients in one morning, too many of whom leave with a good Bible text and the wrong medicine. Correct diagnoses are not attempted; important early diseases —cancer, tuberculosis, and the like—are overlooked.

Eventually a young missionary with rank and pay equal to his own is sent to assist him. The new-comer looks the situation over, and soon either demands a separate field or returns home. Meanwhile patients have been accumulating who because of the progress of their diseases, or thanks to other doctors, have discovered the inadequacy of the medical service they received, and who wonder if the doctor's Gospel message was not as erroneous as his treatment. Gradually his crowd begins to dwindle. Finally he is ready to retire. Since no one has been trained by years of service in that same locality to succeed him, the mission board has a difficult problem on its hands. Such is the one-man hospital which the non-medical members of the mission may praise, but which the Commission feels should not be tolerated.

The mission hospital should have a well organized staff. Only a unified group of men who divide the professional field between them and who are trained to focus the well coordinated attention of all to the needs of each patient, can handle creditably the professional problems which arise daily in a small hospital or dispensary. Such an institution can, in addition to its ward service, undertake prophylactic work and the education of internes, nurses, midwives, and dispensers. A business man responsible to the medical staff should have charge of the physical plant, and non-professional services.

How many of the staff of doctors and nurses should be westerners, and how many nationals, cannot categorically be stated. The best man should be chosen whatever his race, and the race line should never be drawn within the hospital community. Nevertheless, we suggest that in India devolution should be gradual. The principal reason for this is that the premature nationalization of the many government hospitals makes it the duty of mission hospitals to keep professionally as strong as possible in order to maintain sound standards. In

China, on the contrary, devolution might well be as rapid as is practicable.

The mission hospital staff should not only attempt quality rather than quantity service but should plan to make its work self-propagating. The school for nurses should train those who later will serve as hospital supervisors, and as directors of child welfare and public health stations, as well as those for ordinary institutional nursing. The hospital laboratories, including the X-ray department, should be adequate not only for the needs of its staff but for assisting the general practitioner and contributing to public health work in the district.

Such a hospital, particularly if located in a smaller city from which country villages can readily be reached, should create around itself a zone of lesser institutions which can further both curative and preventive medicine; dispensaries, each under a resident physician; health centers with graduate nurses; all under the supervision of, and assisted by, the hospital staff. At least one mobile dispensary also, with a staff from the hospital which makes regular visits to these out-stations, should be added. In this chain of dependent institutions there might well be a small leper colony and a small tuberculosis sanitarium, each with a resident physician, intimately related to the central hospital staff. This series of auxiliary units, radiating into rural communities, but bound together, in professional unity and control, with a central hospital, constitutes as far as we can see the only sound method of medical approach to the rural needs of India. Parts of this plan are already operating successfully in a few places. Wherever a comprehensive program dealing with rural life is established, medical service should be linked to it, in some such fashion.

In general medical missionaries seem to be too interested in major surgery. While good surgical work is a wonderful Christian service, it is nevertheless in the care of those with acute infections, diseases with marked functional aspects, conditions of malnutrition, various nervous states, tuberculosis and leprosy, that the peculiar qualities of Christian professional service have, in addition to their own virtue, a definite therapeutic value. It is urged that it is the surgeon by his fees who supports the hospital. Our answer is that, with the exception of a few clinics, this has been much over-emphasized. Good laboratories are now showing the value of modern medicine to those Orientals who formerly recognized the superiority of modern surgery but could not see wherein modern medicine differed much from their own systems.

Malaria, one of the greatest scourges of India, also hookworm disease, deserve far more individual attention for each patient than they now receive in order that the cures may be permanent. These diseases also offer unusual opportunities for cooperation with other missionary and with government forces in the control of such conditions in the community.

Our feeling is that venereal diseases are dealt with very superficially, considering their great frequency and their serious results socially and morally, as well as individually.

Pediatrics, also, is too little developed in the Orient since it is the children who would benefit most by medical treatment. It is indeed surprising how few children are found in the mission hospitals. The reason for this probably rests with the latency of their conditions and the unwillingness of their parents to admit them.

Our plea is that in India especially, the medical workers should pay particular attention to those family customs which have the sanction of society and religion, but which lead to definite disturbances of personality development and to neurasthenic states almost national in their prevalence and of great importance to all aspects of the mission service. Since the influence of a good central mental hygiene clinic working together through the medical centers and the church is almost the only way successfully to combat these conditions, we urge that the need of such a clinic be recognized.

(C) *Personnel.* Mission bodies are calling insistently from the field for more men and money for medical service. Not a few hospitals in China and India are closed because of lack of staff, or of maintenance funds, or both. Candidate secretaries generally feel that the recruiting of missionary doctors is their most difficult task. Three significant reasons for this difficulty are mentioned, among others, in a recent survey of medical missions in India (Christian Medical Association of India, 1929) : the lack of an effective appeal, the absence of ardent motivation, and a general knowledge that the equipment and support of mission hospitals are inadequate. There is no occasion to question the accuracy of this diagnosis: it points to important changes which have slowly been taking place in the attitude of missionary physicians toward their work as well as those to whom the challenge of a missionary career is being offered.

In the first place, there is a general feeling that medicine somehow has a place of its own in the Christian program, and that its worth and dignity are lowered by making it subserve directly the ends of the mission or church. In the second place, there is a growing conviction that if Christian forces are to undertake the maintenance of hospitals at all, they must be hospitals of high quality: to put good doctors in the field without the means of doing work at the level of their training is as wasteful as to send out inferior ones. The excessive turnover of missionary physicians is due in large part to disappointments in the nature and condition of their work. Difficulties in recruiting arise from parallel causes. The young candidates of today want assurance that they can express their professional skill as well as their Christian love and sympathy; most of them are more interested in a broad social gospel than in church doctrines. All this gives no ground for discouragement in our opinion, but it does call for a recasting of policies. What is needed is not a drive to pour men and money into medical missions in China and India, but a clear-cut plan of concentrating effort upon those institutions which can reasonably be brought to a satisfactory condition with the funds now available. The urgency of a sharp focussing of resources is apparent in India; in China, both need and demand for maintaining and strengthening mission hospitals are emphasized by the present weakness of the Government, but until greater political stability appears, it is unwise to counsel expansion.

(D) *Organization.* Three aspects of organization in medical missions deserve discussion in this brief summary.

Christian hospitals in the Orient, if they are to fulfill their proper functions, will have larger staffs to meet the needs of a more comprehensive and diversified program, to cover furloughs, sick leave, and brief absences for special study. The grouping of physicians together for intimate teamwork of this kind is a delicate task. Many mission hospitals have suffered from the casual or fortuitous assignment to their staff of doctors and nurses ill-fitted for the needs of a compact and smooth-working organization. These difficulties, so apparent even to a passing observer, suggest stressing with special care, in the selection of personnel, those personal qualities which make for good team-play and successful social relationships. Short-term appointments may prove particularly useful in some situations.

Medical organizations of a national character, which serve to bring physicians together in annual or biennial meetings for scientific discussions and fellowship, are most important, particularly in the Orient. The Christian Medical Association of India, now integrated with the National Christian Council through a capable executive secretary, is doing a useful work, but much more might be accomplished if a modest addition were made to its working budget. Its secretary should be able to travel widely over the field, to finance conferences of important committees, issue a monthly journal, organize and direct surveys and act as a general clearing agent, in matters of concern to the medical missionary force as a whole.

The China Medical Missionary Association established more than a half-century ago, gave place in 1924 to the China Medical Association with a missionary division, and is now in process of fusing with the National Medical Association—a body of western-trained Chinese—to form a new and comprehensive organization. The support of enthusiastic missionary members and a small grant from the Rockefeller Foundation have made possible for years the services of a full-time executive officer, and a varied program that has produced much of lasting value.

At the home base, several of the boards concerned in this

study have special medical administrators who keep close contact with the field and its needs, arrange for the physical examinations of missionary personnel, help in planning postgraduate work for doctors on furlough, and coordinate as best they can the varied medical activities of their societies. Only the trivialities of denominationalism prevent this important and valuable work from being done in simpler and better fashion.

(E) *The use of nationals.* It is disappointing to find that very few Indians are in responsible posts in the mission hospitals. Assistants holding frankly subordinate places at small salaries, without prospect of advancement, are in practically every hospital: these men and women are usually subassistant surgeons, the product of low-grade medical schools. In one or two mission hospitals only there are fully qualified Indians recognized as partners in the enterprise. Devolution is being hampered in India in numerous ways, some of which can be identified easily:

1. Scarcity of available candidates. Mission hospitals are required either to meet the salaries of nationals from local income, or to pay them with reference to the status and pay of pastors, teachers and other trained mission workers. The earnings of the hospital seldom permit the payment of comparatively large salaries to highly qualified nationals, even if the principle is approved by mission authorities, and mission boards as a rule do not put nationals upon a basis of compensation equal to that of missionaries. As long as the number of thoroughly qualified Christian Indian physicians is small, and well-paid government posts are open to them, devolution will be discouragingly slow. What effects a strong Christian medical college might have on this problem will be considered later.

2. Social and administrative handicaps. The sharing of administrative and financial responsibility is complicated by the fact that the foreigner because of his detachment from the pressures of Indian family and social usage can do many things without criticism that his Indian colleague finds it all but impossible to undertake. Social barriers, also, sometimes

frankly conceded, sometimes rationalized, often stand regrettably in the way of genuine equality and many missionary physicians express doubt as to the wisdom of going far in devolutional changes under present conditions.

In China, by contrast, comparatively large numbers of nationals are taking an important share in the conduct of Christian hospitals; there appear to be more and better trained ones available, and there are no obvious social distinctions involved in the sharing process. This devolutional progress has come about largely through the abrupt decrease in missionary doctors at the time of the intense nationalist disorders in 1926-28, and although there has been some loss of efficiency professionally, it is outweighed by the advantages of prompt nationalization.

(F)   *The training of nationals.*   India's need for a Christian medical college of high grade is being strongly agitated by missionary forces, on the grounds that the government colleges furnish no idealistic and spiritual influences, that the quality of their teaching is declining, and that admissions are so apportioned among Hindus, Mohammedans, and other religious groups in accordance with numerical ratios to the entire population, that Christians have few places open to them. On the other hand the lack of well-trained nationals in mission hospitals is keenly felt, and the call for physicians in rural areas is urgent. The only institution under Christian auspices now available for the medical training of men is below college standards, and its weaknesses, financial and organizational, are such that it cannot meet the needs of today, although it has served in the past with fine devotion and reasonable effectiveness in the training of hospital assistants.

While in the main the arguments for a superior Christian college free from the impediments which hamper government institutions, are valid, the Commissioners are not disposed to commend its establishment as an integral part of the missionary enterprise, for the following reasons:

1. The investment required would be very large, and would almost certainly divert funds greatly needed for other phases

of Christian program. If the plan is carried further, it should be financed from sources not otherwise accessible to missionary appeal, and only in case endowment sufficient to cover minimal operating costs at an adequate level is in hand.

2. A college of this type cannot be successfully organized and maintained without a degree of secularization entirely out of accord with the hopes and plans of the promoters.

3. It is by no means clear that such an institution would meet the needs of rural areas, or demands for a higher grade of hospital assistant.

4. Christian candidates of high promise are few, and likely to form only a small fraction of the student body.

5. Even if missions were to take no financial part in founding and maintaining the proposed college, its success in training Christian students would imply heavy additional expense for the missions utilizing its graduates. Christian boys would have to be subsidized throughout the course, and paid much higher salaries in subsequent mission work, whether in existing hospitals, or in new rural enterprises.

Mission medical education for women has progressed to the point, in South India, where the union institution at Vellore, with a new and modern plant, is seeking to attain college status. This should be done if funds sufficient to guarantee proper maintenance of staff can be secured; but other steps are no less desirable—the relinquishment of government subsidy, the reorganization of the governing body and the securing of a closer relation between clinical and pre-clinical units than now exists.

The situation in China, where government medical education is still very weak, and where a private Christian college (Peiping Union Medical College) dominates the higher ranges of professional education, is strikingly different. There are six missionary medical schools, in five of which the boards concerned in this study are participating: the Hackett Medical School in Canton; St. John's and the Women's Christian Union Medical School, both in Shanghai; Cheeloo University Medical College in Tsinan; the West China Union University Medical College at Chengtu in Szechuan; and Mukden Medical College in Manchuria. The latter is maintained by a group of British societies.

These institutions have contributed in no small measure to medical progress and enlightenment in different areas of China. They provide better instruction than can be had in any of the government schools. The maintenance of five colleges of medicine in one country, however, is a heavy burden for missionary societies to carry for an indefinite period, and some of them should be liquidated when indigenous institutions, governmental or private, begin to develop strength and stability. In the meantime their work should be conserved by focussing all available resources upon them. Hackett would be immeasurably more useful if it could unite with Lingnan University and the Canton Hospital in a co-educational program.

In Shanghai the present picture reveals two struggling schools, incompletely staffed, with fewer students by far than they should have, restrained by controlling agencies from the obvious and sensible step of amalgamation.

Cheeloo carried an intolerable burden of clumsy and inefficient organization. The school has made a gratifying contribution to medical missions for fifteen years; it has a good staff and student morale, but its work is being done at present under circumstances which cancel any chance of developing into a first-rate medical school. A fresh design of union organization is needed here, if one of the best efforts of the missionary program is to produce what it should.

Nursing education. Nursing education in the Orient has given thousands of women not only an economic advantage which otherwise they could not have had, but a sound preparation for home life. The results of mission work in this field have been notably successful in China.

Social and religious barriers have made the task much more difficult in India. It is felt to be degrading to perform services that involve close personal contact or are menial, and this attitude makes it difficult to secure promising and intelligent candidates. The age limit for probationers is too low, on account of early marriage; the moral hazards of exposing young girls fresh from the seclusion of school to the freer life of hospital work and of community service, preclude general hospital training for women. The Commissioners urge that in mission hospitals properly staffed and equipped for doing so, intensive efforts be made to develop training on a rising scale of requirements and standards. Not every institution should attempt it; only those having unusual resources of plant and personnel can do a significant work in the education of nurses.

(G) *Professional control.* Our hope is that in the future the work of the medical missionaries will come more and more under professional supervision. Only a medical man can judge accurately of medical work. The missionary in charge of a hospital has in the past tried to serve in two capacities—as evangelist and as doctor. One result has been that in his efforts to reach as many persons as possible, he has tended to admit to the wards, but especially to the out-patient department, far more patients than he could adequately care for. Another result, and several of the best of medical missionaries have admitted that this is a temptation which they must stoutly resist, is that they have allowed their evangelistic efforts to serve as a substitute for their much more difficult medical and surgical work and for the studying necessary to keep themselves abreast of the progress of their profession.

(H) *Finance.* The evidences of diffusion in medical work and resultant financial waste are inescapable both in China and India. Apart from unnecessary overlapping and duplication, there has been a tendency to multiply hospitals without board support in areas where local maintenance is not feasible because of the poverty of the clientele. Certain generalizations may properly be made:

1. As a principle, patients able to do so should pay something, however small, in money or rice or manual labor, for service received, and no distinctions should be made between Christians and non-Christians. But no needy person should be turned away because he has nothing to give.

2. The degree of local self-support should not be determined as a general policy, but by local conditions.

3. Only those hospitals with fully effective professional standards should be financed as may be required by foreign funds. Others should be closed, and their staff utilized elsewhere, if necessary, in a program of vigorous concentration.

4. Such a policy can be carried out only by reconsideration and action at the home base.

5. Endowments should be encouraged for teaching hospitals only. For service hospitals a central fund might well be established.

(I) *New work.* The need and usefulness of additional activity in fields of health education, preventive medicine, and public health nursing is obvious. With the reservations that much of this type of work is properly a function of the state, that it is a costly enterprise, for which little local financial return can be expected, and that it can be handled properly only in hospitals financed and staffed for such marginal work, the Commissioners are convinced that if a consistent policy of concentration be enforced, much that is worth while can be done in these newer lines. In particular, efforts in health education should be focussed upon school children and mothers.

CHAPTER X

AGRICULTURAL MISSIONS

The spirit of agricultural missions. Work for the improvement of agriculture and village life in the Orient is an integral part of the missionary enterprise. It is a method of functioning in these villages as Christians. Nearly all of the agricultural missionaries whom we came to know hold the view that "we do agricultural missionary work because we are Christians, not because we want to make Christians." Done in this spirit it exemplifies the life and teachings of Jesus, and is, in and of itself, mission work of a high order. The whole endeavor loses its true meaning, however, if carried on as a bait to draw people into the church, or primarily to provide a basis for the self-support of the church. Such motives as these would not deserve the approving words, "Inasmuch as ye have done it unto one of the least of these my brethren, ye have done it unto me." The agricultural missionary seeks to bring fullness of life to those with whom he works. Approached in this spirit, there is a great future for agricultural missions. But there are distinct limitations which need to be recognized. While there are examples of splendid work, the task is difficult and much of the energy, human and financial, now being spent is going to waste. New plans and new methods of administration must be devised. This calls for a careful study of the problems involved.

Characteristics of Oriental agriculture. The task is not so simple as it may appear to the novice. It is not a matter of showing the oriental farmer how to use western methods, for these very methods have grown out of conditions radically different from those obtaining in the densely settled areas of Asia, and cannot as a rule be applied in the East. In the agricultural life of America there has been an abundance of fertile land and a shortage of available human labor. The pressure of circumstances has been in the direction of discovering how the maximum results may be attained through a small expenditure of human strength. The invention and use of labor-saving machinery has revolutionized our agriculture. A large emphasis has also been placed on animal husbandry as a means of converting grain and forage into marketable forms, which in turn has tended to give a relatively large place in the American diet to dairy and meat products.

In India, China and Japan, on the other hand, there is a relative shortage of arable land and a very great oversupply of labor. The farm population of these three countries is roughly estimated at six hundred million, or about twenty times that of the United States. The area of crop land from which these oriental farm folk live would have to be increased fourteen-fold before the area per capita of farm population would be equal to that of the United States. It is unwarranted and unpromising to introduce American machine and livestock methods of farming into the Orient. The way to be helpful is to start with what is and seek methods of improvement.

The agriculture and the mode of living in the rural areas of these countries seem to have been handed down from a time when no great benefit could be gained by the tillage of more land. In these days local self-sufficiency was the rule, and the elements in the standard of living of the people were restricted almost solely to the things which could be produced right at hand. Each family, or at most each community, had to adjust its consumption to the possibilities of local production. This set limitations on the amount of land required per farm family. The fact that for climatic, religious or other reasons they lived largely on a vegetarian diet further restricted the land requirement per family; hence these countries were long ago densely populated on the basis of very small scale farms and low living standards. The limited elements in the standard of living appear to have been looked upon as inevitable until the development of trade brought many new items of food, clothing and adornment. This stimulated the desire for larger incomes with which to buy the great variety of things which commerce puts into the market. To secure the articles of commerce, something must be produced to exchange for them, but when these farmers desire to produce for the market, they find themselves restricted by the size of their farms. Obviously they do not have space in which to utilize farm machinery, nor to develop the types of animal husbandry used in the West as a means of producing a surplus for the market.

In China and old Japan dairy products are rarely used by village people. The soy bean, not the cow, is the foster-mother of the race in these countries. Bean curd, bean soup and soy sauce are used everywhere. These, supplemented by other varieties of beans and a limited amount of fish and poultry products, give the protein content to the diet. In China there is a wide use of pork in small quantities, but in Japan its use is negligible.

Cereals constitute the basic staple of the diet in all of these three countries. With the present ratio of land and people in these countries this highly vegetarian diet is unavoidable. If the grains were to be converted into animal products in these countries, as they are in America, their power of supporting human life would be reduced to the point of producing famine. In so far as animal industries are based on the by-products of grain, oil and fiber production, they prove a boon to farmers. In India milk production, largely from the buffalo, is based upon such by-products and a considerable amount of grazing. Buttermilk and *ghi* (pure butter fat) are important items in the diet of many Indian villagers but peas of many varieties are the major source of protein.

In addition to the differences in agriculture between the East and West, due to size of farms and density of the farm population, there are radical differences in climate which place significant limitations on the degree to which western methods of farming can be applied in the Orient. Because of prevailing climatic conditions the major crops of India, China and Japan are generally different from those which dominate western agriculture. Rice is the outstanding cereal in the Orient. The millets and grain sorghums are next in importance. Wheat, it is true, is a major crop in the Punjab of India and in parts of North China, but the varieties are different from those produced in the West and the conditions require different methods of culture. Some of the industrial crops, particularly the production of silk cocoons, are entirely out of the line of American farm experience.

The growing of two or three crops a year on the same land adds greatly to the difficulty of introducing improved varieties with larger yields or better quality of product. The new varieties must not only be suited to the soil and climate but must also fit the exacting time schedule of tandem cropping.

Western science and Eastern agriculture. These differences between the East and the West should not discourage those interested in helping oriental farmers through the application of science to agricultural production. While the methods of farmers in the West cannot be transplanted, the fundamental principles as they relate to soils, plant and animal improvement, plant disease and insect control and crop combinations are applicable to the Orient. But they can be applied only by those who, in addition to being scientifically qualified, are also thoroughly familiar with local conditions. The latter is a qualification which the agricultural missionary must acquire in the field.

Work by various agencies is in progress. The application of science to the improvement of agriculture is making headway. A more efficient use of the land through improved seeds and improved methods of cultivation is receiving attention. The limits to the possibilities will not soon be reached, but even when they have been reached the farmers of the Orient will still be relatively poor and unable to possess many of the elements of a modern standard of living unless the ratio between land and land workers can be improved to the point where commercial agriculture may be more generally introduced. When the time came for changing to commercial agriculture in the United States there were vast areas of land, better than those previously in use, which could be had for the taking up.

This made the readjustment in size of farms a simple matter, but in the Orient the settlement of all the desirable land was completed long before commercial agriculture was thought of. The Punjab, Hokkaido and Manchuria have been opened up, it is true, and the farms in these provinces are much larger than those in the older regions. These outlets have not proved great enough, however, to reduce the pressure of population in the older provinces.

A modern commercial city in the Orient, with its many new occupations, provides the economic basis for the development of higher standards of living. But commercial agriculture, the basis of economic betterment in the country, comes slowly. Certain cash crops, like cotton, tea and silk, help toward a prompt economic adjustment, but in the old lines of farming there is little change. This situation results in vast rural populations being left behind in the economic progress of the world. In some regions conditions have been aggravated by the fact that some of the supplementary phases of the rural occupation, such as the production of cloth, have been taken over by the commercial centers without the compensation of increased agricultural incomes as a basis of buying materials for clothing. So long as the unfavorable ratio between farm land and farm people stands in the way of expanding the size of the farm business, any analysis which may be made of farm incomes as they are or as they may become in the Orient through the application of science, will make a bad showing, in comparison with the budgetary demands of the modern living standards of the West.

Life ideals and rural improvements. The things which can be done to improve the living conditions of rural people do not, however, lie solely in the field of technical agriculture, but partly in the realm of ideas relating to individual, family and community life. It is doubtful, for example, whether the ratio between farm land and farmers in the Orient can be greatly improved until the ideas of the farm people have been changed to the point where the desire to improve their living standards and the desire that their children may have better opportunities in life than the present generation can hope for will not only cause large numbers of them to leave agriculture for other occupations, but will impel those who remain in agriculture to limit the size of their families.

So long as the rural birth rate is so high as to maintain the density of the farm population in spite of emigration, there is no relief in sight for the problems due to overpopulation in the villages. In Japan, for example, the last three decades have shown a vast movement of population from country to city. From 1898 to 1925 the population in towns and cities having more than ten thousand inhabitants increased from 8,040,000 to 21,800,000, or an increase of 172.5%.* But during this same period there was no reduction in the population of towns and villages under ten thousand. The number of farm households has continued to increase. In 1930 the number was 5,599,670— 46.1% of the total number of households in Japan. This was an increase of 3.4% over the number of farm households in 1910. During the same period the area of arable land increased only 3.8%. The ratio of land to farm families is therefore essentially unchanged, although the new farms in Hokkaido are larger than those in old Japan. In India the results are similar. Since the British went to India and increased the crop land area by developing irrigation projects and helped to increase other employment through the expansion of commerce and industry, the main result has been an increase in population, rather than an improvement in the quality of the life of the people. This does not look hopeful. The need is for new seeds of life which may thrive under Oriental conditions and from which may spring up in the hearts of men and women new conceptions of life and a new dynamic that will give the people the impulse to strive for higher ideals. Changes in attitudes and ideals of rural people in these regards might, in the course of a few generations, bring about a reduction in the rural population, an increase in the size of farms, and in the use of suitable labor efficiency devices which would result in an important increase in farm income.

Fortunately the improvement of the quality of the life of

* H. G. Moulton, "Japan, An Economic and Financial Appraisal," p. 330.

rural people is not entirely dependent upon increased income. Family budgets are not the full measure of living standards. Much that adds to the richness of life is the product of a "way of living" and is largely independent of economic income. Once the basic needs of food, clothing and shelter have been provided, the ideals of the people, their mental and spiritual outlook, their appreciation of the beautiful, the attitude of members of the family toward each other, and the personal relations of neighbors, are more important than the things which money can buy. These non-economic elements in the living standard are invaluable factors in the culture of a people. The people of some of the villages of these old countries have a culture which surpasses in some respects the culture of rural people in certain parts of the West, where the economic standards are far higher. Yet in all these old countries there are phases of rural life inherited from the distant past which are drab, and others which are repugnant to those who know of the family and community institutions and customs in other parts of the world.

Thus the problems of agriculture and country life which the agricultural missionary must face are complex and difficult. There are technical problems relating to agricultural improvement which will yield only to the scientist who can adapt himself to radically different conditions from those with which he is familiar in the West. Furthermore, he must not be impatient if progress is slow. There are economic and social problems deep seated in the customs of the people. These will yield but slowly to new ideas, but they are as basic as the technical improvements if the more abundant life is to be attained.

The approach to the task. The above statements of conditions and problems are not intended to discourage those interested in agricultural missions, but rather to make clear that this challenging task demands men and women of the best talent and the best fundamental training in the basic physical, biological, economic and social sciences. It is important not only that the missionary approach the task with an understanding of its difficult nature, but that those who support and those who administer missions shall have these conditions clearly in mind, in order that they may appreciate the necessity of giving the agricultural missionary scope and time to develop the work in a fundamental way. One of the most pitiful things in the Orient is the plight of the missionary who has a clear vision and a profound conviction with regard to the way to do effective work but who in order to keep in harmony with an uninformed home board must turn with a heavy heart to doing things which he believes to be ineffective.

A careful analysis of the agriculture and the rural life of the Orient is needed as a prerequisite to the formulating of general plans of procedure. Then every specific undertaking should be preceded by a scientific study of the people, their practices and their environment. Such research should lead to an understanding of the forces and conditions which have led the people into the paths they are following, and should provide the basis for determining whether or not there is prospect of securing beneficial results from certain possible changes. Once this method has developed working hypotheses the next step is experimentation, but this experimentation should not be undertaken until all available results of indigenous experience and research have been fully utilized. To introduce machinery which does not suit the economic needs of the people, to introduce breeding animals with an objective out of line with the desires and necessities of the people, to introduce varieties of cereals and other plants without knowledge of their suitability for the region, or to propose plans for home or community improvement without an understanding of the people and their institutions, is simply to court disaster and to insure the discrediting of the enterprise. These things are mentioned because they have too often characterized the agricultural work of missionaries. The work, to succeed in the Orient, must be built upon scientific knowledge and a thorough understanding of the regions where the recommendations are to be applied. Work based merely on hopeful emotions and a surplus of courage is to be condemned.

Agricultural research.   A survey of the three countries leaves one with the impression that the government agencies in Japan and India are making excellent progress in solving the technical problems of plant production, and that agricultural missionaries are not needed for this purpose. But in China the situation is different. The best agricultural research work is being carried on at Nanking and Lingnan Universities, both Christian institutions. While a plan is on paper for the development of a comprehensive system of federal and state colleges and experiment stations, and some good work is being done, there will for many years be a real need for the leadership which can be supplied from Nanking and Lingnan. In these institutions the work has been scientific in method and practical in application. In cereal selection and breeding, horticulture and forestry, plant pathology, economic entomology, sericulture and economic and social research, the work has been of a quality to command the respect of the scientific world. The extended usefulness of this research awaits the further development of regional tests and extension methods, in which missions can make important contributions through regional demonstrations.

The work in animal breeding has not met with great success in India or China. It is suggested that before missionaries undertake further experiments in cattle breeding, the problems involved be carefully analyzed by a committee consisting of a live-stock geneticist, an animal nutritionist, a veterinarian, an agricultural engineer, and an agricultural economist. In China practically nothing is being done in this field. In India livestock breeding presents enticing problems, and there is a desire on the part of certain of the agricultural missionaries to enlarge their work in this field. However, the government agencies have already spent more money on cattle breeding than the missions can hope to command for this purpose, and have enlisted the services of some most excellent men. The results up to date are disappointing, but adequate to show that nothing short of a large scale (at least a thousand head of cattle) and long-time (at least a hundred years) experiment, under the best genetic, nutrition and health experts, working on a plan in harmony with the economic needs, is likely to yield dependable results. Since this would be a large undertaking as a mission project, perhaps out of line with what can be hoped for in other fields of agricultural mission work, it would likely prove best to establish an experiment of this order on an independent foundation. Such an experiment would render an invaluable service to the people of India and incidentally throw light on many problems of life in a vast region where live the greatest mass of civilized people anywhere under the tropical sun.

Economic and social problems. While government agencies in Japan and India have gone far in meeting the need for research work in the physical and biological sciences in their relation to agriculture, and work in this field in China is making excellent progress, the economic and social phases of rural life require further attention in all three countries. Sir Horace Plunkett formulated his program for agricultural betterment in Ireland in the phrase, "Better farming, better business and better living." It is the "better living" phase of this program which needs to be particularly stressed in all three of the Oriental countries under consideration. This needs to be emphasized in order that the economic results of better farming and better business may be transmuted into better living, also in order that the habits, customs, institutions, ideals and aspirations of rural people may be improved. Some are inclined to leave this phase of the undertaking entirely to the specialist in evangelism, in the belief that a knowledge of the teachings of Jesus will best serve to eliminate the sordid aspects of existence and enrich the lives of the people. It is our belief, however, that right here the agricultural missionary can be especially helpful, first of all by making a study of conditions and ultimately by sharing in the development of practical programs in harmony with Christian ideals.

Much of the practical work along this line will need to be done with the women of the villages. The women, far more than the men, hold the key to changes in living standards, in family and social customs, and in the finer cultural qualities of home and community life. Much of this country life work in the village can be carried on to best advantage by women workers.

Those interested in improving the living conditions of rural people in the Orient will find themselves confronted with many difficult economic problems. For example, improvements in land tenure and agricultural credit, with the hope of relieving the tillers of the soil through more favorable rental or interest conditions will continually come to the attention of the agricultural missionary. As a matter of fact, tenancy appears to be no more common in the Orient than in the United States, but its legal status is less well defined, and the tenants are as a rule living much closer to the subsistence level. Under these conditions the desire to improve incomes by securing reductions in rents is ever the occasion of strife. Some progress has been made in Japan, in particular, in adjusting tenancy problems through arbitration boards for the settlement of rent disputes, but when the Orient as a whole is considered, improvements in tenancy do not give promise of early results in increasing the income of the tenant farmer.

The credit problem involves even a higher percentage of the farmers of the Orient. While government controlled cooperative credit associations have been generally introduced in India and Japan, and experiments are being tried in cooperative credit in China where the clan and guild systems have been playing an important role, there remains in all these countries a large demand for credit beyond that which the cooperatives in their various forms have been able to meet. This demand is being met by private money lenders at very high rates of interest, which become heavy burdens upon large numbers of rural people.

The struggle for lower rents and lower interest rates cannot but make a strong appeal to the Christian workers. How much chance there is for the agricultural missionary to make an important contribution in this field cannot be answered at this time. Certain it is that he should not take sides in the heated controversies between landlord and tenant, but rather seek ways and means of improving their relations through a better mutual understanding leading to more sympathetic relations, through better methods of renting land, or by pointing the way to reduction of tenancy through measures attractive to both parties. Without full information of the specific circumstances and a broad understanding of the elements involved in the problem recommendations should not be offered. The same rule holds with regard to the relations of borrower and lender. Here are important problems, which should be studied with the hope that ways may be found which will gradually improve the economic status of the oriental farmer. Fortunately these and similar economic and social questions are being studied at Nanking University. This work should be generously supported. The universities of Japan are giving more and more attention to this important field of work. Something needs to be done to stimulate more work along these lines in India. An example of effective work of this type is that of Dr. Lucas of Forman College in Lahore, whose results have stimulated the government of the Punjab to project extensive studies in the economic and social life of the village.

Agricultural education. In India and Japan the government agricultural colleges are equipped to provide training in the sciences relating to agriculture but they need an influence which will lead students to look with favor upon opportunities for lives of service in rural communities. Fortunately there are a few Christian men on the faculties of some of these institutions who may do something to foster such a point of view, but more work is needed in this field. This spirit of service to rural people is well developed among the students at the Allahabad Agricultural Institute, at Nanking and at Lingnan Universities. In China the basic needs are for financial resources for the agricultural colleges of Nanking and Lingnan Universities, and for a succession of mature western men, masters in their special fields, who will each devote a few years to helping the Chinese deans and professors realize or advance their ideals and develop strong departments of research and education. The cooperation which Cornell University has given Nanking University by sending specialists in agronomy has proved most valuable. While there is still place for a limited number of highly trained agricultural missionaries who will give their lives to work in these institutions, the preponderant part of the work is and should be carried on by well trained available Chinese, prepared for the work through training at home and abroad.

Secondary schools with farm work and agricultural training conducted in a rural environment provide one of the most promising means of producing leaders who will devote their lives to the improvement of village life in India and China. Some excellent mission schools of this kind were visited in India. A high proportion of the graduates of these schools return to the village and become useful in various forms of community leadership. Some of the best pieces of village reconstruction work noted in India were the spontaneous results of the ideas of persons who had gone back to their home communities and interested their people. In China a few schools of a similar character are rendering valuable service. In Japan government schools are supplying the need. There are openings in them, however, for western teachers of the English language, who may help develop the spirit of service in these schools and thus make them of greater benefit to rural life.

The education of girls is just as important to rural progress in the Orient as is that of boys. If new ideas of home and family life are to penetrate the villages of India, China and Japan they must first be understood and desired by the wives and mothers.

The carrying of the results of technical agricultural research to the people is well organized in Japan. India has a system of agricultural extension specialists and demonstrators reaching out toward the farmers, but unfortunately the farmers are not organized or motivated as in Japan to reach toward the experiment stations for needed information, and owing to the anti-government feeling many farmers are not in a frame of mind to call upon these agencies for help. However, in parts of India, as well as in Japan, the arm of the law has reached in and made the results of scientific research effective. For example, in India certain varieties of cotton are designated for specific regions and all the seed that is planted must be obtained from government sources. In Japan a similar method of control is applied to the production of silk worms, resulting in a greatly increased yield of raw silk of superior quality.

The "rural reconstruction units" in India. The agricultural and rural life aspect of the "rural reconstruction unit" which has been much in the foreground of the thoughts of all interested in rural missions, deserves more attention than can be given to it in the space allotted to agricultural missions in this volume. In India there are five classes of people working in this field:

1. The Y. M. C. A. secretaries, under the leadership of the late Mr. K. T. Paul, a national, have developed the idea of making an approach to the villages of India, comprehensive in two senses: It interests itself in all classes of people, and endeavors to minister to all of their needs, educational, medical, economic, social and religious.

2. Modern Indians like Tagore, Devadhar and Bhagwat, are making a comprehensive and intensive approach to village life and are conducting studies with the view of finding how this work may be successfully done.

3. Certain India Civil Service men, because of their Christian interest in human welfare, are carrying on significant rural reconstruction.

4. One Christian worker visited in India who does not fall into any of these categories sees the need of rural reconstruction, feels that no one as yet knows how best to proceed, and is therefore approaching the problem in a purely experimental manner, with the hope of learning how to approach and carry out the task.

5. The Protestant missions are giving much thought to rural reconstruction work since the visit of Dr. Butterfield to India in 1930. This is resulting in suggestions for the reorganization of agricultural missions in India.

Hitherto, the work had been focussed primarily upon the depressed classes. This came about in a most natural manner, following a mass movement about a generation ago which brought hundreds of thousands of the depressed classes under the care of the missions. An effort was made to improve the economic wellbeing of these people. Land settlement was resorted to, particularly in the Punjab, where new lands were being brought under irrigation. This gave the Christians of the depressed classes a chance to improve their status in fact as well as in name. The possibilities in land settlement, however, were limited and for the majority the hope lay in finding ways and means of improving their condition in the villages where they were.

The agricultural missionaries who undertook work with the depressed classes found that as a rule their parishioners had little or no land. They were farm hands, family servants or village artisans or scavengers. However, they quite generally kept chickens, goats and pigs. Hence these forms of livestock have assumed a large place in agricultural missions. While some attention has been given to such lines as improved gardens and fruit growing, the chicken, as a rule has held the center of the stage.

The movement for rural reconstruction implies that the agricultural work of the missionaries is to be put on a more comprehensive basis. The services will be made available to all the people of the village and the agricultural worker is to go hand in hand with the physician, the nurse, the school teacher and minister to help all who are in need without regard to religion or caste.

This new approach will of necessity shift the center of thought of the agricultural missionary from those phases of agriculture carried on solely or largely by the depressed classes to the major enterprises of the farmers, and their economic and social relations. This larger task will call for a thorough knowledge of the physical, biological, economic and social sciences in their relation to the improvement of agriculture and rural life. It will also require a thorough knowledge of the conditions which have determined the types of farming, methods of culture, forms of crop utilization and social and economic customs in the region in which the worker is located. In India the position of the geographically isolated agricultural missionary can be greatly strengthened by a close association with the government system of research and demonstration. The government of India looks with favor upon missionaries who will organize the farmers to reach out toward the experiment station for aid.

The maintenance of a little exhibit of chickens, pigs, goats and rabbits at a rural mission center as a means of making contacts with the village people should not be mistaken for an agricultural mission, which must deal with the major problems and opportunities of farm and village life. Neither should the suggestion of western substitutes for eastern crops, animals and equipments be indulged in by the novice. A western agriculturalist now working in the north of India pointed out to a number of this Commission an indigenous plow of the better type, and said, that for seventeen years he had been trying without much success to displace this moisture conserving, digging plow with a soil drying turning plow, but that now he is much attached to the old plow and believes that it serves the purpose of dry farming far better than the one he had been trying to introduce. In this he was doubtless correct.

A rapid expansion in the rural reconstruction work before the best methods have been thoroughly established by experiment along agricultural, social, medical and religious lines would endanger the ultimate success of the undertaking. The desire to reach all classes in the Indian village is highly commendable, but the missionary who has hitherto devoted himself to the depressed classes is thereby handicapped in approaching the head man and the caste people in the same village. A new method of approach should be sought in such villages. Efforts should also be made in fields that are entirely new. But until more is known of the methods and problems, the undertakings should be experimental and limited in number, and the whole effort should be under competent direction.

Such information as we now have in hand indicates that the approach to the caste village of India should be made by persons genuinely Christian in character, who will be able to enlist the best talent of the village in the performance of services which benefit all classes of people, particularly those who are less advantageously situated. Such leaders will be willing to proceed by various methods to exemplify the life and teachings of Jesus by cooperating in the improvement of the quality of the life of the village, without asking the people to become members of the church. They will leave to the villagers the determination of the form of fellowship which they will adopt, once they have been motivated by the life and teachings of Jesus, as revealed to them through exemplification, through their own participation in service with the people of their own villages, and through such teachings as they themselves shall have elicited.

Rural work in China. In China the need for rural work is as great as in India, but the situation is different. The caste problem, fortunately does not exist, but a comprehensive system of agricultural research and extension such as is available in India to give scientific aid in the undertaking is lacking. The Christian colleges are providing the background in education and research for a limited development in this field. Certain examples deserve particular mention. One experiment, largely on a self-supporting basis, is under way on Honan Island, near Canton, under the auspices of Lingnan University and the Bureau of Agriculture of the Province of Kwangtung. Another, located at Wukiang (thirty miles up the river from Nanking) appears to be well organized, and gives promise of success. This project is under the supervision of the extension department of Nanking University. Another project, Christian at heart but not under missionary auspices, is that at Ting Hsien, under the direction of leaders in the Mass Education Movement in China. These efforts are looked upon as experimental by those who have them in hand. They are under good management and should be supported, with the hope that in time they will point the way for more comprehensive undertakings by the Government, if not by the missions.

The lone agricultural worker, depending on what he knows and what he himself can learn about agriculture, is in a very weak position. In the past there have been in China many lone workers. As a rule they have failed to render valuable service. They have stumbled along from one mistake to another and the majority of them have become discouraged and have left the work. The remaining scattered agricultural missionaries should be connected up with the Christian colleges or other centers of research. As a rule mistakes of these lone workers have been on a small scale, but there are not lacking examples of mistakes involving large sums of money and much discredit to the enterprise of agricultural missions, caused by failure to secure the guidance of available experts at one of the centers of research.

Japan. The boards have sent no agricultural missionaries to Japan, but through the influence of foreign Christian laymen in the government educational system, and as a result of the teaching and way of living of mission educators, there are many Christians among the agriculturalists of Japan. There seems to be a real need for Christian missions in rural Japan, but for the technical agricultural missionary as such there is obviously no need. Secular agencies are already doing so much to serve the varied interests of the rural population that there seems to be no need for rural missions to set up "rural reconstruction units" in Japan.

Any effort on the part of missionaries and of the national Christian leaders in Japan to develop a technical agricultural service independent of the government agencies is a mistake. The agricultural work of the Christian enterprise in Japan should focus upon the problems of country life, rather than upon efficiency in technical agriculture. There is a large field for service here, but even in this phase of the work cooperation with and stimulation of those working under government auspices may prove the greatest opportunity for rendering service. Whatever is done should get into the major channels. There are more than eleven thousand government extension workers, and there is prospect of the development of a corps of home demonstration agents. With all this extension work in progress, it is highly important to inject right into this main

current of thought and action the ideas and purposes which
Christian missions seek to put into rural life.

Rural life associations.   A line of activity needed in all three
countries is the development of a comprehensive country-life
movement. This involves the bringing together into one organization of all persons interested in rural welfare. The purpose is to stimulate those lines of thought and action which
will put the life of village people on a higher plane. This is a
need much felt in Japan, as well as in India and China. The
objective of this country-life movement might be briefly described as follows:

(1) To give direction to thought and action in the self-
help movement of farmers for better living conditions and
happier relations in their economic activities, in their homes
and in their communities.

(2) To develop and disseminate ideas relating to sound
community and national policies as they affect the life of rural
people.

(3) To develop interest in the better living side, as distinguished from the production and marketing side of agriculture, on the part of persons in the public services organized
for the purpose of helping farmers; to encourage the development of agricultural research and extension where it does not
exist; and to encourage the movement for home demonstration agents to supplement the work of the agricultural adviser.

Such a country-life movement is needed in India, and if
broadly planned to include in addition to the Indian Christians and missionaries, the leading Hindus, Mohammedans
and other Indians, the British Indian Civil Service men and
others interested in rural life improvement, a great movement
could be started.

Although the organization of such a movement in China
would not be easy, it is much needed. There is a nucleus of
personnel to start with, and in time it might become one of
the most important methods of mission work in rural China.

Japan is far riper for this movement than either India or
China. Fortunately there are outstanding men in Japan, such

as those in the Department of Agriculture, in the Universities and among the agricultural leaders who are capable of providing excellent leadership for a country-life association. (Many of these eminent men are Christian in fact if not in name.) While it is highly desirable that men of this type should be in the foreground in the organization of an association for the improvement of Japanese country life, there is also an important place for members of the National Christian Council, missionaries interested in improving rural life, local ministers, lay leaders and others.

The list of persons to participate in this undertaking in India, China and Japan should include prominent leaders among the women. The strategic importance of village women as a factor conditioning progress cannot be too strongly emphasized. Women must have an adequate place in the planning of rural work.

Any important development along these lines must be rooted in the soil. If the undertaking is to be a success, those who work directly with the farm people, and many of the farm men and women themselves must play an important role in the rural life association. This being the need, what can be done to meet it? A suggestion which may commend itself is as follows: Organize an International Committee to promote a world congress of Country-Life Workers, to be held eighteen months or two years hence. This congress could be used as a background for stimulating the organization of country life associations in the various countries in the world, and especially in India, China and Japan. These national associations would be basic to representation in the international conference; hence with the congress in view, the central international committee could effectively stimulate organizational activities in the various countries without appearing to intrude in their affairs.

A world congress of rural-life workers, carefully planned and effectively carried through, would stimulate and give direction to country-life improvement activities in the various countries represented. It would bring to the attention of rural leaders in all lands that which is best in country life in other countries. In these ways it would help bring to pass results agricultural missions have had in mind, and should also prove a beginning in international thinking and good will on the part of farmers and farm leaders—a basic necessity, if international agricultural competition is to be put on a higher plane and if world peace and good will in international relations are to be secured.

Recommendations

Our recommendations with regard to agricultural missionary work are of two orders: one relates to the character of the work; the other to its administration:

I. With regard to the character of the work, the following recommendations are proposed:

A. In India the major attention of missions should be given to three lines of endeavor:

(1) The development of agricultural middle schools in rural environments, devoted primarily to the training of agricultural and country-life leaders;

(2) To experimentation in the development of coordinated rural services in which the leader of the project gives especial attention to organizing the people of the rural area to make use of the agricultural extension services, the public health and medical services, the educational services, and the religious influences which are already available or which may be provided, in improving the quality of the life of all the people in the village or group of villages which may be enlisted in this common undertaking;

(3) While research in the physical and biological sciences relating to agriculture is well developed, a stimulus is needed which will promote the further development of basic research in economic and social problems relating to agriculture and rural life.

B. In China there are three lines of agricultural missionary work which need special attention:

(1) The development of research and the training of re-

search workers is fundamental. The backward condition of scientific research in the government institutions of China makes it imperative for the present, and for some time in the future, that basic research and collegiate education in the physical, biological, economic and social sciences relating to agriculture and rural life be given first consideration. The work which has been done at Nanking and Lingnan is commendable, and should receive increasing support.

(2) The stimulating of the growth of middle schools in rural environments, for the training of agricultural and country-life leaders is also important.

(3) The experimentation in agricultural extension service, properly coordinated with the various missionary and government services which minister to rural life must not be neglected.

C. In India, China and Japan a country-life movement is needed to bring together all workers connected with rural life to stimulate an intelligent interest on the part of all and to develop the spirit of service in those who administer rural affairs. This movement should also create in the hearts of agricultural students a desire to work for the improvement of country life.

II. With regard to necessary changes in administration, we believe that none of the above proposals is likely to be adequately fruitful unless attention be given to the development of a better system of administrative control of this whole undertaking. To secure best results all the agricultural missionaries in any given country should operate under one management capable of planning and coordinating their work. The necessary basic research should be unified in plan and coordinated in execution. The results of indigenous experience and research should be fully utilized. The organization of the work should be such that those rendering service in local areas will be in close touch with the research centers, indigenous as well as missionary. The fields of work in the various countries have also many common problems requiring administrative supervision which can be successfully performed only by persons thoroughly grounded in the sciences related to agriculture and well acquainted with conditions in the mission fields. No individual mission board can command the technical ability required for the effective administration of its own agricultural work. The work today lacks both expert direction and unity in planning. This is resulting in wasteful uses of men and money. In order to overcome this unhappy situation, it is recommended:

1. That the mission boards, recognizing the technical character of agricultural missions and the need of their coordination under scientific planning, join together in establishing an agency to plan and supervise their work in this field. Ultimately this agency should be a section of a unified mission board organization, such as is proposed in Chapter XIV of this report.

2. That the mission boards be asked to consider the advisability of utilizing the Agricultural Missions Foundation, possibly with some readjustment in its organization if found desirable, as the agency to plan and supervise their agricultural work.

3. That the Agricultural Missions Foundation be asked to draw up and submit to the boards a comprehensive plan for the re-direction and future development of agricultural missions. This plan should include a statement of objectives, a formulation of methods of procedure, a list of specific pieces of work to be undertaken, a list of the qualifications of the various kinds of workers needed, covering both missionaries and nationals, and suggestions for the coordination with the new plan of the work now going on.

CHAPTER XI

MISSIONS AND THE DEVELOPMENT OF INDUSTRY

1. *Introduction*

MR. R. H. TAWNEY in his book "Equality" says, "An agricultural society, with its scattered household and unspecialized economic life, is normally both unconscious of requiring elaborate social services and incapable of providing them. Nor on its first plunge into the world of great industry does it realize their necessity. Carrying the habits of the peasant into its new urban environment, it proceeds for a generation to poison its body and starve its soul, before it realizes that what is innocuous in a village is deadly in a town . . . The result is the paradox of rising pecuniary incomes and deepening social misery . . . which has emerged in all industrial revolutions, to the confusion of those who forget that the timid staring creature, man, is so compounded as to require not only money, but light, air, and water, not to mention such uneconomic goods as tranquillity, beauty, and affection."

This striking paragraph may serve as an introduction to a study of the relation of missions to the problems of industry. These problems are modified by conditions of climate and social environment which it is well briefly to review.

2. *Climate*

Climate is one of the most important factors in molding the activities of men. A moderately cool and moist climate has generally been considered best for developing industry.

There is, in the West, little manufacturing in hot coastal climates. But in India some of the largest factories are in the areas of Bombay, Calcutta and Madras where the weather is hot and the summers long and enervating. Trying hot weather puts an undue strain upon the operative, because it favors the rapid spread of disease-bearing organisms, and tends physiologically to make the factory worker slothful and inefficient. This means that the average operative in India does not work as near full time as does a worker in a cooler climate. A given operation requires a larger supply of operatives with the result that wages are lower because each operative produces less. Wages are also kept down because in the Orient the supply of labor is large. The benefits of industrial life are lessened and the task of coping with the social problems which develop is increased.

While parts of China are warm and humid, labor conditions generally are not so adversely affected by climate as in India.

Japan has by far the best climate for manufacturing of any Oriental country. Cool and moist, except for a few trying months of the year, it is admirably adapted to manufacturing all sorts of textiles and miscellaneous products. Whatever may be her industrial problems—and they are many—they are not made more serious by her climate.

3. Social Environment

The social environment of the Orient has been more modified by congestion and poverty and has been cast in molds more fixed by family, clan and status than has been the case in the West. The family is the most important social group in India, China and Japan. Through its sons it is considered a unit running from generation to generation. Family property is pooled and administered by family heads. Members do not think of themselves as individuals but as parts of a group to which they are bound by the closest ties. Family custom places a heavy burden upon a financially successful member to aid relatives who are less fortunate. To help support relatives in a village is perhaps the commonest reason why a son or daughter enters industrial employment. But on the other hand the family receives the factory worker in time of sickness or distress and takes the place of the bread line in times of unemployment. After the recent bombardment of Chapei at Shanghai over 300,000 helpless people, who had lost their homes, were as a matter of family custom eventually absorbed back into their family and clan. The chief burden placed upon the community, so far as the refugees were concerned, was that of temporarily feeding them and transporting them to their family seat.

The clan is the larger unit of the family. It comprises groups of families sprung from a common and recognized family stock. It is usually, although not always, local and frequently dominates a village or portion of a city. The clan has a larger membership and gives the individual greater legal and financial protection and support than is possible in the smaller unit of the family. It provides a medium for common political action and creates and maintains the family in its social position. It is a cooperative entity but it stifles initiative and develops nepotism.

The status of an individual is fixed in India, China and Japan. In India status has developed into a peculiar stratification known as the caste system. A caste is a group bearing a common caste designation and often having the same traditional occupation, so linked together by the tradition of a common origin, and by the same social background, ceremonial observances, and family priests, that its members are regarded as single homogeneous community.

The economic results of caste are for the most part bad. It is true that it is sometimes an advantage for a man to have an hereditary occupation. On the other hand a man must, whether he like it or not, follow his traditional calling, not the calling which he would prefer. Caste is responsible for great wastes in consumption. Each caste must eat special food, and social customs, such as marriage, birth and death ceremonies call for large expenditures frequently leading into debt. Debts incurred in this way are often the immediate cause of a person's seeking employment in a factory.

Many factory employees are "outcastes". They have the lowest place in India's social system, are generally denied entrance to Hindu temples, cannot draw water from the village wells used by caste people, and are burdened with menial and degrading tasks. They are the most ignorant element in India's population, the poorest in mind and estate. They are, however, a product of caste even though they are not actually a part of the caste system.

4. *Western Contacts*

It remained for western impacts of trade, politics, education, and religion so to run athwart these old traditions and customs as seriously to endanger their supremacy. Western business men engaged in shipping, trade and banking are established in all the great cities of the Orient, and less frequently in interior points. Their influence has been a potent factor— not usually friendly to missions—in introducing western business methods and western business codes of ethics. In India, the industrial factory system is perhaps the greatest single force in breaking down the hampering restrictions as well as the protections of caste. But in breaking up the old safeguards there is the danger that the individual may flounder helplessly, like a fish out of water, in the highly rarefied air of an industrial environment. Unless remedial palliatives be applied, the glamor of the new life may so react on the individual that, while striving for tranquillity, affection, and security, he may suffocate and die.

There is no reason to believe that the old regime can be continued in the Orient. Modernization has arrived. Cotton mills, silk filatures, steel works, ship yards, cement plants and many other industrial enterprises indicate that factory life and its problems have already come to Japan. New ideas in industry are being eagerly welcomed in China, where cotton manufacturing is already far advanced in certain areas. In India, coal mining, steel works, cotton manufacturing and jute making, employing over one million operatives, are competing with the old household arts and handicrafts. The rise of literacy, the circulation of newspapers, magazines and books, the transportation of goods and ideas, the possibility of travel and the ever widening knowledge and use of western languages and literature are evidence that it is impossible to turn back the hands of the clock. And most of all, the pressure of poverty continues to force the agricultural worker to seek employment in factory areas. The trend toward industrial development is irresistible.

Efforts are being made in certain mission areas to develop handicrafts in the rural homes and village work shops. In India, a powerful stimulus to such activities has been given by Gandhi in his advocacy of home spinning and weaving of cotton. While home industry in rural China does not produce much in cash earnings its benefits in terms of family well-being are considerable. By the production at home of various articles of clothing—such as cloth, shoes, stockings and grass hats,— the living cost of the family is considerably reduced. Missions and other agencies have encouraged domestic industry, pottery, lace making, drawn work, wool carding, cotton spinning and weaving for the market, and certain forms of metal working. Where such home industries can find a profitable outlet for their product because of quality or excellence of design, this Commission believes they should be encouraged. When, however, home industries strive by hand to compete in the markets with standard factory-made products, they are doomed to fail.

5. Will the Evils of the Western Factory System Be Repeated?

The question now naturally arises, will the problems attendant upon western industrial society be repeated in the Orient? Before attempting to answer this question it will be well to state briefly what changes have been wrought in western society by the development of industry. These changes can be most easily reviewed in England where the first factory developments began. This so-called Industrial Revolution in England brought about great increases in the production of goods and involved new problems of distribution. It developed a new group of wealthy men, whose fortunes were based on the profits arising from industry, and brought great inequalities of wealth between owners and workers. The population increased beyond the capacity of the land to support it. There came also detachment from the soil and crowded and unsanitary living conditions for large numbers of people.

A study of conditions reveals the fact that most if not all the evils attendant upon the development of industry in the West are already developing in the Orient. There is the same problem of over-production and the necessity for finding new markets. There are the same new inequalities of wealth and the shifting of economic control into a few hands; there is also the removal of the individual from his environment with more far-reaching possibilities for difficulty because of the tight bonds which hold the Oriental to his family, village, clan and caste.

This is especially marked in the great industrial cities of India—Bombay, Cawnpore, Ahmedabad, Calcutta and Madras —where there is a constant ebb and flow of population from rural areas to the cities and back again. In China such movements are noticeable in manufacturing districts like Shanghai and Tientsin. In Japan, in addition to what may be called normal migrations from country to city, there is also a special problem connected with the system prevailing for recruiting women workers in cotton factories. Girls from rural communities are brought in large numbers to mill areas for a period of on the average three years. They are lodged in factory compounds and are subject to certain factory discipline and restrictions. Their living conditions are sanitary and probably food and care are better than the average worker gets at home. The dangers come—along with a certain beneficial stimulus—from a too sudden uprooting from the homes and an artificial and restricted life in the city.

It is evident that the development of industrial life in the Orient has brought problems similar in character to those which accompanied such development in the West—intensified in some regions by a hot climate and a social environment burdened by congestion and poverty.

6. *What Has Christianity to Say?*

It is now pertinent to inquire as to what Christianity has to say. Can it bring helpful suggestions from its experience in the West to help ameliorate industrial evils in the Orient? Can missionaries help to introduce scientific methods in improving industries already in existence and bring scientific methods to bear in bettering the living and working conditions of the industrial employee? Can a plan for economic betterment be developed which can be advocated by organized Christianity? Any such plan is extremely difficult to formulate. Christianity, not as an organized body but acting through individual Christians, has profoundly affected social problems in the West. Christians have led in such reforms as the abolition of slavery, the control of the liquor traffic and the sympathetic and humane treatment of prisoners. Christians have been leaders in general education, profit sharing, in fostering high ideals of citizenship and in the freedom and emancipation of women. Christians may be equally influential in the Orient.

The approach of Christianity to any social problem has usually been through the personality of some individual. By the illumination of his soul this individual has lead the way on to social betterment. This makes the development of such individuals Christianity's supreme task. Such a program consistently followed tends to make the Christian group individualistic, democratic, free but collectively ineffective. Its strength lies in its efforts to ameliorate certain specific and usually local evils by such means as schools, hospitals and social settlements. These can be founded and controlled by one personality inspired with a spirit of service. Its weakness lies in the fact that busy with the development of the individual it has not concerned itself with broad programs for human betterment. It has not tried to remove the causes of social conflagrations. It has busied itself with trying to put out local fires after they have started.

It has become increasingly evident, however, in the Orient as well as in the West, that to work exclusively for the regeneration of the individual or merely to ameliorate bad local situations is not enough. Leaders of the Christian Church must also have an intelligent interest in social and economic questions, and sympathetically understand the implications and significance of the new relationships between employer and employee. An attitude of indifference to social problems, although dangerous in an agricultural community, becomes evil and even vicious in an industrial community—an attitude which in the interest of social well-being must be changed. Few missionaries are competent to deal with industrial problems. Many do not know they really exist. Too many still live in a world where creedal statements seem important and affirmations like "The iron did float" or "The sun did stand still" seem significant.

It is disappointing that with great industrial problems in the Orient confronting the missions with their challenge and opportunity, there is hardly a social worker to be found in the whole roster of missionaries trained to deal scientifically and intelligently with human beings trying to adjust themselves to new factory environment.

How can missions then act wisely if the trained and intelligent personnel is not there, for after all a mission is not an entity in itself but only the sum total of the missionaries. Recently a Christian group drew up and published a social creed which illustrates this lack of trained intelligence.

Among other things they asked for the enactment of a law making Sunday a public rest day *with the expectation that wages will be paid.* Does this mean that men be paid for observing Sunday?

Again, they asked for "the promotion of national prohibition." The Church might perhaps advocate temperance or total abstinence, but in view of the differences of opinion regarding the success of prohibition in the West, no group ought hastily to commit the Church to the use of public law to secure the self-control which all Christians desire.

They also asked for "the enactment of a minimum wage, peasants' welfare and social insurance laws, and for legislation and equipment promoting public hygiene," and for "the enactment of a higher progressive tax rate for incomes and in-heritances." These proposals may or may not be sound. But the questions suggested call for research and study before pro-nouncing on any panacea for the evils of maladjustment of wealth. They indicate particularly the difficulty in trying to formulate a social Christian program covering questions where there is such an opportunity for wide divergencies of opinion among equally conscientious people.

Action such as that taken by the group just mentioned does, however, indicate an interest in social questions which is ad-mirable even though it is not well informed. In general there has been too little real knowledge of social and economic questions by the missionaries and the indigenous Christians. This is due in part to the lack of adequate teaching by earlier missionaries who were not only quite ignorant of social pro-grams but who felt that they should stress individual evange-lism above everything else. It is also probably a residuum in the native church from Buddhism, or Hinduism or other reli-gions. These religions have not been in the past concerned with economic or social questions. There is also what may be called "industrial immaturity" in the Orient which makes it oblivious to social needs.

The problems arising out of the development of industry are so new and intricate that there is great difficulty in developing a technique to deal with them. It is discouraging but not sur-prising that missionaries with a few notable exceptions remain startlingly insensitive to the social needs around them.

7. Advantages in Christianity

However, it will not do to dwell too long on the obvious shortcomings of both mission and indigenous church in social matters.

It is well to remember that Christianity has assets of great importance which can be drawn upon in meeting the challenge of the Orient. These assets have a special value in industrial relations.

First and foremost the ideals and ideas of Jesus when presented free from western bias and conventions, make a deep appeal to the oriental mind. The concept that God is a loving father and that all men are brothers grips the imagination even though orientals realize that such concepts are rarely carried out in the lives of western people.

Christianity also brings motivation to ethical conduct. Other great religions teach a noble code of ethics. In a unique degree Christianity provides the dynamic, the will, the urge to achieve a life based on a strict moral and ethical code.

Christianity stresses the supreme value of the individual and teaches, as indeed does Islam and some forms of Buddhism, that the individual may come into immediate and direct contact with the Divine. In Christianity this value of the individual is extended not only to all men but also to all women. Woman, in the Orient, especially if she be a wife and mother is personally influential. Although necessary as a bearer of sons and useful in certain field and household tasks, her status generally has been inferior to that of man. Under Christianity, however, she achieves a new dignity and a new worth not merely for what she may *do*, but also as an individual for what she *is* or may become.

To men and women torn from their natural protective surroundings by the lure of industry, Christianity, by its insistence on the value of personality, bears a message of hope which brings the tranquillity and peace which the lonely soul so sorely needs.

8. *What Should Be Done*

The question now presents itself, how can these and other great and peculiar assets of Christianity be realized? Can the teachings of Jesus be made a practicable rule of life? The same problem exists in the West. The application of his principles through individuals would cure most of the evils of the world both West and East, under any social order which prevailed. Can men in the Orient be made to see that their happiness consists not in the number of things they possess? With the exception of a chosen few, men have not yet learned that lesson in the West. It is not sufficient merely to affirm the Golden Rule. Christ's teachings must be demonstrated in life. They spread more by contagion than by precept. A St. Francis is worth a million men who preach and do not practice.

The trend of modern political policies has been for nations to establish trade barriers such as subsidies, tariffs, spheres of influence, and trading privileges devised under the pressure of political and economic necessity. These have frequently resulted in economic reprisals, boycotts and counter activities which not only disturb the peaceful avenues of trade but also tend to stir up racial and national animosities. Missions have a unique opportunity to develop understanding and serve as interpreters between East and West. To do this requires missionaries of unusual intelligence and comprehension. This Commission has observed a few who can qualify for such exacting work. If missions can continue to recruit men of such intelligence it may well be that in the bewildering complexities of the present, one of the chief functions of missions will be to serve as ambassadors of good will between the West and East.

Missions should recognize and teach that a well ordered community cannot exist when there are too great inequalities of wealth and economic privilege. With extreme poverty comes fear and blighting social conditions which do not permit the individual to develop his own abilities nor achieve tranquillity and peace. Extreme wealth frequently leads to selfish indulgence. Christianity can speak clearly on this point and can wisely attempt to modify any social order which unduly accentuates economic inequality and privilege.

Inequalities are greatly ameliorated when individuals touched by the spirit of Christ feel it their duty and obligation to use their powers not merely for their own advantage but also for the good of others. This should be emphasized as part of the very essence of Christianity. The Christian Church must always stand opposed to selfish indulgence. The economically privileged should feel a corresponding responsibility toward developing the common good. This does not mean to aid the common good merely by charity. The responsibility goes deeper and means that the Christian employer should have it as his first concern not only that he himself should make money and his family live in comfort but also that his employees should receive a fair and adequate wage and should be safeguarded in so far as possible against the hazards of illness and unemployment. The Christian employer should try to see to it that his employees do not require charity from himself or anybody else.

The present economic system has recognized the right of every individual to all of this world's lands and possessions which he could legally acquire and hold. It has laid down rules and regulations as to how the activities of the individual should be conducted and restrained but his right to acquire all he can has never been challenged. It is the privilege and duty of the Christian Church to point out another limitation to men in pursuit of wealth which has not yet become operative in the western world. That is that no man shall seek or use material goods in a way, as has happened in some countries, to nullify the right of every other man to an opportunity to share in the products of nature and the products of social effort. This is particularly important in the Orient where such a protective right has long been recognized in many so-called "primitive social groups."

In addition to the protection in the oriental countries which we are considering, every man has been entitled to a living, the responsibility for which has been the common responsibility of the family, clan or guild. Modern industry, as we have seen, has cut across and weakened these old sanctions and loyalties, but it has not assumed the responsibilities of the old order for the economic sustenance of every member in it. Missions may well stress the principle that Christianity should seek to develop a social program which will provide for every man the chance to secure the income necessary for health and social and ethical development, not as a charity, but as a right.

Another emphasis which could well be made is that all social institutions should be planned to emphasize and strengthen not the differences which divide mankind but the common humanity which unites them. Industrial life tends to develop differences between employer and employee, the leaders and the led, the capitalist and the wage-worker. The Christian Church may by its common worship and common aspiration develop a spirit of harmony and unity much needed in industrial relations.

Christian schools, colleges, and high schools—especially schools for dealing with industrial and social subjects—should give deep attention to exhibiting to their pupils by precept and example, the real significance of the social problems of the day. The distressing fact is that schools—Christian, government, private—do not study actual conditions enough. It is not an exaggeration to say that none of them as yet deal adequately with social questions. Neither mission nor non-mission schools are doing their duty in this matter. They do not work enough from facts and as a result their teachings are far too theoretical to be of great value. Settlement houses at a high state of efficiency should be continued not merely for the immediate good of ameliorating suffering but as experiment stations for use in pointing out to humanity ways toward a better social life.

There must be constant study and effort toward improvement in the operation of these agencies. It is regrettably true that schools and settlement houses, under Christian auspices, with a few conspicuous exceptions, do not as yet meet the social needs of industrial life.

9. *Recommendations*

1. *Research.* In addition to such immediate methods for dealing with social problems in schools and settlement houses, missions should cooperate with universities and educational associations and with nationals, both Christian and non-Christian, adequately to formulate more far-reaching programs. In neither India, China nor Japan have missions studied carefully the problems of industry. It is true, however, that some significant beginnings have been made. At Lingnan University certain departments are applying scientific methods to problems such as sericulture and pottery. A missionary in China

has been working for several years on the use of modern methods in the manufacture of woolens. In the department of Industrial Chemistry at Forman Christian College at Lahore, India, scientific aid is being given to industries such as soap making, sugar refining, porcelain manufacturing and brickmaking.

However, it can still be truthfully said that nowhere in these countries have missions made any notable or significant contribution to the solution of social or economic problems nor presented a program for their amelioration except in local situations. Such a program may involve a number of social groups and may call for action over wide areas. To do this effectively, different boards and missions must work together. One form of cooperative effort which seems absolutely essential is the establishment of a new school or schools for social and economic research, or in strengthening and utilizing any existing school. Trained research investigators must be recruited. Christians should adopt the scientific attitude toward the facts of social development. It is necessary if ill-considered action is to be avoided to have data accurate enough and recent enough to serve as a basis for any plans which may be made. There is particular need for such schools in both India and China, and it is of vital importance—superfluous as this suggestion may appear—that boards and missions pay much more attention than they do to research studies in formulating their social programs.

Such a school should eventually have an extensive program extending into many areas of social exploration. Among other things the following are essential:

(a) Studies of social problems at close range and accurate statements of what they are;

(b) Tests of the practicability of various measures of relief before such measures are adopted;

(c) Close touch and cooperation with government and other social welfare agencies, not only locally but all over the world;

(d) Bulletins and exchange of information on valuable

solutions of social problems and also of failures with reasons why;

(e) Publishing economic and social data on such subjects as family income, indebtedness, rates of interest, labor unions, etc.

The Commission recommends the establishment or strengthening of such school or schools.

2. *School for social workers.* To do careful research work is one thing, to carry out programs of social rebuilding is quite another. For the latter trained social workers are needed of a type hardly known as yet in the Orient. To provide training in the Christian approach to such problems, existing schools should be strengthened and new schools should be established where necessary. The need for such trained social workers becomes increasingly evident as social problems grow more acute and baffling.

If missions can have the assistance of a school of research and the advice and counsel of trained and devoted social workers, they can then begin to define their attitudes with intelligence and in detail on social questions on which their position is now confused and halting. It may be that opinions and attitudes will change from time to time. Different mission groups may attempt different solutions working from the same data, but their action, such as it is, will be more intelligent than it can possibly be under the present system—or rather lack of system.

This Commission recommends that such schools be strengthened or new ones established where necessary.

3. *Relations with business men.* The Commission has observed with deep regret that there seems to be a great gulf fixed between most European and American business men and the missionaries, especially in the largest cities. Whatever may be the reasons, this is unfortunate for both. It would be a splendid thing for business men could they come to know better the missionaries and their families and learn accurately about their problems and their aims. It would also be a splendid thing for the missionaries if they could recruit business

men not only as friends but also as trustees associated in the control of hospitals and schools. The Commission saw many business men of high character in the Orient. It would be most helpful not only to the cause of religion but to good relations generally with oriental people, if more American business firms would take pains to send out as their representatives only men of the highest type.

4. *Relation with labor unions.* There are now great social movements stirring in all these Asiatic lands. One is the development of labor unions. This is a movement inside the capitalistic system. Labor unions generally represent the saner and more conservative groups in labor circles. While the strike is a weapon they use, they are opposed generally to revolution and the more violent methods of adjusting inequalities in the social and economic order. In earlier days missions were more closely related to labor than they are today. The first labor union in Japan was organized in a Christian church. But now there is a real danger that missions and the indigenous churches which have been nurtured by them will remain out of touch with labor unions and their aspirations. Labor union leaders of the present generally do not work with missions nor indigenous churches. They do not find the people interested in their problems or in sympathy with their aims. Without in any way committing the mission or church to a labor program, we believe that more intelligent effort should be directed toward understanding the questions at issue in labor organizations.

This Commission recommends that missionaries make the acquaintance of labor union leaders, endeavor sympathetically to understand their aims and ideals, and to merit their confidence, and in general cultivate cordial relations with them.

5. *Attitude toward capitalism, socialism and communism.* While it is true that missions have been made possible by donations from countries operating under the capitalistic system, there is no reason why for the Orient at least capitalism as a social order should not be objectively appraised. Missions

should not lay themselves open to the criticism that they are acquiescent to the evils of the present capitalistic regime. If they believe in capitalism as on the whole the best social order for the production of wealth and the development of individual initiative, as doubtless most of them do, they should be particularly fearless in attacking the evils of capitalism and in endeavoring to correct them—especially those evils which have to do with the economic exploitation of human beings, a preventable evil which so frequently attends the production of wealth in capitalistic countries.

Toward socialism the attitude of missions has never been defined, nor in fact has the attitude of organized Christianity in the West. It ought not to be. But at least socialism should be better understood, especially with relation to previous social organizations in the Orient, as in many of its motives it is essentially Christian. It should be appreciated as an effort to devise a plan to cure some of the most glaring evils of the modern industrial order. The issue between individualism and socialism turns on the type of structure under which society will operate. The tendency of the times seems to be away from uncontrolled individualism to combinations. If combinations are great enough, operate on large enough areas of human activity, and are controlled by the state for the common good, they are then a part of a socialistic system.

Communism has usually been considered by missions and the Christian churches in China, India and Japan as something sinister to be fought by every means available. This feeling in large part grows out of attacks by certain kinds of communists on Christians and on religious faith. The Christian often fails to distinguish communism as a social order from the acts of violence which have so frequently characterized the attempts of its followers to overturn other systems. Communism also must not be confused with banditry. Careful discrimination should be made between different types of communism, from the Russian type with its violence and anti-religious antagonism on the one hand to those milder forms which are little more than a pooling of economic resources for protection and support on the other. There should be a careful study made of communism, and its strong and weak features should be carefully appraised. Its history, like that of socialism, should be studied. A world organization of missions with its sympathies and contacts extending to many lands should not in the view of this Commission be the advocate of any particular economic order. Missions should consider it their duty and privilege to be informed about all economic orders.

This Commission recommends that missions should maintain in so far as possible friendly relations with leaders of every variety of economic thought—capitalist, socialist and communist. They should maintain an open mind in approaching the problems of each and in their attitude toward the claims of all three. Individual Christians and individual missionaries should be allowed the greatest freedom within the church in their personal views, if such views represent a sincere effort to come at the truth.

10. *Conclusion*

In dealing with the problems which have to do with industry, the Christian Church as an organization must deal with general principles and not with particular solutions and should harbor within its capacious and sympathetic borders persons of widely divergent views on social problems and their relief. Missions and organized Christianity should consider it their duty to stimulate thought, never to suppress it. If one man by the honest study of Christ's teaching becomes a communist, another a labor union leader, another a socialist and another a capitalist, none should find himself excluded from fellowship or prevented from trying to win other Christians to his point of view. The church should not by ecclesiastical or majority action try in any way to coerce him or to force him from its membership.

This study may end as it began with the reminder that the primary function of the Christian Church is to cherish that timid staring creature, man, and to assist him in every way to realize his longings for peace, tranquillity, beauty and affection.

CHAPTER XII

WOMEN'S INTERESTS AND ACTIVITIES

The changing status of women in the Orient. The East to-day represents a radically different environment for women, from that which the pioneer women missionaries, or those of even a later period, found when they came to the Orient. An Indian Mohammedan woman a delegate to the Round Table Conference in London in 1930 and 1931; Chinese women delegates in the National People's Assembly in Nanking in May, 1931; a team of Japanese women athletes competing in the Olympic Games in Los Angeles in August, 1932, are all high lights of the change which is sweeping over the eastern world, vitally affecting the position of women.

In India, where vibrant nationalism has been a powerful ally, the emergence of women has become perhaps the most significant fact of the present day. Political equality, demands for equal educational opportunity, social legislation against child marriage, protests against purdah (literally a curtain symbolizing the veiling and seclusion of women), the active participation of women leaders in the national struggle, and the mobilization of a self-conscious, intensely alive group of women leaders in national movements like the All-India Woman's Conference, are indications of the dawning of a new day for Indian womanhood.

In Burma there is no such distinctive transformation. Free from the deep shadows of child marriage and purdah, and on an already accepted basis of social and economic equality with men, the life of Burmese women presents naturally no black and white contrasts of change such as one finds in India, but only a slow, steady growth of enlightenment through education. Burmese women leaders are becoming increasingly conscious of their opportunities and responsibilities in national life.

The forward movement of Chinese women is less spectacular than that in India but no less significant. The dissolution of the old family system which is the result of many forces, is liberating the women of China from the traditions of family dependence into the expanding freedom of an individual life. New concepts of betrothal, marriage and the home, more freedom of social relationships, a growing urge for economic independence, the active participating of women in national affairs are mile-stones of progress in the life of women in China.

The changing situation in Japan has produced a paradoxical combination of remarkable progress and retarded development of Japanese women. In economic pursuits participating more fully than any other women of the East; in educational advance, judged on the basis of literacy, equal to the women of any western country; in the widespread process of westernization sharing freely, as is shown in the increase in western styles of dress and modes of living—in all these phases of life, Japanese women have stepped out of the eastern frame. But in the lack of legal privileges—divorce, inheritance and property rights—and of political equality, Japanese women are, as one of their prominent leaders expressed it, "still in the feudal period of Japan." Full equality for women in Japan cannot be secured without the organized effort of Japanese women themselves. A mass meeting for women's suffrage held recently in Tokyo attended by representatives of all the women's organizations, women leaders of all types of society and of different religions, demonstrates that Japanese women are beginning to recognize the power of collective action. Women's suffrage obviously cannot be achieved without the sympathy and cooperation of men since they control the decision. Although there is little evidence of any general masculine dissatisfaction with the status quo, a few leaders have included women's suffrage in their political platforms.

The current of change moving through India and Burma, China and Japan has as yet had very little effect on the great

masses, the inarticulate, illiterate millions of women in rural
Asia. But there are signs that the process of change has begun.
However slowly the tide may be moving, even remote areas are
being reached by new currents of thought. Urban and rural
life are gradually being drawn together. What is happening
today in the cities will eventually find its repercussion in the
life of their villages. It is a hopeful sign for the future that the
needs of rural Asia are entering the consciousness of men
prominent in public life as well as the small but powerful
minority of women leaders who constitute a very potent factor
promoting the advance of women in rural life.

Perhaps the most convincing evidence of the emergence of
women throughout the Orient is the All-Asia Women's Conference, assembled at the call of India in Lahore in 1931. Illus-
trating the awakening of oriental women to the realization of
their power and opportunity, this was the first expression of
an inter-Asian consciousness among them, bridging the differences of race, nationality and religion, drawing them together
in the common quest of progress.

Task of readjustment for Christian missions. In this forward movement of eastern women, Christian missions have
played a significant role, a fact admitted without reserve by
leaders of the Orient like Dr. Muthulakshmi Reddi, who repeatedly voices the feeling that "the women of Asia have been
placed under a deep debt of gratitude to the missionary
agencies for their valuable contribution to the educational
uplift of Indian women."* The pioneering effort of missions
in work for women has led the way for later developments
under government and private enterprise in educational advance, health service, social and religious reform. Through a
composite of direct and indirect influences Christian missions
have steadily exerted pressure against the stifling tradition of
the past and have opened the doors of opportunity to women
for the future.

Today the new situation, which in no small measure may be

* Dr. (Mrs.) S. Muthulakshmi Reddi's Presidential Address, All-India
Women's Conference, Lahore, January 1931.

considered an achievement of Christian missions, constitutes one of the most serious problems of the missionary enterprise as related to women. The very fact that women in the East are beginning to live on a different educational and social level, creates new needs and makes new demands on missions far more exacting than those that were made in earlier days. The changed and steadily changing East necessitates readjustments. The ability of missions to make these necessary changes will in large measure determine their future effectiveness.

Concretely, what are the readjustments needed in the various fields of mission effort for women in Asia? Although these countries differ widely in their environmental factors, there is a remarkable degree of uniformity in the fundamental principles of missionary policy, and in the lines of change needed in order that the mission program for women may gear into the new situation in the East.

Education

Throughout all Asia the pioneering period of far flung extension of mission girls' schools has passed. From Colombo to Kashmir, from Rangoon to Mandalay, from Canton to Peiping, from Nagasaki to Sapporo, mission schools for girls have established in the eastern consciousness the value of girls' education. So well has that task been accomplished that now those mission schools are no longer the only educational institutions, as the facilities for education for girls under government and private agencies are widely spread throughout the Orient.*

* The proportion of mission education for girls to the total education for girls in India is shown by the following table:

	Per cent mission schools to total schools for girls	Per cent enrollment in mission schools to total enrollment of girls
Primary	4%	8%
Middle	33	31
High	45	44
Colleges	50	56
Teachers' Training	48	53

(Data from R. Littlehailes' "Progress of Education in India," Vol II)

In China and India, in view of the disparity of educational opportunity for girls and boys, there is little question of the continued need for mission girls' schools and colleges.* In Burma the situation is no less urgent as mission schools are carrying the major burden of secondary education. Judged in terms of literacy, these three countries make a strong appeal for Christian education, since the literacy of women in India is only two per cent; in China it is probably no higher, and in Burma nine and seven-tenths per cent. To deal with the whole problem of literacy, however, is far beyond the power of missions to solve; it is essentially the function of government. Japan, with universal elementary education, and a rapidly spreading system of high schools for girls, and furthermore a literacy of over ninety per cent for women as well as men, raises a serious question as to the educational necessity for Christian schools.**

In all these countries under review, the growth in the number of schools and the improvement of standards demands that Christian education emphasize quality not quantity in the future.*** A policy of concentration is imperative in order that

* In the 700,000 villages of India, there is only one girls' school in every nineteen towns or villages, compared with one boys' school in every three towns. 10% of the girls, 49% of the boys, have school facilities, or one village girl to every 600; one boy in every 100. In Burma there is much less disparity between the education of boys and girls. 2.6% of total female population compared with 4.1% total male population are under instruction.
(Hartog Report. Also, R. Littlehailes' "Progress of Education in India." Vol. I, p. 156)

** In 1928 the percentage of children of school age attending schools in Japan was 99.49% for boys and 99.43% for girls. By "the children attending school" is meant those who were of school age and were attending ordinary elementary schools, and also those who had completed the course of such schools but were still under fourteen years of age.
(General Survey of Education in Japan, p. 12)

*** The growth in girls' schools and in the enrollment, in British India, between 1922-1927, is shown by the following chart:

	Schools	Enrollment
Primary	17%	25%
Middle	15	35
High	16	39
College	35	101
Teacher Training	99	12

Christian schools may continue to render valuable service. Furthermore, they must have some distinctive character and not be merely additional schools duplicating government institutions. In the beginning they set the pace for government education; today, through conforming to government regulations many mission schools in the Orient are in danger of being bound in a strait jacket of conventional method and stereotyped curriculum, which tends to destroy creative originality and educational effectiveness. There are, however, outstanding examples of Christian institutions for girls which although following the regimented system, have maintained their distinctive quality. These exceptions show what may be accomplished if teachers are capable of adapting the system to serve the highest needs of education.

Mission schools for girls, to be justified in the future, must contribute more vitality to the preparation of the eastern girl for her life situation. The Indian bride, a high school graduate, who deplored her lack of knowledge of home and child care is only one of hundreds of girls today leaving mission high schools throughout the East with very little preparation for their future careers of home making. Mission education has given too little attention to the seventy-five per cent who will shape the home life of the future, and has focussed on the needs of the small minority who are preparing for college.

In emphasizing the necessity for a wider range of secondary education, the need for higher education is not forgotten. Mis-

---

(Hartog Report—Auxiliary Com. of Indian Statutory Commission, Chapter VII)

The contribution of mission education for girls in Burma is shown by the following facts: 4 out of 10 middle schools; 20 out of 23 high schools; and 1/6 of the teacher training schools are mission institutions. 9 out of 10 girls in high school are in mission high schools. (R. Littlehailes' "Progress of Education in India," 1922-27, Vol. II). Total enrolment of women students in mission colleges in China has steadily increased from 115 in 1920, to 867 in 1931. The enrolment of women in mission colleges is approximately 5% of the total enrolment.

In 1895 Christian high schools in Japan represented approximately 70% of the total; in 1930 the Christian high schools (38) represented less than 5% of the total government schools (731). The number enrolled in 38 Christian high schools in 1930 was 18,157, with 3,154 graduates. (Christian Education in Japan, pp. 85, 86)

sion effort must continue to promote higher education for women which is still a distinctive field for mission endeavor in the East.* This is peculiarly true of Japan, even though the average educational level is very high, since the government has not as yet fully recognized the necessity of senior colleges for women and has only sparingly admitted women to university privileges.

Mission higher education for women offers significant illustrations of the benefit of building mission-effort on a broad non-denominational base. The insecure financial condition of the union institutions, however, is an evidence of the failure of mission boards to take the cooperative efforts with sufficient seriousness. Unfortunately, when financial retrenchment is necessary the union enterprise is usually the first to be sacrificed. The hope of the future lies in concentration of mission effort in union institutions. But their existence must be financially secured. These women's colleges, training the future women leaders of the East, Christian and non-Christian, merit continued mission support. In Japan this support, although an urgent immediate necessity, should be planned on a decreasing scale since a supporting constituency can be developed more rapidly there than in China or India.

The paucity of women teachers is one of the basic educational problems in the Orient.** In India the training of vernacular teachers is essential for the promotion of village edu-

* Christian colleges for women in the Orient include: in India, Isabella Thoburn, Lucknow; Kinnaird College, Lahore (union); St. Christopher's Training College, Madras (union); Women's Christian College, Madras (union); in China, Ginling College, Nanking; Hwa Nan College, Foochow; and ten coeducational colleges; in Japan, Kobe Women's College, Kobe; Women's Christian College, Tokyo; and twenty-three junior colleges (the two senior colleges having junior colleges are included in this number).

** The paucity of women teachers is illustrated by the fact that there is only one teacher for every 100 girls (under instruction) in India, and only 100 women inspectors for 28,000 schools covering over a million square miles, an average of 280 institutions and 10,000 square miles for each inspectress. In contrast to India, the profession of teaching in Burma is overstocked, there having been 1,900 teachers unemployed in 1930. In China it is estimated that it would require 1,200,000 primary teachers to give primary education to the 37,000,000 children of school age. (Fact-finders' Report on China in loco)

cation. Isabella Thoburn College in Lucknow and St. Christopher's Training College in Madras are rendering valuable service in training women teachers of the higher grade. The latter, a union enterprise, should be better supported by the cooperating boards. In Burma the government has taken over Anglo-vernacular teacher training and will later doubtless assume vernacular training also.

The situation in China is complicated by the government attitude that the training of teachers is in general not the function of private institutions. Missions can only develop training centers if in harmony with the Government. A solution seems to be the development of training departments in existing schools; as, for example, in Hwa Nan College in Foochow and Bridgman School in Shanghai. The Union Normal School in Canton, if the government relationship is satisfactorily adjusted, has an opportunity for real service. It should, however, receive more adequate support or be closed, as it is at present on an unsatisfactory basis.

In Japan the Government has assumed full responsibility for training teachers for regular elementary and secondary education; the missions have no opportunity in this field. They are, however, rendering service in training teachers in special fields —such as English, music, and domestic science. The vocational needs in these lines should be carefully studied so that Christian schools may not train more teachers than can receive employment.

One of the most serious problems in mission schools and colleges for girls is the danger of westernization, which has doubtless been a natural development, since mission education has been established and promoted under western leadership. This tendency merits careful consideration. It is evident in standards of living, in dress, in types of amusement, in foreign forms of worship and in foreign music and art. Following western patterns of thought too exclusively, many institutions fail to appreciate oriental values. This westernizing influence can only be counteracted by a conscious attempt to emphasize the customs and culture of the East. The increase of Indian leaders in positions of larger responsibility should help to solve this problem.

Allied with this danger of westernization is the tendency of Christian schools to segregate girls from normal community life, protecting them like hot-house plants in the "purdah" atmosphere of a boarding school. Large mission compounds are a world removed from real life. To a certain degree segregation is inevitable; safety from social and moral dangers in the environment must be assured. For this reason Christian parents, especially in India, are glad to leave their children at school even during vacations. Non-Christian parents have not as a rule favored long periods of boarding school life.

The extra-curricular program offers aid in solving the problem of segregation of mission schools and colleges through field surveys of social problems and special welfare projects carried on by students. Some of the women's colleges which are fortunate in being located near men's colleges, are attempting to widen the interest of their students through joint debates and social and religious activities.

The tendency toward segregation affects India and Burma especially, and China less, but in Japan the thousands of school girls daily commuting into Tokyo, rubbing elbows with the world, vividly demonstrate the passing of the boarding school danger of segregation.

In emphasizing this tendency in Christian boarding schools for girls, the very great value of the boarding school, in developing Christian character, is by no means underestimated. It has offered the most constructive field for Christian influence in the Orient. It is therefore to be regretted that the decline of the need for girls' boarding schools in Japan practically marks the end of the special opportunity for such Christian service as only boarding schools, because of their intensive character training, are successfully attempting to render.

It is strange that religious education, which is one of the essential reasons for Christian schools, should not have been

regarded as a field needing teachers of more specialized training. Requirements in this field have been much less definite
than in the regular academic subjects. There are very few
teachers who have had any training in religious education.
Furthermore, in the great majority of girls' schools and colleges, religious education is interpreted only through conventional media of Bible teaching and formal religious services,
bearing little relationship to the students' environment, and
showing little awareness of the correlation of Christian teaching with major social problems and with the development of
a fuller life. There are a few outstanding exceptions, schools
with a vital creative religious education program related to
the life situation of the student. But the general lack of a
constructive religious and social emphasis in Christian schools
in an era of marked social change is nothing short of tragic.

Opinion in the West may differ as to the values in co-education but this is a subject which merits the consideration of
Christian educators in the Orient. In India, government education officials regard co-education, especially in elementary
schools, as an ultimate necessity in the solution of the disparity in education of girls and boys, and would welcome the
promotion of co-education in Christian schools, because the
Christian school is eminently fitted to emphasize moral training and character education. Co-education is in harmony with
the present temper of modern China. It has been endorsed by
the national Government as a definite policy for colleges, but
has not been introduced in secondary schools. Christian colleges such as Lingnan and Yenching, are attempting to contribute constructively to the development of the social values
in co-education, fully recognizing, however, the difficulties in
the situation.

Japan has built elementary education on the basis of co-
education, but has not endorsed it for the secondary stage, and
has admitted women to only a few of the universities. Aside
from Doshisha University in Kyoto, and Aoyama Gakuin
Theological Training School in Tokyo, Christian education

has made little contribution in Japan to the problem of co-education.

Viewing the situation as a whole, Christian education for girls throughout the Orient compares very favorably with Christian education for boys. Especially is this true in the type of faculty and students and in the Christian atmosphere and influence.* Furthermore, in comparison with government schools for girls, the Christian schools for girls hold a favorable position; whereas mission institutions for boys are often inferior to the government institutions. It is, however, only a question of time before Christian education for girls will find itself in the same critical competition which now confronts Christian education for boys. It is therefore imperative that the present situation of each Christian institution for girls be studied in order that the standards may be raised.

One can write with enthusiasm of the contribution which Christian education for women has made in the Orient. Many of the women leaders of the four countries under review have been educated in Christian schools. The permanent values of Christian education for girls, however, can be measured only in terms of a distinctive service for the future—a test far more exacting now than in the pioneering period. To meet this test, Christian education should rise above the dull mediocrity of an uninspired highly regimented system; it should be centered in the actual life interests of the student; it should give scope for creative self-expression in the spirit of service; and should aid in the development of Christian character. Only if it can meet this increasingly difficult standard will Christian education for girls render a distinctive service in the future.

* The proportion of Christian and non-Christian teachers and students in boys' mission schools and girls', is significant; In India, results of a questionnaire study of 71 middle, high and training schools show:

Boys' schools—34% of students Christian, 62% of teachers Christian
Girls'   "   69% "   "   "   87% "   "   "
In Japan:
Boys' Jr. College 27%   "   "   71% "   "   "
Girls' "   "   65%   "   "   81% "   "   "

In China: proportion of Christians in girls' schools (teachers and students) is higher than in boys' schools. It averages well over 50%.

Health

A chain of mission hospitals throughout the length and breadth of India and China illustrates the extent of mission medical service for women in these two countries.*

In Burma four mission hospitals, one distinctly for women, and in Japan two—one woman's hospital and one general mission hospital—constitute the mission medical service in these two countries. There is no way of evaluating in terms of human lives the ministry of healing of the mission doctors and surgeons to the millions of women who have passed through these medical institutions, or of estimating their effect in breaking down superstition and conservatism.

There are certain differentiating features in the mission medical service for women in these countries under review. In India social and religious customs, especially purdah, have caused the development of the separate medical service for women and offered women missionary doctors a remarkably rich field for service.** Although the purdah is slowly lifting, the woman's hospital will long continue to meet a distinctive need for Indian women. Restrictive social and moral customs have also limited the development of nurses' training and the nursing service to the care of women patients.*** However, changes in social standards are now making it possible under careful guidance for some government and a few courageous

* The extent of mission medical service for women, in India, is shown by the fact that out of approximately 400 women doctors in hospitals, 150 are women missionaries (Simon Commission Report, Vol. I, par. 69); out of 183 zenana hospitals in 1927, 93 were mission hospitals (Dr. Margaret I. Balfour and Dr. Ruth Young, "The Work of Medical Women in India," p. 82).

** The proportion of 98 hospitals for women, 78 for men and 17 unclassified, shows the importance of the mission medical service for women, in India. In 1930 foreign workers in the mission personnel include 210 women and 133 men doctors. (Christian Medical Association, Prayer Cycle, August 1930)

*** According to a recent Directory of Hospitals, there are 1,070 Indian women nurses out of a total of 1,455 in hospital service in India. Handbook of Trained Nurses' Assn. of India, edited by Mrs. E. A. Watts, S.R.N., published by Trained Nurses' Assn. of India 1931, pp. 84-105.

mission hospitals to introduce general nursing. In the interests of professional efficiency and the development of wholesome moral standards this plan must be more widely adopted by mission hospitals.

Burma offers no special problems in the medical service for women since there are no social handicaps. Women's hospitals, although greatly appreciated, are not a necessity since women can go to general hospitals and receive medical care from men doctors. Nursing is on the normal basis of women nursing both men and women patients.*

In China the mission medical service has made a very great contribution, larger relatively than in any other country. The medical service in China has not been limited by restrictive social customs, characteristic of India. Hence the woman's hospital is not a necessity and the trend toward union of women's hospitals with general hospitals is logical. Since the nationalist movement in 1927 there has been a trend toward a general nursing service. Limiting the nurse to women patients is inefficient and unnecessary in modern China.

In Japan the training of nurses in the St. Luke's International Medical Center and in St. Barnabas Hospital at Osaka, has followed American lines, which are distinctly different from the prevailing Japanese nursing standards. The training of public health nurses at St. Luke's Hospital is a unique service, recognized with appreciation by the government.

To these mission hospitals for women in Asia may be credited the development of the nursing profession there. Christian nurses, most of whom were trained in mission hospitals, still constitute from eighty-five to ninety per cent of all the nurses in India. In China nine-tenths of the nurses are Christian, practically all of whom are products of missionary training.** In these mission institutions nursing has been lifted from the level of menial service, with the implication of low moral

* Ellen Mitchell Memorial Hospital in Moulmein has nurses in training from twenty different centers in Burma.

** The need for nurses' training in China is illustrated by the fact that there are only about 2,000 trained nurses in China, or one for every 200,000 people. The United States has one nurse for every 4,000. In 1931 there were 256 nurses in mission hospitals and 82 women physicians.

character, to the dignity of a profession with definite standards of technical effectiveness and high moral character.

Mission medical schools in China and India have laid the foundation for medical education for women.* In India the need for the future is a higher type of training of college grade, as Christian medical education at the present time limits women to the lower standards of training. In China medical training would be developed more effectively if the separate training facilities for men and women were combined. Medical training for women is of great importance in the East because of the need and opportunity for women doctors. Perhaps in no country have they been needed more than in India, as has already been mentioned, because of the prevalence of purdah. In China the women doctors do not have, as in India, the monopoly of medical service for women, but share equally with men doctors the medical field. The equality of professional opportunity for Chinese women doctors with men in the profession is significant of modern China. In this respect women doctors in America have a less favorable position.

The day of expansion of mission hospitals and training centers in the East is past. The situation requires today a concentration in the interests of quality and a shift of emphasis to preventive medicine and health education. Hundreds of women and children daily appearing in the mission hospital clinic perhaps make a far greater human appeal and afford

* Medical education for women in India includes: 4 women's medical schools (2 government, 2 mission—Ludhiana and Vellore), 1 college, government medical for women (The Lady Hardinge at Delhi), and 13 coeducational medical schools and colleges.

The number of Indian women doctors and nurses studying in mission schools is steadily increasing. Out of the total number of women medical students in medical schools in 1928-29, 43% were in mission institutions (179 in mission schools and 234 in non-mission schools). No later figures were available. (Report of Countess of Dufferin's Fund, 1929-30.)

Women medical students constitute about 8% of the total number of medical students (683 women and 8,937 men students) in India. (Fact-finders' volume on India and Burma in loco)

China has 6 mission medical colleges: 4 co-educational and 2 women's colleges—Hackett Medical College, Canton; and Women's Christian Medical College, Shanghai.

Japan has no mission medical colleges.

more impressive statistics of hospital service than preventive medical work could make. But the emphasis on preventive medicine in building better health conditions will produce more permanent results than the purely remedial service can hope to accomplish. Since the mission schools offer the field for most effective health teaching, a closer coordination between mission hospitals and schools should be effected.

Social and Industrial

A vital emphasis on the social gospel has not characterized the work of Christian missions in the East. The social emphasis in the mission program has been conspicuously absent aside from a few well directed social centers, such as the Naigaum Social Center (Y.W.C.A.), and Nagpada Neighborhood House (American Board) in Bombay, the Social Center in Vellore (Reformed Church of America), the Ai Sei Kan Settlement House and Ai Kei Gakuin Social Settlement in Tokyo (Methodist), the Zenrinkan Social Settlement in Osaka (American Board), and the two institutional church centers, the Moore Memorial Methodist Church in Shanghai and the Baptist Tabernacle in Tokyo. Few missions have allocated special funds for social service programs. Mission boards have appointed few professionally trained women social workers; in the four countries under review there are perhaps not more than a dozen women missionaries with special training for social work, definitely recruited by the boards for social service. Moreover, Christian agencies have also had very little contact with industrial problems affecting women and children and have exerted little influence in educating public opinion. The keen interest of the Young Women's Christian Association in social and industrial conditions throughout the Orient is a noteworthy exception.

Although there is an unfolding opportunity for women workers trained in social and industrial welfare, there are as yet very limited facilities for training in social work offered either by private or by government agencies. The Social Service Training Center for Women (a union enterprise) in

Bombay, and the Social Training Course in Yenching University, Peiping, however, should be mentioned. The provision of such training is a service which demands the attention of the Christian forces. More emphasis on the social sciences combined with practical field experience in social work should be developed in the Christian colleges of the Orient, which serve as the main source of supply for women leaders of the future. Mention should be made in this connection of the splendid training and field experience in hospital social service offered at St. Luke's International Medical Center in Tokyo, and at the Peiping Union Medical Center in Peiping.

The need for an active promotion of the social ideals of Christianity is obvious in the present period of transition. The Christian forces can no longer follow a policy of isolation. The lack of a social gospel has tended to alienate from Christian influence some of the keenest students of the Christian colleges. The divided, uncertain, often timorous presentation of Christian social principles fails to inspire young men and women who are attracted by courageous social programs. It is often feared that the emphasis on the Christian social message might mean a loss in the personal religious appeal. On the contrary a strong social motivation should strengthen and vitalize the religious expression of the individual.

The present period of transition throughout the East with its increase in freedom and breaking down of old traditional moral controls—changes which are especially apparent in the large cities—presents a problem to which Christian leaders should give serious consideration. Under the pressure of many varied influences youth needs guidance in the careful selection of new standards of action. For the great majority the home offers no assistance in the adjustment to modern conditions, as parents and children today in the Orient belong to different social systems and speak a different language. The cleavage between the younger and older generation in the Orient is not merely the difference in ideals of youth and age, but the distance between the social conditions of the East and West.

There is a widespread craving among youth in the East for social relationships. Commercial interests capitalizing on this desire have multiplied amusement facilities of the western type in the large cities of the Orient. Christian agencies, however, have been slow to respond to the social needs of youth and have given very little constructive aid to the problem of social relationships. These should be afforded through mixed activities in church life and through community centers, which offer a program along social, recreational and educational lines. The efforts of the Young Men's Christian Association and Young Women's Christian Association in this field should be especially commended.

The mere provision, however, of social facilities for modern youth will not build new standards nor develop moral stamina to meet the pressure of a changing age. Christian leaders through their personal influence should seek to awaken in youth a deeper sense of personal responsibility and moral control. They must help young people to realize the spiritual values of life and the need for personal religion as a source of power.

Religious Program

The program of direct religious work among women has always absorbed a large proportion of missionary personnel on the field and has constituted a major appeal in women's societies in America. India furnished a striking illustration in 1930 with 1,030 women missionaries listed as evangelists out of a total of 1,730 women workers.* It should be remembered, however, that the term evangelist does not mean necessarily full-time workers, and probably includes many missionaries' wives. These foreign workers are far outnumbered by the large number of Bible women (the term commonly used for the indigenous women evangelists) who since the beginning of missionary effort have played an important part in the evangelistic program for women.

Whatever may have been the value of their earlier contribution, the urgent need for improvement in the work of Bible women is everywhere apparent. In India their number is im-

* Fact-finders' Report for India *in loco*.

pressive, a total of over five thousand, but their work is distinctly depressing as one views the whole field. The present prevailing type of elderly untrained, often uneducated woman carrying on a stereotyped program of routine visits in zenanas, reciting Bible stories and singing hymns, is not justified for the future. There are a few splendid Bible women, notably two in the Methodist Mission in Lucknow, an outstanding woman religious worker in the United Presbyterian Mission in the Punjab, and several in the Church of Scotland Mission in Calcutta and Madras. However, these few really effective Bible women in India made the ineffectiveness of the prevailing type even more conspicuous. Many missionaries counsel discontinuance of Bible women altogether unless a radical improvement is possible.

The training schools in India have been seriously handicapped by the intellectual caliber of the students.* The training, furthermore, has been inadequate, too narrowly centered on evangelism without a social message or an emphasis on the vital issues of modern life. The situation however is not hopeless, as the problem is recognized at least by a few, and efforts are being made to recruit younger, better qualified students to enter evangelistic work. There is also an attempt to develop more diversified training. In order to attract young people of ability to enter religious work, it is imperative that the service be presented on a higher plane and given more professional recognition.

In Burma, younger, better educated Bible women, free from social and religious customs which would prevent independent village work, present an entirely different situation from that of India. The great weakness in Burma, however, as elsewhere, is the narrow type of training and the limited interpretation of the work.

The field of religious work for women in China illustrates opposing trends of conservatism and change, but on the whole

---

* In India there are four regular Bible training schools and a number of short term courses and institutes, also special courses of a simple nature in several theological schools for the wives of the theological students. (Fact-finders' Report)

the situation is distinctly better than in India. The untrained, meagerly prepared, narrowly evangelistic, older Bible woman still predominates but is slowly being replaced by a better qualified religious worker for a more general type of work. The conventional program of the old fashioned Bible woman will eventually be carried on by lay women on a volunteer basis. As women church members grow in responsibility, there will be less need for the paid Bible women on full time service. Toward this end notable progress is being made in some missions, especially in China, in the recruiting and training of lay workers. Another encouraging sign of progress is the fact that religious education as a specialized field is receiving emphasis and attracting educated young women as a career.*

"The Christianizing the Home Movement" promoted under the National Christian Council by a young Chinese woman leader in cooperation with a missionary colleague, also shows distinct advance in the field of religious work for women in China. The concentration of attention of several women missionaries, specialists in religious education, on the preparation of materials adapted to Chinese environment also merits attention as a special type of missionary contribution which should be further promoted. The Religious Education Conference near Peiping in April 1932, attended by men and women leaders from all over China, demonstrated the growing interest in this field.

In Japan the work of Bible women is of a distinctly different type from elsewhere in the East, due to the higher general educational level. The need for home education work, such as zenana visiting in India, and mass education programs in China, is non-existent in Japan. The difference in educational level has also affected the type of worker. Women evangelists in Japan are for the most part young women, of high school education or the equivalent, with additional preparation in

---

* The China Mission Year Book for 1931 gives 3 Bible teacher's training schools of higher grade, 2 schools of a lower grade and many schools requiring only primary school education. Ginling College, Cheeloo University and Yenching University Schools of Religion, Canton Theological Seminary and the Central Union Theological Seminary, have women students in religion. (Fact-finders' Report)

Bible training schools. Several of the schools urge higher entrance requirements than high school graduation. Evangelistic work for women in Japan presents certain distinct disadvantages, as elsewhere; low salaries, lack of professional status, and an undefined and unsatisfactory relationship to the church. These handicaps have too often deterred young women of ambition and ability from entering the service. A new field of work, however, which is beginning to attract well-trained college graduates is religious education supervision in schools and churches.

The Bible women's training schools in Japan illustrate strikingly the need for concentration in the mission program. Ten schools with a total of only two hundred twenty-three students, with an annual foreign subsidy per pupil in 1930 of ¥265 represent an unwarranted diffusion of mission effort.*
A reorganization of the Bible women's training schools is therefore urgently needed. The relative amount of mission subsidy applied to general education for girls and to the training of women evangelists is a further proof of the need for drastic reorganization in the field of religious training: the mission cost for each high school girl is ¥32, for each college girl ¥83, and for each student in training for religious work ¥302. The disproportionate subsidy for evangelistic training is not justified.

The question of the justification of the extensive mission kindergarten development in Japan should be raised in connection with the religious program. Many missionaries regard the kindergarten as a valuable means of evangelism because of the contact which it offers with the community. It can

* There are at present, according to the Christian Education Association survey, ten institutions in which women are given training in religious work, with an enrolment of 223 students in May 1930, with 64 graduates in 1930—39 Japanese teachers and 15 foreign teachers. The total subsidy from foreign sources for general expenditures for training religious workers for 1929 was ¥59,088 ($29,544), and for salaries of foreign workers ¥8,360 ($4,180). The Japanese gifts for 1929 reached a total of ¥2,000 ($1,000). In addition to these schools and special courses, women are admitted to Aoyama Gakuin Theological School in Tokyo and Doshisha University. In 1930 there were 35 women students. (Christian Education in Japan p. 113)

scarcely be justified on the educational basis alone, except for a few experimental kindergartens. The combination of courses for religious work and kindergartens seems logical if kindergartens are maintained as an open door to evangelism.

Throughout the Orient in the field of direct evangelism women missionaries should be replaced by trained oriental leaders as rapidly as is possible without detriment to the work, since eastern women, because of language equipment and understanding of folkways, can carry on the work much more effectively. This policy of replacement is obviously hindered by the dearth of trained oriental leadership but should be persistently pursued. Japanese women are already assuming major responsibility, but more are needed. In Burma the general situation is favorable for indigenous leadership. In India and China the withdrawal of the foreign workers from the direct evangelistic program will be retarded by the lower educational level, and to a certain extent by restrictive social customs. This is especially true in India, where it is difficult for the indigenous woman leader to work independently in rural areas. However, for all four countries the primary function of the foreign religious worker in the future should be the training and counsel of eastern women leaders, who themselves must assume the responsibility for the direct religious program.

The program of religious work for women in all the countries under review needs recasting. Two types of training far eastern women in religious work should be provided: the training of general religious workers for home, community and church work with a definite social emphasis; and the training of supervisors of religious education for schools, colleges and elsewhere. The greatest need for the improvement of the whole program is a higher type of woman worker. This can be achieved only by giving religious work the recognition of a professional career worthy of well trained women.

Considering the prevailing status of eastern women, their position in the church is surprising. In many churches in the Orient women have equal voting rights, hold the position of elders and deacons, assist at Communion and serve as ushers.

In Japan there are two licensed women preachers in the Presbyterian Church, one of whom is taking examinations for ordination. Women in the Orient are members of provincial and national Christian councils and may act as church delegates in most of the churches. In their official status women have received more complete equality in many churches in Asia than has been accorded to women in churches in the West.

Although eastern women have these official rights and privileges, actual equality is very often not accorded to them by conservative pastors, who dominate the situation. The conservatism of the pastor is a serious handicap to women religious workers, often making their position untenable. The question of equality is less serious for lay women as they carry on their varied church activities freely and make a real contribution to church life in many ways. They are noted for their active efforts in raising funds, a service much appreciated.

We have spoken of the religious influence and work of missions in terms of a definite program. There is, however, a field of unexplored possibilities for fellowship of Christian leaders with women of non-Christian faiths. With the awakening of eastern women has come a sense of common spiritual need, which has drawn women of different religions together. Missionaries should be in a position to give and share richly in this spiritual quest. They have much to learn from the oriental quality of deep devotion and the eastern genius for meditation.

In the presentation of the Christian message to the women of the East there is need for a basic change in appeal. Christianity can no longer center its emphasis on the social handicaps of non-Christian faiths, such as child marriage, Hindu widowhood, and purdah, since non-Christian leaders also are repudiating these evils and are undergoing a process of social reform from within, slowly accommodating themselves to the idea of freedom of women. Christianity must base its claim to the women of the East as also to the women of the West, on its deeper spiritual appeal embodied in Christ's message to the woman of Samaria—"The water that I shall give shall be a well of water springing up into everlasting life."

Rural Emphases

In the preceding discussion of different phases of mission work for women, no specific mention has been made of women in rural life. Although missionary effort through a variety of channels—health, education, social welfare and evangelism— is exerting an influence on the life of village women, the mission program as a whole tends to be primarily directed to urban life. In future mission planning the needs of village women should be given more adequate consideration.

"The welfare of village Asia is closely bound up in the welfare of women"—the opinion expressed by Malcolm Darling, a British official in the Punjab—reflects the growing recognition of the importance of women as the key to rural progress. The social lag of the village is inevitable as long as women are under-privileged and suffer under heavy handicaps. In India and China illiteracy, ignorance and superstition have weighted the scales heavily against the welfare of women. Village women in Japan are on a higher educational level than are those in other Asian countries. But the women of rural Asia are all alike burdened by grinding toil and frequent child-bearing, which leave little strength for constructive home-building or the care of children. Hence, the life of rural Asia can rise no higher than the level of the village woman.

Christian missions should recognize the pivotal importance of rural women in oriental life and include plans for their welfare as an integral part of all mission programs. Essential to adequate rural welfare is the inclusion of women leaders in all of its phases. They should have a part in the planning of village welfare, and trained women workers should be included in all rural projects. Only women workers can cover the needs of women because of the social conservatism characteristic of the Orient.

The needs of village women should be regarded as a whole and efforts must be directed toward lifting the entire level of life. The narrow evangelistic approach seems futile. Only an inclusive Christianity will be productive of lasting results. One woman evangelist with her one Bible woman covering a thousand villages, unable to make more than perhaps an hour's visit every three years, demonstrates, it is true, devotion and sacrifice, but wasted effort, as ineffective as trickles of water lost in the desert sands.

Such an illustration of diluted evangelistic effort demonstrates forcibly the necessity for a policy of rigid concentration in rural work. The vastness of the needs makes delimitation of the field imperative. The missionary enterprise cannot assume the responsibility for solving illiteracy or curing the ills of the women of rural Asia. But it can stimulate others to action and contribute to the solution of rural problems through demonstrating certain definite lines of rural welfare.

Missions are carrying on various types of rural efforts which tend to lift the whole level of the village women's life and invest it with richer meaning. Commendable examples in India of such efforts in rural work affecting women are the Lucy Perry Noble home-life industrial school in Madura, the vernacular training center for teachers in Ongole, the village center near Nagpur, and the roadside clinic carried on by the Vellore Hospital. In China, the Christian Institute of Industrial Arts in Foochow (union enterprise), a number of mass education efforts under missions, projects for raising the economic level of village women, such as a wool-weaving project in Shansi, and the four experimental rural centers of the Young Women's Christian Association, illustrate effective rural work. Although mission work in Japan has been distinctly urban-centered, there are a few significant rural efforts along the line of village institutes for farm women and social evangelistic work.

Missions can make an outstanding contribution to rural life by recruiting and training students in schools and hospitals for village work. Too few mission institutions emphasize rural needs and inspire young women to enter rural service. It should be the chief task of foreign workers to discover and train potential women leaders who will devote themselves to improving the conditions of rural life. In actual programs of village welfare, for a number of years foreign women workers of specialized training and experience will be needed for cooperation and counsel with indigenous workers. Oriental leaders themselves, however, must eventually assume full responsibility for the rural task.

Further Special Problems of Readjustment

We have briefly touched on certain definite readjustments needed in the various fields of missionary endeavor affecting women. But there are fundamental changes which underlie all other details of change. Inherent in all of these specific suggestions is the need for general reorganization in the missionary enterprise which will make possible an improvement of quality through unity of effort and more specialized centralized supervision of different lines of work. All phases of the mission program for women will be greatly benefited if the plan for reorganization of the missionary enterprise as a whole, discussed in detail in Chapter XIV is realized.

A special problem affecting women's work which must be considered in relation to this proposed plan of reorganization is the question of the separate women's mission boards. It is not within the scope of this discussion to do more than merely state the problem. The separate boards undoubtedly have the distinct advantage of insuring the steady growth of women's work with adequate finance and freedom of control. The disadvantage consists in the fact that the separate administration often engenders rivalry and a spirit of divided loyalty and also sometimes results in a lack of balanced proportion in the mission program. It is to be hoped that the reorganization of the missionary enterprise as a whole may lead to a closer relationship of women's work with the general program which will be beneficial to the further development of women's interests.

A problem which affects the whole range of Christian missions, but especially work for women, is the reorientation needed in the missionary point of view. The emergence of eastern women has come with a surprise and even a shock to many missionaries who have built their service and technique on the concept of Indian women behind four walls of the zenana, or of Chinese women with bound feet and bound minds, or of Japanese women sitting passively at home. As one pioneer woman doctor in the Punjab said, "We missionaries stand appalled before the answers our prayers have brought. The first prayer I heard offered in India just before I reached this field forty years ago was that God would break down the walls and let the women free. The walls are broken. We did not have any idea what it would mean to India." To shift mental gears suddenly to the concept of the women of Asia in a changing environment, enjoying the privileges of a new freedom and likewise exposed to its dangers, is very difficult. But the foreign workers cannot fail to recognize this change in environment and welcome the eastern women into larger responsibility.

There is perhaps even greater need for reorientation in the point of view of the American constituency and boards than of the missionary in regard to the changing situation of eastern women. In fact in her readjustment to the changing environment the missionary is often handicapped by the prevailing psychological attitude of the mission public in America, whose mental picture of eastern women, especially in India, is heavy with shadows of the depressed, illiterate masses, almost unrelieved by high lights of progress or by any conception of the outstanding leadership developing among oriental women, both Christian and non-Christian.

The primary task for the future, in all phases of mission effort for women, consists in the training of leaders and withdrawal of the foreign worker from specific tasks as rapidly as this can be achieved without sacrificing the essential values of the Christian program. Whether in education, health, social work, or evangelism, the foreign worker must concentrate on the objective of making her own work unnecessary.

Mission work for women has moved slowly in the transfer of responsibility and control. The difficulties in the women's field, as already suggested, are unique and admittedly great because of a number of factors inherent in the situation: the general social environment of the Orient which retards the development of women; the paucity of trained eastern women ready for major responsibilities; and the impermanence of women in professional life, due to the high percentage of marriage in the Orient. However, admitting all of these deterrents to devolution there has not always been a persistent promotion of this objective. Too often the distinctly possessive attitude of women missionaries toward their institutions—in a real sense the measure of their full devotion to their work—has made it very difficult for them to relinquish responsibility. The fear that the effectiveness of the Christian enterprise might be impaired by a transfer of authority has also retarded devolution. Furthermore, the missionary's maternalistic attitude of affectionate protection has hindered the development of fully responsible indigenous leadership.

Today the enlarging freedom of the women of Asia has loosened the ties of their dependence and has made possible and even inevitable the transfer of responsibility. The stage of development is different in the four countries under review but the fundamental principles are the same; the future of the Christian movement depends on the discovery and training of eastern leaders in all lines affecting women.

In emphasizing the contribution of the missionary in training oriental women in various fields of effort, care should be taken not to set up western standards as the norm for the East. In the eagerness for development according to the western idea, there is a danger that certain special eastern values may be sacrificed. If these special qualities of the oriental woman can be conserved, a modest plenty of western efficiency may well suffice.

In preparing eastern women for posts of major responsibility the value of scholarships for study abroad in America or elsewhere, should be recognized, and mission funds allocated for this purpose. The success of such a plan would depend in large measure on the careful selection of mature, qualified students and equally careful guidance given to them during their period of foreign study. In order to make this possible it might be necessary to divert some funds to scholarship expense, which are now used for foreign personnel. Judged in terms of the ultimate objective of preparation of women leaders this seems a wise measure.

In emphasizing the need for a concentrated effort on developing leadership the achievement of missions in the past in this field is by no means forgotten. The most convincing evidence of the contribution of Christian missions to the progress of eastern women is the number and quality of the leaders, both Christian and non-Christian, who had their early training in Christian schools and colleges. The range of the contribution made by women graduates of the Christian colleges in Asia shows how widely the influence of Christian education has radiated through all the various professional careers entered by women as well as through home life and in civic and national affairs.* Such outstanding Christian women as Cornelia Sorabji and Dr. K. M. Bose in India, Dr. Ma Saw Sa in Burma, Dr. Yi Fang Wu and Shu-Ching Ting in China, and Michi Kawai and Mrs. Ochimi Kubushiro in Japan, inspire the hope that missions may continue to participate effectively in the development of eastern women.

With the increase of women leaders of the Orient in ad-

* The Who's Who for China 1930-31 shows that 16 of the 21 women mentioned were educated in mission schools. Thirteen of the 16 are active in Christian work.

A study of women graduates from some of the mission colleges in the Orient shows the influence of mission education; they represent a fair cross-section of trained leadership:

India: Of 411 graduates (339 Christian, 72 non-Christian) from 6 women's colleges (5 arts colleges and 1 medical school) 252 are in professional life, 39 have studied abroad.

China: Of 333 graduates from 4 Christian colleges (2 medical and 2 arts) 215 are in professions, 41 have studied abroad (26 of these in America).

Japan: Of 305 graduates (180 Christian, 125 non-Christian) from two arts colleges, 125 are in professions, 21 have studied abroad.

In the professions represented teaching leads in all three countries with a number of government inspectresses and college presidents. A considerable number are in the medical profession in India and China, but only one in Japan. The small number in religious and social work is striking: In India 5; in China 11; in Japan 15.

ministrative positions, the number of missionaries will naturally diminish. Eastern leaders, however, express the desire that there may be permanently a certain number of foreign workers in Christian institutions for the sake of international contact. There is also an opportunity for an undefined type of service which foreign leaders can render with eastern women through personal contact with both Christian and non-Christian, and through an active participation in civic and national women's movements. Oriental women are just beginning to extend the range of their interests and have a growing desire for international friendship. The East today offers rich possibilities for informal contacts and cooperation.

Not all women missionaries can be of service in this special field. The few, however, who are specially fitted by training, experience and personality to make such a contribution should be released from institutional routine in order to devote themselves to these informal friendly relationships. Strangely enough the value of this type of service has not been fully recognized as a definite part of the woman missionary's work, although the fabric of life itself is woven of such influences far more than of the direct self-conscious effort at human betterment which has largely characterized the mission approach.

It is needless to say that the present situation in the East makes difficult demands in the choice of women personnel. The successful woman missionary of the future should present technical training and experience in some special field of service, she should show an eagerness and an aptitude to understand and appreciate foreign cultures; she should reveal sympathy and insight as to human relationships; she should possess deep spiritual resources; and above all else she should radiate a contagious Christian personality. The strength of the mission enterprise for women in the past has been measured by the women missionaries who fearlessly pioneered and gave themselves with full devotion to their task. The changing conditions affecting women throughout the East still call for a spirit of pioneering to help in the difficult readjustment. The future still offers opportunity for consecrated Christian service.

Summarized Recommendations for Mission Activities Affecting
Women in India and Burma, China, and Japan

The recommendations for mission activities for women in India, Burma, China and Japan follow the same general lines, with however a certain amount of divergence in emphasis determined by the difference in environment and stage of development reached in mission effort in each of these countries.

Education. 1. It is recommended that in India, Burma, China and Japan Christian education for women continue to receive the support of mission bodies with the objective of improving the quality of existing institutions rather than increasing the number of schools and colleges.

a. It is recommended for Japan:

(1) that concentration of effort be the condition of continued support to Christian high schools for girls and that this support be on a decreasing scale;

(2) that the policy of a gradually decreasing scale of support be applied also to senior colleges for women although temporarily increased financial aid is required.

b. It is recommended for China and Japan that in the interest of educational efficiency the unification of high schools of the same grade, or the specialization of program in different schools be effected where there is more than one junior or senior middle school for girls in the same center.

2. It is recommended that Christian secondary schools in India, Burma, China and Japan introduce more elasticity of curriculum, emphasizing (a) vocational training and a home science program centered in the life situation of the student, (b) experimentation in method, offering more scope for extra-curricular activities, (c) more appreciation of the cultural values of the Orient, and (d) closer contact with the general community, in order that the Christian schools may be more intimately related to life.

3. It is recommended that greater attention be given in

girls' schools and colleges in India, Burma, China and Japan to the development of a more vital religious education program planned with insight and imagination for the building of Christian character; and that trained leaders of inspiring personality be secured to direct the program.

Health. 1. It is recommended for India, Burma, China and Japan that mission medical service for women (a) stress preventive medicine and health welfare especially for women and children, and (b) more closely coordinate Christian hospitals and schools in the promotion of health education and social hygiene.

Social and industrial. 1. It is recommended that the Christian agencies in India, Burma, China and Japan include in their future planning,

a. An emphasis on the social program and facilities for training women leaders in social and industrial work;

b. An intelligent interest in social and industrial conditions especially as affecting women and children;

c. A serious consideration of the social and moral problems of youth in the present period of change, by providing for normal relationship—social, educational and recreational—for young people through activities in church and community centers.

Rural needs. 1. It is recommended that the mission program in India, Burma, China and Japan give more attention to the needs of women in rural life—in education, health, economic and social improvement and religious nurture:

a. Through an emphasis on welfare work for village women in all rural reconstruction projects;

b. Through the presentation to women students in Christian institutions of the needs and opportunities for rural service;

c. Through the inclusion of women leaders in the planning of all rural welfare programs.

Religious needs. 1. It is recommended that in India and Burma, China and Japan two types of full-time worker be trained for religious work: (a) a more general type of religious worker for a combined program of social and religious work with women in the church and at home; and (b) specialists in religious education as teachers and supervisors in schools or churches.

2. It is recommended that in Japan reorganization of the Bible women's training schools be effected (a) through a unification of these institutions in reference to the needs of geographical areas, (b) through an improvement in their quality, that such reorganization be the condition of continued financial support to be based on a decreasing scale.

Leadership training. 1. It is recommended that in order to prepare eastern women for positions of leadership, scholarships be established for study abroad in America or elsewhere for women students, preferably of experience and maturity; and that during the period of foreign study they be given educational and social guidance.

Conclusion

It is impossible to evaluate separately the many factors that are influencing the lives of oriental women, opening to them the doors of a wider freedom and a larger opportunity. The emphasis which Christ places upon the supreme value of the individual, making no distinction between men and women, has left its impress on the East. Christianity has much to offer to the women of the Orient today in the deepening of their personality and in the interpretation of their new freedom as a high responsibility for service.

PART III

ADMINISTRATION

CHAPTER XIII

PROBLEMS OF ADMINISTRATION

1. *Missionary Personnel*

Critical importance of the problem. The history of Protestant missions is a story of the influence of personality upon individuals and communities. The selection and preparation of missionaries is therefore the critical point of the entire enterprise. During the hundred and more years since the work began, the process of selection has been profoundly altered. In the first place, the great growth in the volume of the undertaking has tended toward rigid and mechanical devices for the purpose. Secondly, the increasing diversity of the missionary program has widened the range of qualifications upon which selection is determined. In the third place, a gradual change in the attitude of Christian people toward the purposes and functions of missions has been reflected in the number, type, and motivation of candidates for missionary service.

Changing motivation and diminishing supply. The results of rapid growth and increasing complexity will be discussed later in connection with simplification and unity in organization. The questions of changing motivation and diminishing supply call for comment here. The candidate secretaries of the several boards have been faced during the past few years with a startling decrease in the number of men and women offering themselves for missionary service. The falling off of funds which has necessitated a reduction of the missionary force has obscured the extent of the decline, but it is none the less real.

The Student Volunteer Movement is dying out of the great colleges and universities. The records of the Movement justify the conclusion that "the mission boards of North America assuredly can no longer depend on these outstanding institutions for the growing of missionary conviction that will fructify later, in life service abroad."* In the main, boards now depend upon their denominational schools and colleges for recruits, and the great majority of candidates for the foreign field come from these sources. It is easy, though hardly safe, to assume that religious indifference and secular influences in the great universities are undermining the appeal to Christian service, and that denominational schools are the natural centers of constructive religious teaching. The evidence indicates that this is at least not a complete explanation. An altering outlook on conventional religion and on our relations to other peoples and nations, together with new views of social responsibilities and tasks, is apparent everywhere, and particularly in student groups which have been brought in touch with the stimulating intellectual life and freedom of the universities. To dismiss these as symptoms merely of a loss of religious aspiration is to disregard a change of fundamental importance. There is no lack today of passionate moral and social idealism among young people, but there is a growing impatience with some of the concepts of religion which are traditionally dear to an older generation.

There is no doubt that the changing outlook and views of the younger generation have been operative in the decline of missionary interest in the past few years. They have affected the offering both of money and of lives for foreign service. In a study recently presented at a foreign missions conference,** some of the probable causes of the decrease in the number of students offering themselves as candidates for the mission field are suggested as follows:

a. Students question whether the national or "younger" church groups in foreign lands are inviting missionaries or whether they are being sent in spite of national opposition. Some students from the Orient have represented their people

* Charles H. Fahs, Fact-finders' Report, Home Base.
** Study of the Distribution and Classifications of the Missionaries of Twenty-eight Societies, Leslie B. Moss, January 1931.

as being hostile to the missionary forces; in fact, a considerable number have emphasized the values in their national cultures to such an extent that they have raised doubts in students' minds as to whether Christianity has any vital contribution to make to them.

b. Students are suspicious of organized Christianity and do not see that the Christian message is being applied in a practical way to the whole of life. They hesitate to subscribe to the creedal and doctrinal statements which they think they will be required to accept when they apply for service, and which seem to them outgrown or overemphasized.

c. Students want a life-work where they will find ever widening opportunities for service. They have seen many missionaries return after short periods on the field and have come to wonder whether missions offer a real job for life.

d. There is in their minds an uncertainty as to the Christian message, a vagueness of conception as to the place of Jesus Christ, the character of God, and the effectiveness of prayer.

e. There is confusion as to the place of the missionary enterprise today in the minds of many people to whom students are looking for religious leadership.

f. They seriously question whether their contribution to this generation can best be made through foreign missionary channels. There are many other openings for Christian service: there are broader conceptions of its scope.

g. The failure of the boards to let candidates know the possible types of service in advance, so that they may prepare themselves adequately, has deterred volunteering.

In this summary, there is a clear call for a reinterpretation of missions. Such a reinterpretation is offered in another chapter of this report. We earnestly hope that if a challenge of the missionary's opportunity is rightly presented to the young men and women of today in the terms of a new aim and purpose, the response will be adequate to meet the need; but in any case we are convinced that unfit men and women should not be sent out, even if existing positions must otherwise be abandoned or existing institutions closed. The case is preeminently one in which quality is more important than quantity. Indeed, it is not too much to say that upon the quality of personnel, far more than upon any other factor, or all other factors combined, depends the real and permanent success of the missionary enterprise.

Qualities essential to the missionary's success. The task of the missionary is an extremely difficult one. It calls not only for a self-sacrificing spirit and an utter devotion, but for moral courage, a high order of intelligence, and a love of adventure. Perhaps more than for any of these it calls for the capacity truly to understand and genuinely to love and sympathize with the people among whom he works. A distinguished missionary has said that "foreignness" is the greatest handicap to the success of the missionary enterprise. Men differ widely in their ability to overcome this handicap, but it is clear that no one should be sent out who does not give promise, upon examination, to rise to true leadership through a readiness to serve rather than to command, to win the confidence and affection of the people with whom he is to live and work, and ever to seek new and better ways of accomplishing his purpose. The quality of the missionary's wife, it should be added, is almost as important as that of her husband.

Competency as observed on the field. In the countries visited, the several members of the Commission have met many missionaries. A wide range of gifts and capacities is to be found among them. A few—but regrettably few—are using the power of a vivid personality to bring fresh and stirring influences into their communities; some, though lacking conspicuous gifts, are diffusing Christian influences by the spiritual excellence and gentle friendliness of their lives; many are devoted, patient and unimaginative people, content with the dull round of a conventional service and so encumbered with administrative routine as to be incapable of thinking freshly and planning wisely; a few, because of defects of health or education, or of unloveliness of personality, have impressed us as entirely unfit for the exacting missionary task of today.

Need of orientation schools.   The Commission feels strongly
that institutions should be established by the cooperative
action of the mission boards for the special preparation of
candidates for service in the respective mission fields. What is
contemplated is something in the nature of an orientation
school in which (to take the field of India as an example) the
history, art, and religion of the country, its political, social
and economic conditions, and the psychology of the Indian
people, would be thoroughly and impartially studied under
the guidance of competent specialists, some of whom should
certainly be Indians. Such subjects as hygiene, sanitation and
the effects of climate and food might well be included in the
curriculum.

The reasons for this suggestion are as follows:

a. In the absence of such an institution, every missionary
must be seriously handicapped at the outset by ignorance of
environmental factors which condition his success.

b. There are missionaries who, because of lack of energy
or preoccupation with more immediate duties, never find the
time properly to orient themselves after they reach the field,
and consequently are at a permanent disadvantage in intercourse with educated nationals and in efforts to serve intelligently the needs of their constituents. It has come to our
attention repeatedly, in each of the countries visited, that few
missionaries have a command of the language adequate to
present their message to intelligent audiences with felicity.
The lack of ability to do so does not necessarily imply lack of
usefulness, but it does indicate a condition calling for serious
attention.

c. We believe that such a training of the candidate, especially if it were to bring him into intimate contact with nationals, would assist materially in the intelligent determination of his fitness for missionary service and would reduce the
wasteful turnover in missionary personnel.

The need of this sort of a training center is obvious. The
method by which it is to be met is a matter for expert counsel.
Whether it can best be developed by strengthening one of the
existing training schools in the United States, or by building

on the foundation of one or another of the language schools in each of the countries, is a question requiring careful exploration. The existing schools in Peiping and Tokyo show promising growth in the directions indicated, and might be further developed for these special purposes.

Need of stimulation in the field.   Greater attention should be given to the intellectual and spiritual stimulation of the missionary in the field, as well as to the more comprehensive preparation of candidates for service. To this end it is suggested that the boards make provision in each country for circulating libraries of modern books and current periodicals, and send out from time to time, for short courses of lectures or conferences at convenient centers, available leaders of American thought in such subjects as philosophy, religion, economics, medicine, modern history, and politics.

The reason for this recommendation is that we have found many missionaries unconversant with the trends of modern thought, both in religion and in secular fields, a condition which we have attributed in large measure to their lack of stimulating contacts and to their inability, with the meager resources at their command, to provide themselves with a reasonable supply of current literature.

Salaries and mode of living.   We have no convincing evidence that missionary salaries and allowances in general are seriously inadequate. It is true, as has been pointed out, that the meagerness of the missionary's financial resources may make it difficult for him to keep abreast with current trends of thought, but we believe this condition can be measurably remedied without increasing the salary scale. It is true, also, that during the past two years the successive reductions in salary, varying from ten to forty per cent, because of marked contraction of board incomes, have resulted in diminishing the margin—at its best pitiably narrow—between comfort and bare subsistence. A favorable exchange rate has helped to soften the blow in some instances, but there is justifiable anxiety as to the future.

The missionary's western style and scale of living subject him to some criticism by nationals and contribute in a measure to the "foreignness" which handicaps him in his work. To the average Oriental, he appears to be a man of wealth, living not only in comfort but in luxury. He does not seem to be leading such an ascetic or self-sacrificial life as the Indian, for example, has been accustomed to expect of a spiritual leader. It seems neither fair nor reasonable, however, to expect the missionary to deny himself the ordinary comforts of life according to western standards, much less to adopt the standards of the poor of India or China. In all probability it would endanger his health and lower his energy without commensurate gain. In the case of a missionary with a family, it would be out of the question.

Many of the missionaries of today are willing to live very simply and to make necessary sacrifices, but in contrast to those of the pioneer period they do not so readily believe that a sacrificial spirit requires them to ignore sanitary conveniences and well-understood measures for the protection of health, such as the screening of houses in malarial areas, or to live in native houses which cannot be properly heated in cold climates.*

It is true that not a few missionary compounds and bungalows are unnecessarily large and imposing. Sometimes they seem unnecessarily remote from the life of the town. Such developments should certainly be guarded against, for they only add to the sense of aloofness with which the missionary at best has to contend. We have seen it demonstrated that westerners can live comfortably in much less expensive and less commodious houses than were formerly thought to be necessary, and we have been greatly pleased to find that in some educational and medical institutions there is no distinction whatever between the houses assigned to foreigners and to nationals.

The matter has been well summed up as follows: "The missionary . . . should make an effort to live, as far as that is within decent limits, on the level of his adopted people.

* Fennell P. Turner, Fact-finders' Report, Home Base.

That he should observe the laws of cleanliness and hygiene, goes without saying. If he can live in a fine house and not be an object of envy, let him do so, but by all means let no missionary carry with him as part and parcel of the doctrines of Jesus the heavy baggage of Occidental civilization."

In conclusion it should be emphasized that friendliness, accessibility, and the spirit the missionary reveals in his work and in his social contacts, are far more important than the external manner of his living.

Furloughs. In many quarters there is serious question as to the adequacy of the provision made by the boards for missionaries on furlough. This refers not only to allowances in money, but to the provision of time for advanced study and training. The purpose of the furlough is three-fold: physical recreation for the missionary and his family; further preparation for his task; development of the interest of the home church in missionary work by personal contact with those from the field. A large percentage of the missionaries in the Orient report that furlough allowances are insufficient save in those cases where they are able to live with relatives during the period of leave or have financial resources in addition to their salaries. Particularly are the allowances insufficient when a missionary is anxious, as so many are, to pursue advanced studies or to overcome defects of earlier training.

Exhausting deputation work during furloughs is an additional cause of unhappiness. There is widespread complaint that missionaries are called upon to do excessive speaking and church visitation and—what is worse—that much of it has to be done under the most haphazard planning by the board offices. Another frequent complaint is that when planning for study during furloughs, missionaries have found difficulty in securing from their boards helpful advice as to the institutions in the home land where they can find the courses of instruction and the facilities they need.

The missionary's children. The education of the missionary's children presents in many cases a serious problem. An effort to solve it by the establishment of special schools at central and healthful points has been made in India, China and Japan, but the expense of tuition and travel often imposes a considerable financial burden. The difficulty increases greatly when the children must be sent home for their higher education. In addition to the heavy expense, this involves long separations at a time when children are going through difficult periods of adjustment to different modes of living, to different countries, and to different peoples. The anxiety and strain of these separations and the financial responsibilities incident to them are very great.* The maintenance of homes for missionary children in the United States has been helpful in meeting some of these trying difficulties, but thus far there has been no adequate solution of the problem.

Turnover of missionary personnel.   On this subject observations and interviews on the field by members of the Commission have been supplemented by a large amount of illuminating material gathered in 1931 by Fennell P. Turner and Trevor P. Bowen.**

The voluntary or involuntary withdrawal of a missionary from the work of his board not only involves financial loss but in many cases implies impairment of morale on the field. A study of the reasons for withdrawals between the years 1918 and 1931—unfortunately an incomplete one—indicates two classes of causes for the termination of appointment: those which are extraneous or non-preventable, and those which have arisen from preventable conditions. With the first we need not be concerned. They include such things as ill health of the worker or his immediate family, political or military conditions in the field, the passing of age limits, the lack of sufficient funds.

The preventable difficulties must be examined. Of the replies from more than seven hundred former missionaries as to the reasons for their withdrawal from the field, the most frequent is dissatisfaction with conditions and opportunities

*Fennell P. Turner.
** Fact-finders' Report, Home-Base.

for work (121). The next in order is friction with fellow missionaries, board officials, or nationals (94). Forty-four note a change of religious attitude or of interest in missionary work. A smaller number record insufficiency of salary, a feeling of insecurity of tenure, or calls to larger opportunities elsewhere.

Problems of personality. Occasional clashes of personality are unavoidable. There are elements inherent in the missionary's life and work which make for nervous tension and instability, and criticism of what may often seem to be un-Christian attitudes will be restrained if we take into account the effects of climate, of assignment to uncongenial types of work and of maladjustment to new environments, upon those who are normally cheerful, wholesome, and companionable people. Nevertheless, it is of the utmost importance that missionary candidates should be weighed carefully for qualities that will weather the host of adversities they are likely to meet. Evenness of disposition, a sense of humor, serenity and patience are as essential to success as fervor and devotion.

While there is no rule of thumb by which personality hazards can be determined in advance by board officials or examiners, there are certain mental trends which are significant, and should be carefully borne in mind when deciding upon the appointment or rejection of candidates. It must not be forgotten, in the first place, that although the normal impulse toward missionary work abroad arises from courage, enterprise and a pioneering spirit, there are persons who are driven in the same direction by restlessness or discontent; that while religious enterprises attract the finest character types, they serve also sometimes as an avenue of escape for the timid, who have been baffled by the problems of life in their home environment.

In the second place, there are various sorts of morbid personalities which afford an index, even in early adolescence, to the possibility, or probability, of a later psychoneurosis. Such qualities as excessive introspectiveness, sensitiveness and "touchiness," egotism and undue self-importance (or its converse of marked self-distrust), all are significant danger signs which would warrant the rejection of any applicant whose personality is marked by them. Emotional people with defective endurance easily break down under the wear-and-tear of monotonous tasks, and are poor risks.*

It is equally important that courage and tact be employed by the boards in dealing with misfits. We have met with many instances in which the harmony and effectiveness of a mission group were being steadily undermined by the unwise retention of persons clearly incompetent or out of place. The removal of such persons is an unpleasant and embarrassing duty, but evasion and delay only serve to increase the difficulty and too often result in bitterness, demoralization and the loss of competent men and women.

Doctrinal discord. Another regrettable cause of turnover is to be found in the presence, in many missions, of individuals who foment theological discord or endeavor to defeat the programs of social reconstruction advocated by their broader-minded associates. The corrosive effects of antagonism so engendered are evident in many stations of the societies whose work we have been studying, and there is no doubt of its sinister consequences in the turnover of personnel. Scrutiny of the questionnaire material in Volume V of the Fact-finding Report (Causes for Withdrawal of Missionaries) fully confirms our observations. We suggest the unwisdom of sending to the field persons who insist upon emphasizing divisive dogmas or who have a narrow and rigid conception of the scope of missions.

Unmarried missionaries. The unmarried woman missionary presents a special problem. Many of them represent the highest values in the missionary field, and in general they appear to be contented in their work and healthfully adjusted to their environment. Even a superficial observation, however, reveals the fact that breakdowns from emotional crises, the

* Vide, A. H. Woods, Special memorandum to the Presbyterian Board of Missions, 1930.

development of neurasthenic states and even more serious disturbances are by no means infrequent.

Some of the causes which lead to those conditions are obvious. The abnormality of the missionary's life in a foreign land is accentuated, in the case of the unmarried woman, by the lack of family ties and domestic responsibilities on the one hand, and of the social and recreational outlets of the professional woman in America on the other. There is little to shift the focus of her attention from routine mission work, and the consequence is a tendency to become mission-centric in a dangerous degree.

These factors should not be ignored. The greatest care should be exercised in the selection of unmarried women for missionary service and in their field assignment. Generous latitude in creating for themselves cheerful and restful living conditions should be given. Independent housing has proved in some cases to be helpful in avoiding friction and annoyance. Opportunity and encouragement should be given to widen the horizon of interest for missionary women, especially by participation in the varied movements which are determining the social emergence of women in the Orient.

In Protestant missions, unmarried men escape most of the social limitations that affect single women missionaries. They are free to come and go, unhampered by the restrictive proprieties that necessarily must be observed by women living in the Orient. In any case the administrative problem of unmarried men is not acute, for they are comparatively few in number, and those who go to the field for life service ordinarily marry within a few years of their arrival.

Uncertainty of tenure. Progress in devolution and the growing sensitiveness of nationals to missionary leadership have created new perplexities for the missionary. He lacks assurance as to his future; his anxiety arises not only from the fact that at almost any time he may be forced to leave a work which has captured his enthusiasm and devotion, but that he may return to the home land after many years of absence in circumstances which will make it extremely difficult for him to find other employment. Years of living on a missionary salary have precluded saving for such an eventuality; the board can furnish little aid; he may have a dependent family, and children to educate; what is he to do? Conversations with many missionaries have brought out these apprehensions clearly, and convey the impression that anxiety and foreboding over the future have brought not a few of them to an attitude of discouragement and defeatism. Assurance of more adequate provision for such contingencies would aid greatly in the maintenance of missionary morale.

The demand for specialists. In the consideration of missionary turnover it should not be overlooked that there are certain types of workers increasingly in demand. There is an insistent call from national leaders, particularly in India and China, and to some extent in Japan, for mature people who shall act in an advisory capacity, even though they cannot hope to acquire a thorough knowledge of the language. There is also an increasing demand for specially or technically trained workers. Particular reference to these needs will be found in the reports and findings on education, rural life, and medicine. In many cases, specialists need not contemplate life service, but may go out for a work limited both in scope and time.

In this connection, brief reference should be made to short-term missionaries, who are being appointed in constantly larger number, especially for service in Christian schools and colleges. While in general the judgment of missionary leaders is that short-term appointments are undesirable, we are of the opinion that in certain situations the practice is sound. It is particularly important to consider sending out for brief periods mature persons of outstanding capacity in special lines. In Japan there is little prospect of permanent tenure. Nationals in that country will insist upon an increasing voice in the selection and withdrawal of missionaries, as well as their return to the field after furlough. The time is nearing when it may be preferable in all fields, to offer appointments on the understanding that they are terminable at the end of a comparatively brief service period. It may be wise, in some cases if not generally, to make term appointments of young men and women in the form of service fellowships.

Conclusion. Summing up the difficult problems of missionary personnel, the Commission is convinced that a much more critical selection of candidates should be made, even at the risk of curtailing the number of missionaries sent out, and that those appointed should have the benefit of a carefully planned training for their work; that great pains should be taken in the designation of these appointees to specific tasks and locations; that whenever possible, nationals should have a voice in their selection; and that, if feasible, the early years of their service should be of a tentative nature. It is recommended that steps be taken to supply missionaries on the field with intellectual and spiritual stimulation through the circulation of current books, and that as far as can be done, measures be devised for more adequate care of missionaries retired from the field in the progress of concentration and devolution. Attention is called to the importance of making better provision for missionaries on furlough, not only in the matter of allowances but in the use of time for study, recreation, and the visitation of churches.

2. Diffusion and Concentration

No one can read the portions of this report which deal specifically with such subjects as evangelization, education and medical work, without being impressed by the frequency and emphasis with which reference is made to the unfortunate results of diffusion of personnel and resources. Here undoubtedly is one of the most obvious and one of the most serious weaknesses of missions in the Orient.

Diffusion takes a variety of forms. In the case of educational institutions it ordinarily means that the number of schools or colleges established in a particular area is out of proportion to the personnel or the funds available for their adequate maintenance, with the consequence that the quality of the service rendered by the institutions is inferior. There are cities in which three or four mission schools under the auspices of as many denominations are struggling along with resources hardly sufficient for a single first-rate institution. Another form of diffusion is found when a particular school or college attempts to do more than it can do well. We recall, for example, a mediocre junior college which has applied for and received a university charter. In medicine, similarly, it means either a greater number of hospitals and of dispensaries than can be carried on at a satisfactory level of efficiency or the sacrifice by a particular hospital of effectiveness to extensiveness of service. In evangelization it most commonly takes the form of an effort to convert and baptize persons in rural areas under conditions which make it impossible to develop a self-supporting church.

Nowhere is the evidence of unwise diffusion more clearly observable than in the field of evangelization in India. There are hundreds of villages in some parts of India where evangelistic work has been carried on with a measure of initial success but where there is no adequate financial provision for the religious and secular education of converts, and no reasonable prospect of developing adequately nurtured Christian groups. The demand at home for impressive statistical results of missionary work, the indiscriminate promotion of "mass movements" by some missionaries, the emotional satisfaction of winning souls, the excessive expectations of financial support from America, are among the causes which have contributed to this unfortunate situation. Recent reductions in mission appropriations have made the abandonment of work in many of these villages inevitable. In many others the outlook for results of permanent value is, to say the least, discouraging. Yet some missionaries feel that they must exert every effort and in the aggregate expend large sums of money in order to maintain the work on what can be little better than a nominal basis.

The conditions we have just described, while extreme, are not unique. The number of weak Christian institutions and of merely nominal Christians throughout the Orient is a reproach to the missionary enterprise. Moreover, they represent in the aggregate an enormous waste of men and money. Denominational interests, institutional pride, and lack of cooperative planning, have contributed to the development of conditions which should no longer be tolerated. We are convinced that one of the most urgent needs of the missionary enterprise is the adoption and rigid enforcement, in all fields, of a definite policy of concentration of personnel and resources. Experience shows that this cannot be accomplished by the missionaries in the field. The forces which make for the maintenance of the *status quo* are too strong for them. Plans for concentration are usually unwelcome to nationals employed in religious work. In situations where they have voice or influence and especially where the boards give discretion to the field in the allocation of funds, the mission-employed workers strongly resist the contraction of established work, no matter how unpromising it may be. Vigorous and determined action on the part of the mission boards in America is imperative.

3. *Devolution*

If the missionaries in a given field are successful the time comes when they are no longer needed. Before they withdraw, however, their duties and responsibilities must gradually be assumed by the Christian nationals. In all of the countries we have visited the process of devolution is already under way. In Japan it ought to be completed within a few years. In parts of India, Burma and China, where educated and competent nationals are not yet available in sufficient numbers to carry on effectively, the period of transition will be considerably longer.

The successful accomplishment of devolution calls for wisdom, patience and generosity on the part of all concerned. It is not surprising that there are many missions in which the process is not working satisfactorily. In some cases, doubtless, this is the result of local conditions. There is a mission in India, for instance, where the difficulty of devolution has been immeasurably increased by the rise of factions among the

Christian Indians of the community. But broadly speaking the difficulties are chiefly attributable to two causes.

One cause is the rapid growth of the nationalistic spirit. The people of the Orient have developed an intense desire to manage their own affairs, and a great deal of confidence in their capacity to do so. This is reflected in the attitude of Christian nationals toward the missionaries. They are eager— sometimes too eager—for positions of authority, and while they nearly always contend that the West's financial assistance is still needed, they commonly believe themselves entirely competent to administer funds as well as to provide intellectual and spiritual leadership.

The other cause of difficulty is the natural reluctance of missionaries to withdraw from fields of labor to which they have devoted the best years of their lives. This reluctance is all too likely to result in the rationalization that the Christian nationals are not yet ready for responsibility, although to a disinterested observer competent native leadership appears to be available. How often we have heard a missionary say in substance: "We finally transferred the job to the nationals, and they have done so well that we wonder why we didn't entrust it to them long before."

What with the impatience of nationals and the reluctance of missionaries, it is not surprising that friction results, that mistakes are made, and that there are differences of opinion both as to the responsibility for bad situations and as to the best way to avoid them. A few general propositions may safely be laid down.

1. Devolution should be real, not nominal. It is strange that this should have to be said, but unfortunately there have been cases in which missionaries have adopted measures which nominally transferred authority and responsibility to nationals, but which in reality had no such effect. We do not mean that there was deceit, but that the missionaries, because of their reluctance to surrender authority or their lack of confidence in the nationals and by virtue of their personal influence over the nationals or command of finances, continued after the transfer of authority to dominate the situation.

As one national put it, "We sat in the council-room, but there were too many missionaries looking in at the windows."

2. In anticipation of devolution nationals should be trained by participation for the assumption of responsibility. There have been cases in which, as the result of a reduction of missionary personnel or resources, or of unwise pressure from the nationals, responsible authority has been abruptly transferred to nationals who were unprepared to assume it. This is neither fair nor sensible. The average Christian national, though he may be a spiritual leader, is unaccustomed to authority and inexperienced in administration. Missionaries should have the foresight to select promising young men and women and to train them carefully for the responsible duties which they will later be called upon to undertake. It is frequently said that one of the duties of missionaries is to make themselves dispensable as soon as possible. Obviously the way to do this is to begin as early as possible to train nationals to take their places. In some missions this appears to have been neglected.

3. Probably the best way to accomplish devolution is not by the "handing over" from time to time of one project or institution after another, but by a gradual coalescence of the missionary and national elements in the control of all the activities of a mission, and the subsequent gradual withdrawal of the missionary participants.

The process of devolution in educational and medical work is governed by special considerations to which reference is made in the chapters devoted to these subjects. The policy of the Chinese Government in requiring that the executives of every registered college, as well as a majority of the board of directors, be Chinese is particularly significant. Perhaps its adoption was premature, though we were favorably impressed by the Chinese presidents of the Christian colleges whom we met. The point is that it clearly reveals the nationalistic temper which prevails throughout the Orient and emphasizes the importance of foresighted and intelligent planning for gradual devolution in every field.

4. *Finance*

Responsibility of the boards.   Money given to foreign missions comes from many donors, scattered over a wide area. The fact that much of it comes from persons who can ill afford to give and who deprive themselves of comforts to do so, puts a grave responsibility upon the boards to see that the money is wisely spent. Donors themselves, with a few exceptions, are not in a position to pass upon the relative value of various types of missionary work, and in general must trust the boards to make the best possible use of the funds contributed. It is difficult, however, for the boards themselves to appraise objectively their distribution of funds, and there is no agency of review to determine whether the work is well or badly done. The only checks are the wisdom and judgment of the secretaries and occasional reports of commissions sent out to study some particular project or type of work.

Distribution of funds.   Money for the work of foreign missions whether given directly or through the boards, is expended under three general categories:

1. Home base maintenance, including salaries of secretaries and office personnel, and general overhead expense.

2. Field maintenance, including missionaries' salaries and housing, the erection and maintenance of service buildings (schools, hospitals, and churches) and miscellaneous overhead costs.

3. Operating funds devoted to the field program of the mission including the salaries and wages of pastors, teachers and helpers, and appropriations made toward the conduct of schools, hospitals and evangelistic work.

With the first two items we are not concerned here, but the third, particularly as it relates to church subsidies, calls for comment. Although some of the churches in each of the countries studied are now self-supporting, and a number indeed have been so from their inception, many have been aided with mission funds over extended periods of time. The practice is very general in China, and prevails to a disturbing extent in Japan and India also. The problem has been brought to the attention of this Commission by many thoughtful missionaries and other competent observers, as being not only unproductive of the good results anticipated but positively harmful in its effects. There has been much discussion of this practice and many warnings by missionaries and secretaries as to its evil effects, but it is so strongly entrenched that none of the boards has had the courage to put a stop to it except when diminishing resources have compelled action.

This Commission believes that the long-continued use of money for local church and pastoral support is unwise and detrimental to the establishment of self-supporting, self-propagating churches and that it not only affects adversely the church as an organization but has subtly deleterious effects upon individual administrators and beneficiaries as well.

The reasons which have led to this conviction are:

1. The recipients of money under those circumstances tend to become dependent on the mission and subservient to the missionaries. Although the use of American money may help to keep better-trained men in the ministry than would be possible if they were entirely dependent upon the local church, it is nevertheless difficult to contribute to the support of men in this way without injuring their self-reliance, determination and self-respect. The greatest trouble with the indigenous church is the weakness of its pastoral leadership. The Commission believes that one of the reasons why the ministry is so commonplace is because it has appeared to be a career where a man could secure an easy—though meager—means of support, free from dependence upon those he was supposed to serve.

2. One of the great handicaps to the mission enterprise in Asia is the fact, to which reference has previously been made, that the western form of Christianity is "foreign." The use of foreign money as a subsidy to the local church implies a subserviency to foreigners extremely distasteful to educated nationals. Partial financing of local organizations by the mission

tends often to defeat its own purpose by repelling courageous and independent members of the community.

3. There has been and still is in India, China and Japan a marked tendency to erect church buildings so large and expensive as to be far beyond the capacity of local Christians to maintain. This is to be condemned not only because it imposes upon local churches types of edifices and forms of worship unsuited to their needs but because it discourages endeavor to achieve financial independence.

4. While the use of western money in these ways permits mission work to be pushed forward more rapidly than it otherwise could, it will frequently be found that work "forced" by subsidy is not of such enduring value as it would have been had the work been allowed to develop along normal lines. This does not mean, however, that funds may not properly be used, temporarily and with caution, for promising new ventures.

It will be some time before the practice of subsidizing churches can be completely abolished, but when money is appropriated for such a purpose the boards should require of the missions a frequent review in detail of the situation. Meanwhile they should improve methods of handling and accounting, not only for money given to the churches, but also for all other expenditures on the field. The checks and safeguards of established techniques of accounting protect both ways: they serve not only to give confidence to donors, but they also protect administrators from suspicion and annoyance.

Allocation of funds. The distribution of foreign funds by the forces on the field depends too often either upon traditional policies or upon the fluctuating moods or interest of the voting majority. The proportion of foreign monies allotted to evangelistic, educational and medical work, for example, varies more widely than the special needs of local fields warrant. No guiding principles as to the relative merits of various types of work appear to have been pursued, and the lack of balanced programs is obvious. This state of affairs is unavoidable in cases where funds are allocated by majority voting, and can be corrected only by unity and reasonable continuity of direction.

Accounting methods. To improve the methods used for handling the resources of the missionary enterprise, it is necessary to go to the root of the difficulty—the accounting methods used by the boards at home. Since there are likely in the future to be more joint missionary enterprises than in the past, it is essential that the boards establish adequate and uniform accounting systems. This does not mean that some systems now in use may not be excellent in themselves. The Commission is asking now not only for individual excellence but also for uniformity in the interests of efficiency and economy. A new and comprehensive system should be established, so devised that board and mission operations can be compared and simplified, and uniform systems of accounting, cost recording and statistical reporting set up on the field.

This should result in very considerable saving through decrease in field personnel and overhead. It should also save the time of missionaries and others who now handle accounts of the various boards without adequate training for such work. It should be feasible to set up in a general mission area one financial office serving all the boards. This would develop logically if the recommendations of the Commission for unification of the work of the boards at home were carried out. Such a reorganization of the accounting methods of the boards together with the unification and simplification of their financial operations in the field would not only greatly increase efficiency but would assure donors at home that useless overhead expense was being eliminated.

It should be adopted as a principle that no money contributed from any source to the nationals shall be allotted by the people who themselves are beneficiaries, directly or indirectly. This could be accomplished by creating control-disbursing groups for China, India or Japan which should assign to a given area the sums of money to be spent on indigenous work. Ideally this disbursing group should be made up wholly of nationals; if for the present this is not possible, the group should consist temporarily of both nationals and foreigners.

Provisions should be made in the accounting procedure for dealing with money received in the field in the form of tuitions, professional fees, gifts from special donors, and the like. Indeed, the system finally adopted should show the entire financial operations at home and in the field, dealing not only with funds coming from the boards or donated through them but also with contributions made through persons or institutions abroad. These accounting methods should be related to an accurate and comprehensive annual budget. It is desirable to require the careful thinking through of a program in advance of asking funds to maintain it, with sufficient flexibility in the budget, however, to allow for unforeseen contingencies or opportunities.

The following excerpts from the reports of Fact-finders who surveyed the missionary administration in China and at the home base* are illuminating:

"One would think that it ought to be easy to discover the total costs of supporting the Christian movement in China and the distribution of those costs between foreign and Chinese sources. But such a supposition is entirely untrue. It is no one's business to keep accounts for the total Christian movement in China. No one has done so and no one can do so in the present state of the bookkeeping of the several agencies. Consequently, the Inquiry cannot state to what extent the total Christian movement in China is self-supporting.

"One would think that it ought to be very simple to take the books of any one of the great denominations and find out precisely how much of the total cost of the denominational work comes from board appropriations and how much from Chinese sources. Again one is dealing with a supposition contrary to fact. The division of responsibility between the boards and the Chinese churches, and other agencies is such that the present systems of accounting nowhere brings into a comparable total the complete respective expenditures from those two sources toward the combined work.

* Fact-finders' Report for China *in loco*.

"Again, one would think that at least it ought to be possible to compare the denominational boards with respect to the work for which they acknowledge responsibility and undertake financial accounting; but neither is this possible. The books of the boards are not kept on the same basis. The boards issue different sets of figures in different connections, which are manifestly made upon different bases. The result of effort to use the different figures is so discrepant and confusing that it is generally not worth while trying. This has been the conclusion of repeated attempts to produce comparability in forms of accounting which are simply not comparable. The attempt has been repeated by the Inquiry with the same result. It simply cannot find out exactly how nearly self-supporting the work of any of the denominational missions is.

"The reports published by the boards are much more exhaustive than those usually furnished by commercial organizations doing a comparable 'volume of business,' but while they are probably well suited to the requirements of board officials, the financial statements contained in them are rarely susceptible, with any degree of certainty, to comprehensive analysis. Often they seem unnecessarily repetitious, while the absence of connecting links makes reconstruction into other forms a lengthy and hazardous venture.

"The different systems of recording and accounting used by the various boards add to the difficulty and the hazard of attempting consolidated or comparative statements.

"While it may be equally dangerous to suggest specific reform in this direction without a thorough study of the various organizational procedures, it seems to be absolutely necessary that many of the forms of procedure and reporting be standardized before the financial setting of the missionary enterprise can be intensively reviewed in the countries covered by this Inquiry."

CHAPTER XIV

REORGANIZATION AT THE HOME BASE

The growth of missions. The Protestant foreign mission enterprise has grown from a small and intensely personal program of carrying the Gospel to "heathen lands" into a complexity involving hundreds of organizations, and related, as far as the denominations represented in this study are concerned, to 57,657 American churches with a total membership of 10,015,366. Excluding bequests, members of these congregations gave, in 1931, an average of $1.41 each to foreign missions. The administrative machinery, which includes devices for interesting the average church member to the point of giving his $1.41 yearly, for transmitting it through appropriate channels to its distribution point on the foreign field, for selecting and appointing individuals for foreign service, and for dealing with the incredibly numerous and varied problems of a world-wide program, is in the nature of the case extensive and involved. On the field the undertakings have spread from simple presentation of the Gospel to a wide diversity of religious, social and technical activities. It is not surprising that such great and rapid growth has resulted in difficulties, especially when it is remembered that the executive direction of these organizations ordinarily has been entrusted to men chosen rather for their qualities of church leadership than for skill and training in business administration.

In an important sense, the conduct of missionary activity is a business; in organization, in financial and executive procedures, the work of the boards closely parallels the running machinery of large commercial concerns doing business on an international scale, and the criteria of administrative practice may be applied as properly to the one as to the other.

In other ways, missions have little in common with business ventures. The various denominations have been re-creating themselves in foreign lands by the projection of their own historical forms, without any conscious, or at any rate ostensible, purpose of competing with each other. It is evident, however, that they are all doing essentially the same work, and as the lines of sectarian and denominational distinction are beginning to blur both at home and abroad, it is pertinent to inquire why non-competitive organizations should not abandon purposeless and wasteful duplication.

Evils of disunion. References to the harmful results of disunion, and the fundamental and urgent importance of reorganization at the American base, appear frequently in the preceding chapters of this report. Costly overlapping, wasteful overhead expenses, the failure of attempts to coordinate programs or to concentrate personnel and resources in such a way as to increase their effectiveness—these and other evils have been emphasized in our analysis of the situation in each of the countries visited and in every field of activity. We are concerned, however, not only with the ineffectual use of money and personnel, but with more vital losses involved in spiritual disunity and in the tacit misrepresentation of Christianity to the people of other lands by these divisions. No one who is familiar with the conditions we have observed can fail to realize the critical seriousness of the situation.

Moves toward union and coordination. Efforts to remedy the evils of multiplicity and duplication have been going on for many years. Out of them have come such union bodies at the home base as the Central Committee on the United Study of Foreign Missions, the Missionary Education Movement, the Committee of Reference and Council, the National and International Missionary Councils, and others. Some of these have independent powers, particularly those which have to do with educational propaganda; others are merely coordinating committees without executive authority, expending energy and money in paper work, negotiations and conferences.

Missionaries on the field have been confronted even more sharply with the wasteful and stultifying effects of disunion and have made efforts to correct them, although with caution and misgivings. Observation makes it clear that the spirit of unity and cooperation is far more active in the field than at home, and that progress toward union there has been retarded by the lack of centralization at the base. Comity agreements, more or less faithfully observed, have assigned certain field areas to the exclusive care of specific denominations, mutely acknowledging that sectarian allegiance is no vital part of the Christian message. Coordinating agencies such as the National Christian Councils have been useful, but because of the lack of executive power their influence is largely dependent upon suasion and conciliation. The watchful and jealous eyes of groups in every member denomination are upon them. Even in institutions where union is endowed with nominal authority there is ample evidence that far-reaching concomitant changes at the home base are necessary to their genuine success.

The point we press is not that union enterprises as we have seen them are unworthy of praise or encouragement, but that because of diversity at the controlling source they are unreal. Instances of this unreality are to be found in every phase of the missionary undertaking where joint programs have been attempted.

Three examples will suffice for illustration:

a. The Associated Mission Treasurers represent a concentration—in part—of the financial operations of boards in Shanghai, where a single office is maintained, and some phases of their work are handled in common, such as buying and selling exchange, transportation, the purchase of certain supplies and the like. Services of this sort done at a small charge for other missions bring in enough to carry rental and office overhead. The Association is not able, however, to departmentalize accounting, or financial records generally, because of the diversity of systems used by the several member boards. Not even furloughs can be handled among their own joint staff: when one treasurer leaves, someone else from his own mission must come in and carry on whether really qualified to do so or not. The question of standardized accounting has been discussed by the Treasurers, but initiative for changes of moment must come from the home base, and thus far there has been no movement from that direction.

b.   Cheeloo University illustrates other problems which emerge from a union which is gestural rather than actual. In spite of a formal charter which seems to provide unity of control, the University represents in reality merely a loose aggregation of societies, which may come in or go out of the responsibilities of support more or less at will. In difficult financial times they are more likely to withdraw men from critical positions on the staff or to reduce maintenance grants than to contract their own denominational program for the sake of a joint responsibility. Such a situation is a constant perplexity to the administrators because of the lack of assurance of regularity or continuity of support, and the uncertainty is embarrassing both for officers of the institution and for responsible members of staff.

A second weakness lies in the fact that appointments to faculty are made primarily by the societies. This tends markedly to limit breadth of selection, balance in the teaching force, and administrative authority within the colleges of the University; it tends to accentuate loyalty to mission boards rather than to the institution itself, and disturbs the University program by removing furlough schedules from its control.

The officers have constantly to conciliate numerous societies and individuals in order to hold their support, or to prevent the withdrawal of contributing boards from the union for minor causes.

c. A union enterprise in South China centering largely around the American Presbyterian Mission, is shown opposite in graphic form to illustrate the widely scattered and remote sources of final reference. The arrows indicate the journeys which must be followed by any proposal relating to policy or general procedure. The time consumed in communicating with numerous distant controls through equally numerous intervening missions, and the administrative lag involved in the process, effectually throttles timely action. Of a dozen measures proposed within a period of two years, it was stated that only one had survived to completed action; most of the remainder had perished during the long transit, or were still en route.

Whatever term may be applied to this administrative grouping it is not a union in a true sense, although it represents an

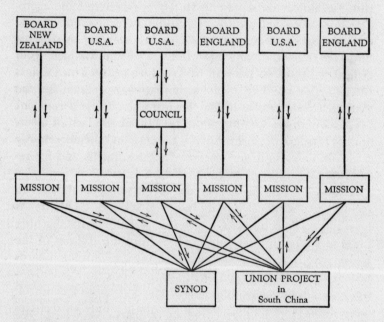

honest and earnest effort of missionaries on the field to work harmoniously together.

It may be thought that we have drawn a picture darker than the facts warrant. We do not believe this to be the case, and it should be emphasized that the picture is presented not for the purpose of destructive criticism, but in an earnest effort to show things as they are from a detached but friendly viewpoint. That noble lives and passionate ardor have been poured into the missionary enterprise is abundantly evident.

It is precisely this which leads us to rebel against a system of administration which hampers and at times nullifies these great qualities. If any indictment be found in the analysis of existing conditions it is against the limited outlook of Christians in America who determine the views and policies of their board officials at home and their missionary agents on the field. Enough has been said to make clear our conviction that decisive action must be taken by these same people if the missionary enterprise is not to deteriorate and eventually to wither into insignificance.

The need of unity on a comprehensive scale.   The time has come for a plan of administrative unity on a comprehensive scale. In the homely but striking metaphor of a missionary leader in the Orient, the old model, which was once regarded as a marvel, will no longer sell. Possibly by making a few superficial improvements and introducing one or two new features it may be made to last a little longer. But certainly the wiser course is to undertake at once, in the light of experience and with a long look ahead, the construction of a new model designed to meet the needs of a new world.

A careful study of the problem in its varied aspects has convinced the Commission that the efforts heretofore made in the direction of unity and coordination have produced few significant results, but we recognize great difficulties of effecting union on a large scale. Denominational loyalties are deeply embedded in emotional religious life, and have dominated missionary effort for more than a century. There are many other intricate and perplexing questions to be solved. We believe, nevertheless, that thoughtful Protestants will not longer insist upon imposing a particular theology and polity upon the Christians of Asia; that they will desire rather to encourage the followers of Christ in the Orient to develop their religious life and their religious organizations in harmony with their own conceptions and their own genius; and that to this end they will be willing to support a far wider and bolder policy of missionary cooperation and union than has heretofore been attempted.

The Commission's proposal. It is not enough, however, merely to take note of these emergent problems, nor to assert the factors which underlie them; we need to ask what can be done. Some constructive plan is called for to meet needs so clearly seen; and apparently so insoluble. The challenge they offer is to be met by a new conception of the administrative conduct of missions, designed to replace the present incongruous systems by a central body, through a series of orderly steps covering a period of years, so planned as to cause a minimum of dislocation in the continuing enterprise. The Commission proposes, therefore, a single administrative unit for the foreign Christian enterprise in place of the complex, costly and duplicative machinery the existence of which is encumbering the great work that Christian good will is trying to do. In view of the complexity and delicacy of the undertaking no detailed plan of unification is insisted upon. If a hearty acceptance of the general principle and a determination to do what is needful, without counting the cost of personal and denominational advantage, can be attained, the task of perfecting a plan may be undertaken with assurance; it will take time for complete accomplishment, but it can be done.

In the judgment of the Commission, as at present informed, the best plan of unification should follow the general course indicated on next page.

1. Denominations willing to cooperate should participate in the organization of a council for the administrative direction of missionary effort in all fields. Where separate women's boards still exist, they should be included, with appropriate representation in the council. Each denomination should be represented by one or two members (in addition to one of its board secretaries in an advisory capacity) and means should be devised for the selection of at least an equal number of members-at-large, chosen without reference to denominational adherence. Wisdom, tested capacity for leadership and wide experience in administrative affairs should determine the appointments to this body.

2. The functions of the council should include the formula-

tion of general policies for their representatives on mission
fields, the appointment of executive officers, field directors, and
by confirmation, of all field personnel.

3. The executive officers should be salaried specialists devoting their entire time to the phases of the program com-
prised under evangelization, general education, religious edu-

CHART OF A SUGGESTED ADMINISTRATIVE REORGANIZATION

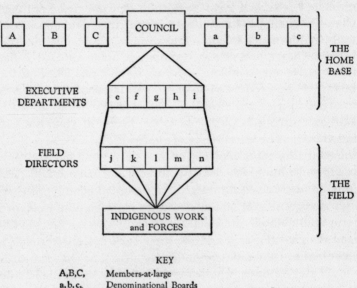

KEY

A,B,C,   Members-at-large
a,b,c,   Denominational Boards
e,f,g,h,i,   Executive Departments:
              Evangelization, Education, Medicine, Rural
              Life, Finance, etc.
j,k,l,m,n,   Field Departments corresponding

cation, medicine, rural life, women's work, and social betterment. They should form a cabinet of executives, exercising
administrative control in their respective divisions, but unit-
ing in the consideration of general policies, projects and
budgets to be concertedly recommended to the council.

4. Field directors should supervise the work of regional divisions, make surveys, and take the initiative in new and experimental projects.

5. Under such a plan, it is obvious that the administrative functions of denominational boards as now constituted would be greatly modified. A duty of critical importance, however, would rest upon them—that of interpreting and promoting the work of foreign missions among their own churches in America, and of maintaining in cooperation with the council the interest and support of these units of Christian people, upon which the vigor and success of Christian work abroad ultimately rests. While it is important that the vision of home churches shall be lifted above obstructive denominational walls, it is equally important to preserve those relationships between individuals or congregations at home and particular missionaries or special kinds of work on the field which create bonds of personal acquaintance and interest. The boards must see to it that the work of Christian extension abroad is kept as a stirring reality close to the hearts of churches and individuals. The enthusiasm of undivided loyalty to a great common task must replace the loss of denominational proprietorship; but close contact with field activities should carefully be maintained through all of the usual channels. Whatever changes it may be found wise to make in administrative form and method, care should be taken to encourage and extend designated giving and the support of projects through a coordinating center, but not independently. The church boards should also continue, when desirable or necessary, to hold title to properties, save as they may be transferred to indigenous holding bodies, and should recommend to their denominations from time to time, candidates for recurring vacancies in the council.

In order to avoid misunderstanding of the foregoing plan and to define clearly its advantages and its limitations, the following comments are submitted:

A. The ends sought to be achieved are those which are revealed by the new conception of the scope and aim of missions presented in Chapter IV, part 1. Among the advantages which ought to result are:

(1) A new view of the functions and responsibilities of the Christian Church: a call to wider allegiances, and a rebuke to un-Christian divisiveness.

(2) An administrative basis, simple, adaptable, and economical.

(3) Centralized disbursement, accounting, and audit of funds.

(4) A body of creative leaders raised above the level of denominationalism.

(5) Experimentation under expert guidance.

(6) A united and coordinated front on the foreign field.

B. The plan relates to the organization of the foreign missionary enterprise alone. It does not suggest the union of denominations in any other field of endeavor, much less in matters of creed, forms of worship and internal organization and policy. What we contemplate is not a unity which would over-ride differences in the home churches, but one which, while recognizing that diversity at home may have its advantages, nevertheless would draw Christians together in enterprises which have for them a common meaning and value.

C. The plan is designed neither to supplant nor control the organization and work of churches located in mission fields or of any other indigenous forces, but to increase the effectiveness of the aid rendered such forces through American funds and personnel.

D. We think it essential to the successful operation of the plan that the council shall not be constituted on the basis of proportionate denominational representation. The ablest and wisest Christian leaders should be selected for the direction of the united enterprise, and to this end sectarian considerations must be set aside.

E. The initiation of changes such as we have proposed may involve a temporary increase in cost; secretaries and other officials who will not be needed after the organization has been simplified must be retired, if necessary, with suitable allowances. The same is true of missionaries withdrawn from the field in the process of concentration and liquidation. After these initial steps are completed, however, and the appropriate consolidations and reductions are effected, we are convinced that the enterprise can be conducted not only on a higher level but at substantially less administrative expense.

The Commission does not contend that the plan outlined in the preceding pages affords the only solution of the defects of administration which are crippling the Christian work now going on in foreign lands and threatening to defeat the realization of its proper aims; as details are weighed, particular consideration may indicate the wisdom of adopting variations in the working out of the principles laid down. We earnestly hope, however, that no measures will be adopted so timid and compromising, so uncertain of meeting obvious needs, as to necessitate the organization of new channels outside of the established boards. We trust that the churches at home will realize that the situation is far too serious to permit further drifting along in disunion; and that they will take prompt and vigorous measures to bring about such a realignment of forces as will evoke creative missionary statesmanship at home and abroad, command the enthusiasm of the finest and most adventurous type of Christian young men and women, and open the way for a more fruitful expression of good will, as followers of Jesus, toward the people of other lands.

Finally, in recommending so complete a reconstruction of Christian missions the Commission records its deep sense of responsibility. Without some such transformation of outlook and method this noble undertaking, so full of significance for the life and hopes of humanity, cannot in our judgment, fulfill its great potentialities.

It is not to be expected that divergence in the conceptions and interpretations of the Christian message will wholly fade as we join in trying to carry to people of other lands the fruits of our religious aspiration and experience. Within the body of this Commission such divergence exists; our differing views are acknowledged with cheerful candor and good will—their existence is neither surprising nor disturbing. The point of high importance is that we are one in the conviction that we, and all like-minded disciples of Jesus Christ, ought to work together in singleness of purpose, with deepening faith and enlarging vision, to the end that men everywhere shall be drawn together in a full and ennobling experience of God.

Summary of Principal Conclusions

An effort has been made, in the paragraphs below, to gather together in a summary of succinct statements the principal conclusions of the Commission. These statements are designed to emphasize issues, which although amplified fully in the body of the Report, appear to the Commissioners to be of such basic importance as to call for presentation in the sharp relief of brevity and detachment. It is to be borne in mind that the conclusions here presented confine themselves, in so far as they are findings and recommendations, to the seven Protestant societies whose program in the Orient was studied by the Commission.

I. The continuance of missions. To any man or church, possessed of religious certainty, the mission in some form is a matter not of choice but of obligation. If there is any truth or value in religion at all, it is for all men. To ask whether missions in essence should any longer go on is like asking whether good will should continue or cease to express itself.

But the essential rightness of the mission idea will not save actual missions from decline or extinction unless in spirit and deed they worthily present that idea. There is real danger lest adherence to aims and methods which impede the communication of living insight may not alone thwart the success of Christian missions, but end their usefulness.

II. Their aim. The message of Christianity presents a way of life and thinking which the Christian conceives, not as his way alone, but as a way for all men, entering without violence the texture of their living and transforming it from within. The goal to which this way leads may be variously described; most perfectly, perhaps, in the single phrase, Thy Kingdom come. That is, and always has been, the true aim of Christian missions.

In more literal phrasing, the aim of Christian missions to-day in our conception would take this form:

To seek with people of other lands a true knowledge and love of God, expressing in life and word what we have learned through Jesus Christ, and endeavoring to give effect to his spirit in the life of the world.

III. Their scope. The point of central importance is this— there must be first of all a new kind of person as the unit of society if there is to be a new society; there is no substitute for the regeneration of the individual units. Nothing can displace, or minimize the importance of, a true and well-qualified evangelism.

But the Christian way of life is capable of transmitting itself by quiet personal contact and contagion, and there are circumstances in which this is the perfect mode of speech. Ministry to the secular needs of men in the spirit of Christ, moreover, *is* evangelism, in the right sense of the word; to the Christian no philanthropy can be mere secular relief, for with the good offered there is conveyed the temper of the offering, and only because of this does the service become wholly good.

We believe that the time has come to set the educational and other philanthropic aspects of mission work free from organized responsibility to the work of conscious and direct evangelism. We must work with greater faith in invisible successes, be willing to give largely without any preaching, to cooperate whole-heartedly with non-Christian agencies for social improvement, and to foster the initiative of the Orient in defining the ways in which we shall be invited to help.

As the mission faces the future it becomes a matter of honor that its standards of teaching, or of medical service, or of art or music or literature or whatever it touches, are higher, not lower, than those of secular performance.

IV. Their attitude toward other faiths. The mission of today should make a positive effort, first of all to know and

understand the religions around it, then to recognize and associate itself with whatever kindred elements there are. It is not
what is weak or corrupt but what is strong and sound in the
non-Christian religions that offers the best hearing for whatever
Christianity has to say.

It is clearly not the duty of the Christian missionary to attack the non-Christian systems of religion—it is his primary
duty to present in positive form his conception of the way of
life and let it speak for itself. The road is long, and a new
patience is needed; but we can desire no variety of religious
experience to perish until it has yielded up to the rest of its
own ingredient of truth. The Christian will therefore regard
himself as a co-worker with the forces within each such religious system which are making for righteousness.

V. The men and women in missions. The task of the missionary is an extremely difficult one. It calls not only for a
self-sacrificing spirit and an utter devotion, but for moral
courage, a high order of intelligence, and a love of adventure.
Perhaps more than for any of these it calls for the capacity
truly to understand and genuinely to love and sympathize
with the people among whom he works.

The Commission is convinced that a much more critical
selection of candidates should be made, even at the risk of curtailing the number of missionaries sent out. Those appointed
should have the benefit of a carefully planned training for
their work; great pains should be taken in the designation of
appointees to specific tasks and locations. Whenever possible,
nationals should have a voice in their selection and retention,
and if feasible, the early years of their service should be of a
probationary nature.

VI. Permeative influence and the wider Christian fellowship.
Christians should count among the best results of their
endeavor the leavening influence of the spirit of Jesus in the
common life of each country.

Ways must be found in which the multitude of those in the
Orient who are followers of Christ, but who cannot be brought

into the body of the Church as now constituted (and perhaps not for a long time to come), may be reckoned as disciples and may come, with each other and with us, into the wider Christian fellowship.

VII. Concentration of effort. The number of weak Christian institutions and of merely nominal Christians throughout Asia is a reproach to the missionary enterprise. Denominational interests, institutional pride and lack of cooperative planning have contributed to the development of conditions which should no longer be tolerated. We are convinced that one of the most urgent needs in all fields is the rigid enforcement of a policy of concentration of personnel and resources. Experience shows that this cannot be accomplished by the missionaries in the field; the forces which make for a continuance of the present status are too strong for them. Vigorous and determined action on the part of the mission boards and the denominations behind them, is imperative.

VIII. Transition from temporary to permanent character. A mission, by definition, is intrinsically temporary; the time comes when established centers of religious life must be left to develop according to the genius of the place.

Missions should now be preparing for the transition from the temporary work of church planting, pioneer work in medicine, education and the training of leaders—to the permanent function of promoting world understanding and unity on a spiritual level through the ambassadorship of relatively few highly equipped persons, and through institutions for the study of theology and civilization, and the emerging needs of the adopted land.

IX. The transfer of responsibility—devolution. The goal of the mission must be the transfer of its responsibility to the hands of the nationals. Answerable for the integrity of its work, the mission cannot realize the idea of the indigenous church by simply letting go. The desire to make himself unnecessary is a mark of the true missionary; but in achieving that end, the transfer of responsibility must follow thorough training of nationals: devolution should be real—not nominal; and gradual—not abrupt.

X. *Administrative unity and cooperation.* The Commission believes that the time has come for a plan of administrative unity on a comprehensive scale, and proposes a single organization for Christian service abroad in place of the complex, costly and duplicative machinery which now exists.

If a new alignment of forces, rising above denominational and doctrinal barriers can evoke creative missionary statesmanship at home and abroad, can command the enthusiasm of the finest and most adventurous type of Christian young men and women, and bring the whole enterprise to new levels of accomplishment, we are convinced that the churches of America will have a great part in the making of a better and happier world, but not otherwise.

Its accomplishment will require a hearty acceptance of the general principles that have been laid down, and a determination to do what is needful without counting the cost of personal and denominational advantage. If these can be attained, the task of perfecting a plan of unification can be undertaken with assurance; it will take time to accomplish, but it can be done.

Index to Recommendations

General Index

Academy of Music, 173
Administration and Organization, committee, xiii
Administrative function, xi, 289-312
  accounting methods, 310-312
  accounting problems, 313
  allocation of funds policies, 309
  career questions and devolution, 300, 305
  charts on unity, 317, 320
  children of workers in the field, 296
  compensation of field workers, 294-296
  demand for specialists, 301
  devolution, 304-306
  diffusion and concentration, 302-304
  distribution of funds, 307
  doctrinal discords, 299
  finance problems, 307-312
  financial responsibility of mission boards, 307
  furloughs, 296
  keeping field workers up to date, 294
  living standards in the field, 295
  morale, 297
  nationals in personnel, 306
  orientation schools for field workers, 102-106, 115, 293
  personality problems, 298
  personnel criticisms, 15-18
  personnel problem, 289-302
  personnel qualifications, 292
  personnel turnover, 297, 299
  reasons for personnel shortage, 290-292
  reorganization at the home base, 313-324
  short term personnel, 301
  special problems of unmarried personnel, 299

Administrative function— (Cont.)
  unity advantages, 322
  varying competence in field, 292
Adventist Mission, 189
Aegean Sea, evangelizing countries of, 82
Agra conference, 1929, 166
Agricultural missions, 214-236
  approach to task, 220-221
  economic and social problems, 223-225
  educational work, 225-227
  relation to evangelism, 214, 223
  rural reconstruction and aid, 227-234
  scientific work, 217
Agricultural Missions Foundation, 236
Agriculture, animal husbandry, 215, 216, 221, 222, 228
  credit problem, 224
  education, 225-227
  oriental, 214-218
  research, 222
  science in, 217-218
  statistics, 219
  tenancy, 224
Agriculture, Department of (Japan), 233
Agriculture and Rural Life, committee, xiii
Ahmedabad, India, 242
Ai Kei Gakuin Social Settlement, 269
Ai Sei Kan Settlement House, 269
All-Asia Women's Conference, 257
Allahabad, India, 165
Allahabad Agricultural Institute, 225
Allen, Young J., 185
All-India Woman's Conference, 255

333

Christian Literature Societies—
(*Continued*)
theological problems, 192
(*see also* Literature: Christian)
Christian Literature Society,
Japan, 188
Christian Literature Society,
Madras, 184
Christian Medical Association of
India, 206, 207, 266 *note*
Chuang, C. H., 160
Church, approach to student class,
96, 110, 111
and labor unions, 252
attitude on industry, 247
doctrine over-emphasized in mission fields, 89, 95
finance and self-support, 307-309
growth in missionary fields, 82
indigenous, as goal, 106-108
in Oriental cities, 97
merits of the indigenous, 82
non-membership among Christians, 111
outstripped by Christianity, 110
peculiar problems in rural Asia,
98-102
relation to missions, 81-115
sectarianism obsolete, 92-94
self-support in Asia, 88
situation in the world-culture, 33
subsidy weakness, 108
training centers for new missionary work, 102-106
transformation needed in mission
field, 91-115
unity movement in mission fields,
93
vital ideal of universal, 27
(*see also* Christianity)
Churches of Christ, in Japan, 88
Church of Scotland Missions, 272
Church-planting, 81-115
abandoned as paramount aim,
109-110
decreased importance in rural
field, 100
denominational confusion, 85-87
historical methods censured, 84-
87
ideal method, 82-84

Co-education, 264
Colombo, Ceylon, xii, 258
Colleges, 164-179
purposes, 164
Colleges: Burma, 165-169
Colleges: China, 169-172
coordination problem, 171
medical, 268 *note*
present prestige, 170
registration and regulation, 171
statistics, 169
teacher training problem, 262
women's, 258 *note*, 259, 261 *note*
Colleges: India, 165-169
devolution problem, 169
medical, 268 *note*
relation to universities, 166
religious exercises, 168
statistics, 166
women's, 259, 261 *note*
Colleges: Japan, 172-176
curricular mediocrity, 174
peculiar difficulties, 174
plan for federated Christian university, 175
statistics, 172, 173, 265 *note*
women's, 261
Commercial Press, 181
Commission of Appraisal, Laymen's
Foreign Missions Inquiry, 91
committees, xii
formation and purpose, xi
Commission on Christian Education, 175
Commission on Christian Higher
Education in India, 166 *note*,
168
Committee of Reference and Council, 314
Communism, 252-254
in China, 154
misdirected education a feeder,
158 *note*
Confucianism, in Japan, 37
renaissance of China, 41 *note*
Congregational Church, ix
in Japan, 88
Cornell University, 225
Country-Life workers, world congress proposed, 233

Japan— *(Continued)*
  devolution, 304
  hospitals *(see* separate item)
  important churches in, 87
  improved missionary methods in, 31
  industrial labor conditions, 242
  industrial research, 249
  industry, 238, 240
  Kingdom of God movement, 63 *note,* 94
  labor unions, 252
  laymen in rural work, 105
  literacy and book distribution, 189
  manner of Christian worship in, 90
  medicine in, 198
  mission need decreasing, 25
  music in Christian worship, 90
  Protestant population, 14
  religious requirements, 39
  Restoration of 1868, 119, 144
  rise of women, 256
  rural culture, 72
  rural life associations, 232-234
  rural population problem, 219
  rural work, 231, 278
  schools *(see* separate item)
  social background of industry, 239
  statistics on women, 282 *note*
  student attitude, 111
  United Church movement, 93-96
  western education in, 118
  women and medical work, 266-268
  women in evangelism, 273-275
"Japan, An Economic and Financial Appraisal," H. G. Moulton, 219
Jerusalem Meeting, 1928, 66
Jesuits, 10
Jesus, xiv, 6, 26, 35, 156, 165, 214, 223, 230, 245, 246, 334
  appeal to non-Christians, 110, 111
  as mission message, 51-52
  basic teachings, 49
  example, 55

Jesus— *(Continued)*
  in non-Christian faiths, 43
  instrument of deity, 58
  missionary as a soldier of, 10
  missionary injunction, 8
  philanthropy and teaching as unity, 60
  Sermon on the Mount, 57
Jones, B. M., 138
Jones, E. Stanley, 47 *note*
Judaism, local stress, 6
  source of Christianity, 37
Judson College, 165
Judson Press, 184

Kagawa, Toyohiko, 94, 188
Kandy, Ceylon, xii
Karen people, character, 136
  Christianizing, 138
  National Society, 138
  self-support in church and school, 88, 142
Kashmir, India, 258
Kawai, Michi, 282
Kennedy, M. D., 119 *note*
Kilpatrick, William, 135 *note*
Kingdom of God Movement, 63 *note,* 94
Kinnaird College, 165, 261 *note*
Kobe, Japan, 172, 173
Kobe Woman's College, 173, 261 *note*
Korea, xii
  Christian publishing houses, 184, 187
  laymen in rural work, 105
Kubushiro, Ochimi, 282
Kumiai Church (Congregational), 88
Kwangtung Province, Bureau of Agriculture, 230
Kwansai College, 172, 173
Kwansei, Japan, 147
Kwanto College, 172
Kyoto, Japan, 149, 172, 264

Labor unions, 252
Labrador, 17, 78
Lady Hardinge Hospital and Medical College for Women, 195